CHILDREN'S CHAR

Early Interve
the St___

Alison Body

C000156498

P

First published in Great Britain in 2020 by

Policy Press
University of Bristol
1-9 Old Park Hill
Bristol BS2 8BB
UK
t: +44 (0)117 954 5940
e: pp-info@bristol.ac.uk
www.policypress.co.uk

North American office:
Policy Press
c/o The University of Chicago Press
1427 East 60th Street
Chicago, IL 60637, USA
t: +1 773 702 7700
f: +1 773-702-9756
e:sales@press.uchicago.edu
www.press.uchicago.edu

© Policy Press 2020

British Library Cataloguing in Publication Data
A catalogue record for this book is available from the British Library.

Library of Congress Cataloging-in-Publication Data
A catalog record for this book has been requested.

ISBN 978-1-4473-4643-2 paperback
ISBN 978-1-4473-4644-9 ePDF
ISBN 978-1-4473-4645-6 ePub

Cover design by Dave Rogers/Double Dagger
Front cover: Urban Road

"There can be no keener revelation of a society's soul than the way in which it treats its children."
Nelson Mandela, Former President of
South Africa

Dedicated to my husband, Tom, and our two sons,

Iden and Quinlan, with love.

Contents

List of figures and tables

Figures

Tables

About the author

Alison Body is a lecturer in philanthropic studies with the Centre for Philanthropy at the University of Kent. Formerly the Faculty Director of Early Childhood at Canterbury Christ Church University, she has long been interested in how the voluntary sector can support children in achieving positive outcomes. Previously a CEO of a leading children's charity and a lead Commissioning Officer for early intervention services for Kent County Council, she has significant experience of working closely with voluntary sector organisations and funders to deliver essential services which achieve maximum impact for children, families and communities. Drawing on over a decade in practice, Alison was awarded her PhD in Social Policy in 2017 from the University of Kent. Her thesis focused on the commissioning of early intervention services.

Since then Alison has become an established academic publishing research focusing on children, charity and fundraising. Her latest publications explore the relationship between third sector organisations and the state, the role of voluntary action in education and how children learn philanthropic behaviours. Alison also holds a number of voluntary positions including Trustee of the Voluntary Sector Studies Network (VSSN), Director of Led by the Wild CiC, supporting children's outdoor education, environmental learning and conservation activities, and volunteers for the Scouts Association as a Beaver Scout leader.

Acknowledgements

While this text is a single authored monograph, largely based upon an updated version of my own PhD study which I submitted in 2016, there must be clear recognition that few academic texts are produced in isolation, and this book is no different. First and foremost, my thanks must go to all the practitioners, professionals, teachers and volunteers who shared their views and experiences, without which this book would not exist.

I am fortunate to work within a small team of inspirational colleagues in the Centre for Philanthropy at the University of Kent. Beth Breeze and Lesley Alborough have been constant sources of encouragement, reflection and motivation in writing this book.

I further am indebted to my wonderful supervisors, Jeremy Kendall, Kate Bradley and Derek Kirton who carefully guided me through the original study and encouraged me to continue that research and write this book. This book also represents my research journey following the completion of my PhD and draws upon further projects, such as the role of voluntary action in education (Chapter 4), which I have been proud to complete with Eddy Hogg.

This book would also not have come into fruition without many long debates with my colleague, Maria Lehane, who actively advised and supported me on structure, narrative and positioning this debate within policy rhetoric. Without her input, especially within the formative ideas of this book, I doubt it would have been written.

Finally, my love and thanks go to my husband, Tom, in recognition of his never-ending love and support, and our two wonderful sons, Iden and Quinlan. They keep me grounded in a challenging world, and for that I am deeply grateful!

Introduction

'This isn't the voluntary sector we once knew, it is a new and challenging landscape, basically a whole new ball game … if you want to play, you need to learn the rules fast.' (CEO, medium children's charity)

Let's start by relaying the experience which inspired this book. It took place in 2016 during an interview with a Chief Executive of a charity tackling domestic abuse. On a blustery winter's day, clutching a hot coffee we sat, wrapped in our warmest clothes, in a freezing cold office. 'I'm sorry' the CEO said, 'we try to only switch the heating on when the clients are here, money savings, you know' she broke off, and then she started crying. She went on say how she had started this charity over 30 years ago, as part of the women's aid movement and as a victim of domestic abuse herself. She passionately believed in holistically supporting women, and particularly their children, through developing play-based early intervention and support. Over the 30-year period they had directly supported more than 6,000 women and children to escape and overcome domestic abuse. The charity had won national and international recognition for their work. Built on their vast experience, knowledge and practice they had developed a specific framework of intervention aimed at helping children cope with, and move on from, the emotional turmoil of living with an abusive parent or carer. Throughout the 2000s this programme had grown, and in the mid-2000s they expanded, becoming dependent upon funding from the local authority. Two days before our meeting she had been informed that under a recommissioning process they had 'lost' the contract, a tender for a service which was based on their 30 years of experience, in favour of a large housing association with no previous experience of delivering domestic abuse support services for children. 'They were cheaper' is the only explanation she was given. She was distraught, not because they had lost a contract, but because she felt, knowing the organisation who had 'won' that all the values and strengths of her lifetime's work would be lost. In her words, she 'was done, done fighting, done grovelling for money, done trying to fight' for the survival of her small but vitally important charity. She finished by saying:

> 'It's all well and good these commissioning documents and compacts that say we will all work together, but the reality is very different, the reality is destroying the local charities which make up the fabric of our communities … but that's a story that is never told.'

Less than a year later this charity closed its doors for the last time, and we felt it was time to tell those stories and experiences, but in a way that did not present them as isolated cases, but instead as a series of shared experiences, contextualised in current and ongoing debates.

This brings us to this book, which presents original research spanning 2008–2018 about the lived experiences of voluntary sector organisations delivering early intervention and prevention services for children and families in the England, and contextualises these experiences in wider social policy, research and debates. Particularly focusing on the relationship between children's charities and the state, we talked to 80 individuals from across 40 micro to major children's charities delivering children's early intervention-type services. To ensure that we gained a balanced insight into this debate we also spoke to 20 Commissioners responsible for commissioning some of these charities' services. Commissioners came from across a range of children's services, including children's social care, health and education, and from a range of public service backgrounds, including the local authority (including statutory social services and early intervention services) and local borough councils. Drawing these 100 voices together we present here the lived experiences of those working with and on the frontline of children's charities.

Why this book, and why now?

The title of this book reflects the motivation for this text: *Children's charities in crisis: early intervention and the state.* The challenges facing children's charities are effectively pushing the sector to crisis point. Propelled by increasingly tough discussions around independence of the voluntary sector (for example, Aiken, 2014; Benson, 2014; Independence Panel, 2015; Milbourne and Murray, 2014; Rochester, 2014) fears of mission drift (Cunningham, 2008), incorporation (Fyfe, 2005) and concerns over bureaucratic powers reducing the voluntary sector voice (Milbourne and Cushman, 2013), commissioning and state-sector relationships require further scrutiny. Policy shifts in preventative services have also raised significant questions about how we conceptualise and support vulnerable children in our society.

Nonetheless while all of this happens, the demand for children's services is increasing. Between 2006 and 2016, the number of child protection enquiries undertaken by local authorities rose by 140% and children subject to child protection plans doubled (LGA, 2018). The complexity of problems facing children and families increases as levels of poverty deepen and inequalities intensify between those who are wealthy and those who are poor. The Local Government Association estimate that by 2025 councils are likely to face a funding gap of £3 billion, this is without costing for increasing demand, which is likely to increase in the face of disappearing early help and early intervention services.

As early help and early intervention support rapidly disappears, children increasingly only get support when at crisis point. According to four of the leading national children's charities, The Children's Society, Action for Children, Barnardo's and the National Children's Bureau, between 2010–11 and 2015–16, local authority spending on preventative services decreased in real terms by 40%, with a predicted further 29% reduction by 2020. As a result, early intervention support services have been systematically dismantled, almost to a point of no return. This has meant the loss of children's centres, family support, parenting help and youth work. By 2016 over 600 youth centres had been closed, and approximately one children's centre has closed every week since 2010. A failure to intervene early means that children are entering the social care system more than ever before.

In response to these challenges, this book brings forth, a not yet fully explored debate about the relationship between voluntary sector organisations working with children, young people and their families (referred to in this book as children's charities), and the statutory responsibility of the state to deliver early intervention and prevention services. This is not a new relationship. The 'third way' driven by the Labour governments of 1997 to 2010, and the subsequent 'Big Society' and commissioning agenda propelled by the Conservative party in the Conservative-led coalition (hereafter referred to as the Coalition) has redefined these relationships and created an altered space, with adjusted rules, within which voluntary sector organisations must now operate. This book aims to examine and explore this space and the relational factors that guide children's charities, drawing together academic literature, social policy and the lived experiences of children's charities navigating these changes over the period of a decade (2008–2018).

Defining the scope of the book

This book specifically explores the relationship between children's charities and the state, particularly in the context of early intervention service provision within children's social services. By children's charities we refer to any formally constituted, not-for-profit organisation with a central mission of supporting children, young people and their families. While the majority of the voices from children's charities which we have included in this book are registered with the Charity Commission, some are not due to size (that is, they are micro, community groups), while another is a registered community interest company, limited by guarantee. We refer to these organisations as children's charities throughout this book to protect confidentiality.

In the context of this book early intervention means services which are established to intervene as soon as possible to tackle social and emotional problems emerging for children, young people and their families, or pro-actively working with a population most at risk of developing problems. Early intervention can happen at any point in the life of a child or young person and can be delivered through both universal and targeted services.

Local authorities have a statutory duty to provide early intervention support, currently provided under a service commonly known as 'Early Help'. This book however does not seek to offer a critique of early intervention, moreover it explores the relationships between the voluntary sector and the state in this policy area. Therefore, this book draws specific attention to the intersection between the state and children's charities in the provision of these services, and indeed the role of wider support services such as schools. Commissioning is the dominant mechanism by which this is managed. Commissioning is the process by which health and social care services are planned, purchased and monitored. Commissioning broadly comprises a range of activities, including assessing needs, planning services, procuring services and monitoring quality. While clinical commissioning groups are responsible for the commissioning of services for the National Health Service, local authorities are responsible for commissioning publicly funded social care services, including children's early intervention services.

Although specific in focus to early intervention, schools and children's charities, due to the focus on commissioning, this book offers valuable insight for anyone interested in the role of the voluntary sector in the provision of public services.

Why is this book significant?

Children's charities play a central part in the provision of early intervention and prevention services. Unsurprisingly, the close working relationship between these charities, schools and the state has come under increasing scrutiny. This book raises and discusses the tension between how the commissioning bodies define early intervention and prevention services, as targeted interventions to support identified 'problem families' (Pithouse, 2008; Dean, 2010), and voluntary sector actors, who on the whole reject this definition of early intervention, citing it as too targeted and too late. Instead, many voluntary sector organisations opt for a more universal approach in which services may address wider social concerns (Hardiker et al, 1991). However, the dominant and more process driven, somewhat transactional commissioning approaches often result in prescriptive and punitive contract management and hierarchical relationships, meaning that some children's charities operate in a constrained space and struggle to act independently and speak out with a critical voice.

In discussing these tensions, three significant arguments are presented in this book. The first is how children's charities have evolved in light of the changing environment, presenting three typologies of responses. We start by suggesting that by engaging in these process driven commissioning processes, some children's charities legitimise this discourse and subscribe to the delivery of more punitive, targeted approaches which would normally be considered as sitting outside of the charities' ethos (Peters, 2012). Children's charities can become more entrenched in this activity, and these behaviours become more self-fulfilling, as the activity continually reproduces itself. The process of commissioning can therefore contribute to hardening the approach on 'problem' families (France et al, 2010), and children's charities become part of the legitimisation of this narrative.

Whereas some children's charities have fallen in line with this narrative, others have rejected it, some precluded by the commissioning process and others as an act of dissent against the hierarchal relationship between the state and voluntary sector (Ryan, 2014). In contrast, other children's charities fall somewhere in between this conformity and dissent. They are, to some extent, part of the legitimisation of this approach as they bend and accommodate contractual obligations posed by the state. Nonetheless, they are also able to utilise social skills and tactics to not only secure themselves more advantageous positions in this environment but also to mobilise their particular ideological bias, that is what they think should be done. The ability to mobilise this ideological bias results in these charities being able to, under the right specific circumstances of more relational driven commissioning approaches, set the agenda for the wider field of activity.

The second of our significant arguments results from taking a closer look at commissioning. We seek to extend our understanding of commissioning beyond the binary divide between process- and relational-driven commissioning approaches. Instead, in keeping with some previous colleagues' work (Checkland et al, 2012; Harlock, 2014; Rees, 2014; Rees et al, 2017), we propose a much more nuanced, richer understanding of the realities of commissioning service provision, which is multifaceted, complex and often awkward, driven by individuals' professional and emotional responses to multifarious situations. Building on this richer understanding of commissioning we hope to have responded to the call for 'further grounded research into the realities of commissioning at the local level' (Rees et al, 2017: 191), using children's services as a case study example. The reality is that Commissioners are largely critical of overly bureaucratic commissioning processes, and often seek to rebalance them through the employment of specific strategies, such as informally supporting and promoting certain charities over others alongside trying to act as buffers against the impacts of austerity. Within process driven commissioning styles this means that Commissioners develop strategies and ways to 'bend the rules', or 'play the game' to ensure that contracts are secured at a local level by children's charities that they have 'faith in' to the deliver the required services.

This leads us to the third significant argument: children's services are in crisis and change is an imperative. Austerity has stripped support to the core and children's charities are struggling to cope with ever-increasing complexities and challenges, with fewer resources. As a result, schools are feeling the pressure and being asked to pick up the pieces. However, they too are in midst of a funding crisis with many schools struggling to make ends meet. Thus, they themselves are turning towards charities and fundraising for support. As children's services come under increasing strain, traditional organisational structures, such as education, health and social care, are breaking down. While this breakdown of traditional institutions and subsequent blurring of the boundaries creates significant problems for vulnerable children, it now provides the 'action imperative' (Hupe and Hill, 2007) to develop innovative commissioning responses which step outside of the traditional and policy 'rule bound' boundaries to find collective solutions. We therefore conclude this book with suggestions about how we can and should move forwards collaboratively.

Structure of this book

The book is divided into four parts, Part I, covering Chapters 1 and 2, focuses on social policy, and how the discourse of the third sector and early intervention has evolved over recent successive governments. Part II, covering Chapters 3 and 4 discusses those on the frontline of early intervention, including charities and schools. Part III, covering Chapters 5 to 7, focuses on children's charities experiences of these shifting landscapes and what this means for both the voluntary sector overall and the field of preventative services. Part IV, Chapter 8, concludes and suggests positive steps for moving forwards.

In Chapter 1 we provide an overview of the concept of prevention within child welfare, particularly under the New Labour government (1997–2010). Coming to power in 1997, Labour placed considerable focus, and financial investment, on reducing child poverty and social exclusion, and increasing universal early intervention support and coordination between services. The role of the voluntary sector became mainstream in the provision of children's services, with the launch of several high-profile initiatives. Focusing on the concept of 'prevention' within child welfare and building on these shifting understandings of childhood and the concerns for children, this chapter explores how social policy operationalised under the Labour government. It discusses how Labour developed strategies to tackle issues surrounding children and young people who are considered disadvantaged, vulnerable or at risk and how they mobilised the voluntary sector within this response.

In Chapter 2 we explore contemporary children's services, and how the persuasive logic of prevention has been adopted in more modern service delivery and the role of the voluntary sector in providing these services. Focusing specifically on the early 2010s, we map the shift from the Conservative flagship project of the Big Society, to the renewed localism project of the Civil Society Strategy (HM Government, 2018b). We draw out the links between the societal hardening in focus, shifting from universal to targeting of preventative services, and discuss the role of the voluntary sector in delivery of these services.

In Chapter 3, we provide a contemporary policy overview – covering the past decade from 2008 to 2018 – and how that has translated into practice. We outline the realities of early intervention policy and begin to look at the lived experience of delivering services on the frontline. What is evident is that practice in children's social care and early intervention is struggling to keep up with the pressure and the diversity of demands placed upon services. Voluntary sector and statutory services are facing increasing cuts as thresholds for defining a 'child in need' increasingly shift up. Children's outcomes and the services available to them are widely varied depending on the type of support they require and where they live.

In Chapter 4, we focus on education and explore how education has increasingly turned to charity in times of austerity. Education is a core service which provides the grounding, qualification and socialisation for children and young people, which will likely have an impact on them for the rest of their lives. A primary tool for increasing social equality, achieving aspirations and supporting children and young people to become active, pro-social citizens, it is unsurprising that this is an area of interest for many philanthropists, charities and voluntary sector organisations. Similarly, as schools face ever more fiscal, performance, recruitment and retention pressures, we see them increasingly turning to voluntary action – that is fundraising and volunteers – to counter resource pressures. This chapter explores this core concept, the relationship between education and charity. Focusing particularly on primary education which concentrates on 4–11-year-olds, we investigate how charities shape and support education, and indeed how schools engage in voluntary action to support their day to day delivery. We consider the implications of this work and what this means for the charitable sector. We finally conclude with what this means for schools, and, what is most important, what this means for the children whom they seek to serve.

Chapter 5, is the first chapter of Part III, concentrating on voices from the frontline and their lived experiences. Within this chapter we focus on the lived realities of commissioning. Commissioning, the central process for managing relationships between the voluntary sector and the state, is one of the most contentious issues for modern day children's charities. Early intervention and preventative services for children sit central to this debate — these statutory services at the heart of local government are often commissioned out to voluntary sector organisations for delivery, and form the very focus of this book. We argue that commissioning in its current form is failing; it threatens the very survival of local voluntary sector organisations seeking to support children and young people, and, rightly so, is coming under increasing scrutiny. High profile cases such as the demise of the charity Kids Company, led by the charismatic Camila Batmanghelidjh, have brought the relationship between the state and the sector to the fore of public and academic debate. In the simplest terms it raises the question of how the state and children's charities should work together to ensure the best possible outcomes for children. In this chapter we begin to unpick some of that debate, examining what has happened over the past decade, charities' experiences and how we may potentially move forwards.

In Chapter 6 we move on to explore the impact of commissioning and policy changes on early intervention and preventative services for children delivered by the charitable sector. The definition of early intervention and preventative services is highly contested and politicised within policy and commissioning processes. This reflects an ongoing debate regarding the shifting paradigm of prevention. As the commissioning narrative has developed, there has been an overall disengagement between the voluntary sector providers and the state. As the charitable sector is increasingly exposed to intensifying marketisation, polarisation of relationships increases. Indeed, the tendency towards this polarisation of relationships is significant in terms of the discussion concerning redefinition of early intervention services, highlighting the apparent lack of voice and agency of children's charities in terms of defining this area of activity. We identify here three 'types' of organisational responses to this ever-changing environment: conformers – those charities who align themselves close to the state and regularly reinterpret their mission to fit state logic; the outliers – those charities which reject state approaches to early intervention and seek to deliver services completely independently of the state; and the intermediaries – those charities which walk between conformity and dissent, working with the state when necessary or to their advantage, and walking away when not. We discuss how these types fundamentally alter children's charities' perspectives and experiences of commissioning and the impact this has on their wider work.

Chapter 7 specifically focuses on how some children's charities are not just surviving in this complex environment but indeed thriving. As the commissioning culture has matured within the public sector, so too have the responses from children's charities. Commissioning and policies regarding the charitable sectors engagement are full of multiple contradictions, confusion and complexity. Within this, we have seen two major opposing schools of thought manifest themselves. One, often driven by politicians and social policy decision makers, advocates for the commissioning and competition agenda as it increases choice and diversifies services by placing them outside of the public sector (for example, Sturgess et al, 2011; Blatchford and Gash, 2012). Another, often pushed by academics and practitioners, which is more critical, argues that commissioning is leading to the marketisation and privatisation of services (for example, Davies, 2008; Milbourne, 2009). Many children's charities, and indeed Commissioners, feel inhibited by these difficulties, however we also identify a group of children's charities, supported by particular Commissioners, who 'play the game', reinterpreting rules, and at times breaking rules, to secure what they consider the best outcomes for children. This dedication to securing their own, individual ideological bias, sets them apart from other actors in the field of early intervention and preventative services. While many children's charities experience significantly negative effects of Commissioning, several children's charities have successfully negotiated a pathway between conformity and dissent. As a result, they have successfully negotiated contracts and tenders to their advantage, or even bypassed commissioning processes altogether, to secure a mutually developed contract. This includes small-scale grants which were considered to 'go under the radar' to large-scale contracts. This survival does not happen in isolation, but instead requires a relational approach in which *some* children's charities deploy a range of tactics to secure additional advantage, while *some* Commissioners 'bend the rules' to facilitate advantage for certain children's charities who they believe will deliver a 'better' service for children. Thus, we conclude that commissioning is neither a fair or rational process and suggest that now is perhaps the time to reconsider this relationship.

Chapter 8, the conclusion of this book, discusses the potential way forwards. Collaborative commissioning as a concept is receiving increased attention from policymakers, practitioners and academics alike. As an emerging idea however it is still an unknown. In this concluding chapter we discuss the potential of collaborative commissioning as a way forwards for children's early intervention services and the continued unknowns surrounding it.

A note about language and definition

According to the UK Civil Society Almanac 2018 (NCVO, 2018) there are over 166,000 charities registered with the Charity Commission for England and Wales. However, of these charities, those with an annual income over £1 million account for 81% of the sector's total income, yet represent just 3% of the total number of charities. In contrast, charities with an income below £100,000 make up 82% of the sector in terms of numbers, but represent less than 5% of the total income. Therefore, the vast majority of the charitable sector is made up of small and micro organisations, while the major and super-major organisations (over £100 million income) dominate the landscape in terms of income and profile. Children and young people are the most common beneficiaries of charities, with 59% of charities listing them as one of their core beneficiaries. Based on submission of accounts to the Charity Commission, this figure does not encompass the vast number of other voluntary sector organisations including smaller enterprises that sit below the Charity Commission's radar: social enterprises, community groups, voluntary action groups and cooperatives.

Identifying a definition of the charitable sector is problematic and widely disputed. Politicians, policymakers and academics struggle to agree a commonly applied name. Consequentially a number of contested terms have emerged. For example, utilising the Wolfenden Committee's term 'the voluntary sector' arguably places too much emphasis upon 'volunteers', thus ignoring the vast number of employees within the sector. Alternatively, to capture both formal and informal activity some actors refer to the voluntary sector as 'the voluntary and community sector'. There is the Labour terminology of the 'third sector' which still resonates today and with it carries a number of political ideologies (Alcock, 2010), or the stricter term for charities registered with the Charities Commission and recognised as such by the Inland Revenue of the 'charitable sector', however this ignores the vast number of voluntary sector organisations who are not registered as charities. Additionally, we could use the Conservative terminology of 'civil society', which is unwieldy in application, or the American inspired 'not-for-profit sector'.

Such debates stem from political ideology, competing social, economic and cultural agendas and the differentiation of the application of criteria for definition. Famously termed as a 'loose and baggy monster' (Kendall and Knapp, 1995) the voluntary sector is a unique combination of service provision, advocacy, fundraising and campaigning, provided by voluntary sector organisations from large professionalised, bureaucratic entities to small networks and informal voluntary networks (Jas et al, 2002). As a sector in 2017, it employed approximately 2.7% of the UK workforce, that is over 880,000 individuals, and achieved an income of over £47.8 billion in 2015/16 (NCVO, 2018). However, definition per se is not the vital factor, what matters is 'adopting a characterisation that is appropriate to the purposes at hand' (Halfpenny and Reid, 2002: 536). In this book, we refer to the organisations directly engaged in the research as 'children's charities' and use the terms 'voluntary sector' and 'charitable sector' interchangeably throughout. This is in order to encompass the vast range of organisations from the formal, professionalised, bureaucratic organisations to the informal networks, while reflecting the need to differentiate it from the for-profit sector, commercial businesses and the state. Such a definition draws upon widest understanding of the voluntary sector and focuses upon the notion of the structural/ functional definition (Salamon and Anheier, 1992). Used by academics such as Billis and Glennerster (1998) and Kendall (2003) this definition identifies the voluntary sector as an assembly of organisations that are: '(a) formal or institutionalised to some extent; (b) private – institutionally separate from government; (c) non-profit-distributing – not returning profits generated to their owners; (d) self-government – equipped to control their own activities; (e) voluntary – involving some meaningful degree of voluntary participation' (Billis and Glennerster, 1998: 81).

PART I

Preventative services and children's charities: policy and paradigm shifts

1

New Labour, children's services and the third sector

This chapter provides an overview of the concept of prevention within child welfare, particularly under the New Labour government (1997–2010). Coming to power in 1997, New Labour placed considerable focus, and financial investment, on reducing child poverty and social exclusion, and increasing universal early intervention support and coordination between services. The role of the voluntary sector became mainstream in the provision of children's services, with the launch of several high-profile initiatives such as Sure Start, the Children's Fund and the Connexions service.

In this chapter we demonstrate that social policy encapsulates child welfare from several alternative perspectives, often corresponding to whatever the current dominant social conceptualisation of childhood and the welfare state may be within that period (Hardiker et al, 1989; 1991). Focusing on the concept of 'prevention' within child welfare and building on these shifting understandings of childhood, and the concerns for children, this chapter explores how social policy operationalised under the Labour government, developed strategies to tackle issues surrounding children and young people who are considered disadvantaged, vulnerable or at risk and mobilised the voluntary sector within this response.

Every Child Matters

Following on from the Children Act 1989, the Every Child Matters Green Paper (DfES, 2003) and the Children Act 2004 enshrined in law a commitment for state intervention in the private realm of the family. The Green Paper covered three principal themes: early intervention and effective prevention, supporting parents and carers, and accountability, integration and workforce reform. Furthermore, it articulated five outcomes that all children should achieve – *being healthy, staying safe, enjoying life and achieving, making a positive contribution*, and *achieving economic wellbeing*. With the aim of improving the wellbeing of all children, this paper set out the requirement for agencies and services to work together, share information effectively and in turn provide evidence against a set of performance indicators. The Every Child Matters Green Paper (DfES, 2003) and the following Every Child Matters: Change for children (DfES, 2004) were built upon evidence suggesting that early intervention would have the best outcomes and most positive impact for the life chances of children, highlighting the need for preventative services.

The Children Act 2004 delivered the legislative changes required to support this new agenda, including the promotion of agencies to work together and integration of education and children's social services within local authorities. Emphasising the need for services to cooperate and share information, the creation of Local Safeguarding Children Boards promoted and monitored the effectiveness of safeguarding among agencies working with children. These legislative changes saw the introduction of several new initiatives including 'Contactpoint', a database to capture the amount of contact children had with statutory services; development of shared assessment tools to support social work practitioners; and updating of statutory guidance for all professionals working with children to understand their responsibilities for the welfare and safeguarding of children. In addition, an existing holistic framework for assessing children in need, the Common Assessment Framework (CAF), was widely embedded and adopted across agencies (France et al, 2010).

Labour and tackling social exclusion of children

The establishment of the Social Exclusion Unit (SEU) in 1997 marked out the newly elected Labour Party's aspiration for change. Employing a range of individuals from across local government, the voluntary sector and business, the emphasis of the SEU was on the importance of joined-up thinking and working together. As such, the SEU defined social exclusion as 'a shorthand term for what can happen when people or areas suffer from a combination of linked problems such as unemployment, poor skills, low incomes, poor housing, high crime environments, bad health and family breakdown' (SEU, 1998). Recognising the multifaceted nature of social exclusion and committed to the idea of universal service provision, Labour sought to tackle this through five broad programmes (Percy-Smith, 2000). These included enabling people to work; dealing with issues such as crime and antisocial behaviour in poorer communities; integrated help for children and young people; access to services for those in the poorest areas; and making government work better.

Arguably, the establishment of the SEU brought social exclusion to the fore of government politics. In addition, Labour's promise to eradicate child poverty by 2020, further cemented their commitment to tackling this issue. A central report published by the SEU in 1997 identified three responses to tackle social exclusion. The first encompassed the 'New Deals' programme which targeted failing statutory services such as schools, health and crime prevention, and provided interventions to support identified socially excluded groups including lone parents, the unemployed and the disabled. The second response provided funding to support regeneration in perceived disadvantaged communities. The third response advocated a 'joined-up' working arrangement involving cross cutting policy teams. One of these policy teams, Policy Action Team 12 (PAT12) (SEU, 2000) highlighted several priorities to focus on regarding children and young people. PAT12 identified gaps in preventative services for children and young people, recommended a greater emphasis on early intervention, identified the need for greater coordination of local provision and recommended increased flexibility in the services provided to meet the needs of children and young people more effectively. In 2006, the SEU merged with the Prime Minister's Strategy Unit under the Cabinet Office. The new Social Exclusion Task Force launched off this platform to provide central government with strategic advice and policy analysis to tackle social exclusion.

With social exclusion firmly positioned as a major policy priority, backed up with a range of government initiatives, and a significant focus upon targeting children and young people deemed to be at risk of social exclusion, the stage was set for the launch of both support and preventative initiatives. Based on the recommendations from PAT12 and in keeping with child welfare reforms, three new initiatives were launched. These initiatives were Sure Start (targeted at children aged 0–5 years) in 1997, the Children's Fund (targeted at children aged 5–13 years in 2000 and Connexions service (targeted at young people aged 13–19 years) also created in 2000, all situated within a 'risk and protection-focused prevention paradigm' (France and Utting, 2005). Arguably all three of these programmes were established to 'reduce risk factors, build resilience, and promote protective factors within the domains of the family, school, and community, or with the individual child, intervening early to reduce the risks of future negative outcomes' (Evans and Pinnock, 2007: 22).

The government founded the Sure Start programme to help prevent social exclusion by targeting families with very young children. Initially specifically aimed at children living in poverty Sure Start facilitated cross-agency funding, in areas of deprivation, to facilitate the statutory sector, voluntary sector, community organisations and parents and families coming together to tackle inequalities at the earliest opportunity (Brown and Dillenburger, 2004). The central aim of this service was improving life chances through increased access to family support services, early intervention services and health advice (Eistenstadt, 2001). As an attempt of continued support through a child's life, established in 2000, the Children's Fund was a national preventative service initiative for children aged 5–13 years.

The Children's Fund initiative aimed to deliver 'preventative services which provide support for young people and their families before they reach crisis, with the aim of reducing the future probability of poor outcomes and maximising life chances' (CYPU, 2001: 7). Like the Sure Start programme, the initial model of delivery centred on locally established partnership setting priorities. Each local authority area had to draw together a local partnership made up of representatives from the local authority, voluntary and community sector, health, youth services, youth justice and other key stakeholders, to manage and oversee the programme delivery (CYPU, 2001). Funded from 2000 until 2008, in three waves, with a total budget of £960 million, much of the funding was ring fenced for the voluntary sector. Funding was released to each of the 149 local authority Children Fund partnerships following the acceptance of a plan by local partnerships. Central to the Children's Fund objective was the requirement, 'to provide additional resources over and above those provided through mainstream statutory funding, specific programmes and though specific earmarked funding streams. It should engage and support voluntary and community organisations in playing an active part and should enable the full range of services to work together' (NECF, 2004). This commitment solidified the relationship between the Children's Fund initiative and the voluntary sector. Unsurprisingly, as a result, the Children's Fund became a major source of funding support for voluntary sector organisations delivering early intervention services.

Central pillars of the New Labour approach

Central to the approach to children's services adopted by New Labour, were two core themes, Children's Trusts, to oversee strategic direction and accountability of services, and children's centres, to ensure universal and targeted access for all. The Children Act 2004 set out instructions as to how services should be governed by local authorities and how services should work together. It enshrined much of what was recommended by Laming (DoH, 2003) and established the statutory duty that required every local authority to work with partners, through Children's Trusts, to devise and implement strategies to improve outcomes for children aged 0–19 years. Children's Trusts existed as local partnerships bringing together the organisations responsible for services for children, young people and families in a shared commitment to improving children's lives.

The Children's Trust governance framework demanded that local authorities show greater accountability for decision making and spending, and involve children, young people and families in decisions that affect them. The aim of the Children's Trusts was to develop, at a senior level across the local authority, responsive and effective health, social care and education services for children (Fitzgerald and Kay, 2008) which was pivotal to the creation of Labour's Department for Children, Schools and Families (DCSF). To meet this demand the local authority had to develop existing services and commission new services (Fitzgerald and Kay, 2008) to facilitate joint planning and ensure arrangements for integrated working between agencies involved in the care and education of children.

Children's centres were established to act as a wrap-around service-hub, designed to ensure 'every child mattered'. At the local authority level children's centres developed from Sure Start children's centres which were based on a family support ethos (Featherstone et al, 2013), whereby children from deprived postcode areas were assured a nursery placement (Eisenstadt, 2011). Sure Start children's centres were located in areas of 'high disadvantage', and provided a service that gave access to 0–5 year old children for 10 hours a day, five days a week for 48 weeks of the year. In areas of 'less disadvantage' the offer provided was a 'drop in' arrangement with hours to 'suit local need' (Barker, 2009). As part of their offer, these centres hosted statutory and voluntary services for children and families including access to Job Centre Plus employment advice, various health services (with access to midwives and health visitors) and education services. In targeted areas further support was available including access to police and legal advice in a bid to tackle domestic violence. The links to employment services for parents included a joined-up approach to training providers, some of whom were also located in some children's centres. Signposting was also part of the children's centres' remit, to include benefits advice along with library services and relationship support, although these services may not have actually been provided on the site of the children's centre (Barker, 2009).

The children's centres arrangement to facilitate multi-agency working was replicated by organisations such as social care services and education that were physically and geographically restructured so that a variety of multi-agency workers shared buildings. New Labour's (1997–2010) intention was that any child who had needs identified under a 'common assessment framework' would be best served at a single point of access, by a lead professional and would have the support of a team around the child, as opposed to the child and their family being seen in isolation by a variety of professionals. Professionals were to share information with the aim to minimise risk by identifying a child's needs and responding to them before they potentially escalated.

Children's centres were 'intended to provide a universal service for families that should 'reflect local need' (Barker, 2009: 82; DfES, 2006), thus creating a governance arrangement that was a hybrid of a targeted universalism within service provision; a 'key component in the ECM agenda' (Barker, 2009: 88). Such support was not to last, between 2010 and 2018 around 1,000 children's centres were closed.

The third sector

Alongside the increased focus on partnership working within children's services, Labour promoted an opening up of public services, encouraging delivery of services outside of the public sector. When Labour first came to power in 1997, they brought with them the concept of 'the third sector'. Anthony Giddens propelled this term into public policy in his work *The third way* (1998). Giddens, a prominent leading British sociologist, suggested the reorganisation of views on modern society and politics (1979; 1984; 1998). The term 'third way' was essentially an attempt at developing a centrist platform which offered voters a potential pathway forwards from across the political spectrum as a balance between the free market economics presented by the neoliberal ideology and the social justice discourse presented from more left-wing liberal ideological frameworks. The term aimed 'to capture a new, and broader, notion of what could and should, be the focus of political and party attention' (Alcock, 2010: 158). Encapsulating this, a series of new institutions paved the way for the creation of the Office of the Third Sector (OTS) in 2006. The term 'third sector' brought with it a further redefinition and reconceptualisation of the voluntary sector. It sought to capture organisations acting within the voluntary sphere by broadening the definition to encompass the legally constituted charities, voluntary groups, faith-based charities, industrial and provident societies, social enterprises, cooperatives, community interest companies and companies limited by guarantee.

During the 1980s and 1990s, several of the threads from which Labour would build the framework for the concept of the third sector were already underway, propelled by the Conservative government. Arguably the most important of these threads was the work of an independent commission chaired by Nicholas Deakin, set up by the National Council for Voluntary Organisations (NCVO), who produced a report entitled 'Meeting the challenge of change: voluntary action in the 21st century' (Commission on the Future of the Voluntary Sector, 1996) commonly known as the Deakin Commission report. The Deakin Commission report mapped out a vision and principles for the voluntary sector over the following decade. However, largely perceived as reflecting the views of a team of 'representative bodies' and lacking in either forward thinking or critical analysis of the sector as a whole, the report was criticised as little more than a consensus document (Lewis, 1999). Although, considering the Conservative government in power at the time of its writing and with a general election on the horizon, it could have been framed as such deliberately (Kendall, 2000a). Nonetheless, the notion of partnership within the report and the suggestion of a 'concordat' as a mode of operationalising this partnership between the state and voluntary sector went beyond any of its predecessors, such as the Wolfenden Committee report. Kendall goes onto argue that with this mind it was more of a 'holding document' and its blend of 'timidity and innovation' could be 'ultimately argued as successful' and 'dynamic in the political context' (2000a).

Further to the establishment of a concordat the Deakin Commission report included several other recommendations which later came to fruition under Labour, including a new legal definition of charities, the establishment of taskforces to develop the concordat (later to be known as the Compact), alongside recommendations around tax issues for charities, capacity building and quality assurance. In total the report detailed 61 recommendations, with approximately half of them aimed at the government for action. Largely ignored by the Conservative government at the time, Labour welcomed these recommendations and they heavily influenced Labour thinking around the concept and politicisation of the third sector.

Therefore, for Labour the third way 'was intended to capture a rejection of public service policy planning that relied primarily on the state (as supposedly was the case with previous Labour governments) or the market (as had been the case under the Thatcher governments of the 1980s)' (Alcock, 2010: 163). Labour were keen to highlight a 'newness' in their thinking which offered a real alternative to previous administrations. Arguably, there was little real change promoting the notion of mixed state and market forces for the delivery of the most effective services possible. The promotion of the 'third way', with the development of the broader sector term of the 'third sector' created the possibility of a 'new space for a proactive role for the sector as a tailor-made alternative to both the state and the market' (Alcock, 2010: 164). The third sector therefore occupied a unique position, as neither state nor private sector; it was presented as a genuine alternative.

This 'mixed welfare' was widely promoted by Labour and thus the voluntary sector was pulled centrally into political and policy debates, a position it had not held before and would give to rise to a new relationship between the central and local government, and the voluntary sector. In his Fabian pamphlet (1998), Tony Blair, then Labour party leader, defined the 'third way' stating that it recognises the need for government to forge new partnerships with the voluntary sector. Blair argued that, whether in education, health, social work, crime prevention or the care of children, 'enabling' government strengthens civil society rather than weakening it, and helps families and communities improve their own performance … the state, voluntary sector and individuals working together (Blair, 1998: 14).

This commitment pulled the voluntary sector centre stage, mainstreaming their activity and engagement, or as Kendall (2009) termed it 'hyperactive mainstreaming' through a number of very proactive moves including the creation of new institutions, commissioning out services, partnership formations and a rise in political status. However, the role of the voluntary sector is underpinned by an economic discourse, which is potentially in a juxtaposition to the social justice discourse presented by the sector itself. As voluntary sector organisations increasingly engage in the delivery of policy, tensions arise between their responsibility to service users and participants versus the need to deliver services in an increasingly competitive and demanding market (Taylor-Gooby and Wallace, 2009).

During the 1980s and 1990s, much of the strategic interface between the state and the voluntary sector took place through the Voluntary Services Unit, located in the Home Office. The association with the Home Office presents this unit as having a remit of social control and policing. Labour rebranded this in 2001 as the Active Community Unit, and expanded its remit and budget significantly, allocating an additional £300 million three-year budget to support an infrastructure development support programme for the sector aimed at improving voluntary activity (Alcock, 2010). Shortly after, the creation of the Civil Renewal Unit focused on community action. The later merger of these two units, with a third unit, the Charities Unit, created the Active Communities Directorate. This expansion of both policy influence and budget remit sent a clear message to the voluntary sector in terms of both defining and mainstreaming voluntary sector activities. Similarly, in the Treasury in 2006, a new Charity and Third Sector Unit formed, and the Department of Trade and Industry (DTI) became the home to the newly formed Social Enterprise Unit (SEU). With the creation of the new institutions, also came the new legal structures. To incorporate organisations in the voluntary sector that traded as businesses, through reinvesting profits in the business and had clear social or environmental purposes, the term 'social enterprise' gained momentum. Partly to incorporate these as a legal form, community interest companies emerged. Community interest companies were introduced as a legal form under the Companies Act 2006. The formation of these new units and legal structures risked constructing a confusing landscape for policy creation and engagement of the voluntary sector. Thus in 2006 this was simplified and consolidated by the creation of the Office of the Third Sector (OTS), which was situated within the Cabinet Office, centralising the voluntary sector within the heart of government (Hilton, 2011) and securing this through the allocation of a Minister for the Third Sector. The creation of the OTS in 2006 confirmed and solidified Labour's deliberate attempts to 'expand the reach of policy intervention into areas not traditionally associated with the voluntary action in the country' (Alcock, 2010: 159). Alcock (2010) argues that one of the most significant features of the OTS was the remit of the third sector, rather than the voluntary sector. The term 'third sector' expands our understanding of the sector to encompass a variety of organisations beyond that of the traditionally understood charitable and voluntary organisations, to include community interest companies, social enterprises, community mutuals and cooperatives.

Further cementing Labour's commitment towards the third sector, the development of several 'horizontal' infrastructure and capacity building programmes, backed with significant investment emerged (Kendall, 2000a). The Deakin Commission Report had made numerous recommendations in light of the relationship between public agencies and the voluntary sector including the suggestion that there should be a governing concordat, a framework of guiding principles to oversee this relationship. This was realised when the Home Office published a national Compact in England (1998), providing a model for the development of the Compact in individual areas. Local Compacts reflected the relationships between separate public bodies, that is, the National Health Service, police, local authorities and the third sector. In a review of relevant policy and political literature, Kendall (2000a) argues that the notion of the Compact was 'completely without precedent, representing an unparalleled step in the positioning of the third sector in public policy' (Kendall, 2000a: 2). As such, this, combined with the institutional changes discussed, represented a 'clear step change' (Kendall, 2000a) for the relationship between the voluntary sector and the national government.

The Compact however was not a legal document; it was a proactive agreement, requiring all parties to willingly and actively participate. This led to several issues arising including different levels of participation by various agencies and third sector organisations due to capacity and ability. In tackling this, the government then set up the Compact Commission in 2007 to oversee the implementation and highlight good practice. As such, the Compact continued to gain momentum and became a key tool of engagement highlighting new government commitment to the engagement of the third sector, recognition of the need to work in partnership and integration of the voluntary sector into the political and economic discourse.

There was growing recognition of the need for infrastructure development within the voluntary sector to facilitate voluntary organisations to participate actively within the principles outlined within the Compact, including the ability to tender for contracts to deliver public services. This brought forth the debate of the marketization of the voluntary sector (Milbourne and Cushman, 2013). Further underpinning this, Labour committed to a number of investments to support the voluntary sector's growth and development, including establishing the Futurebuilders fund, initially £125 million over three years (2005–2008), which expanded to a total of £215 million and extended over a further three years (2008–2011). This funding provided grants and loans to assist voluntary organisations participating in the commissioning process. The delivery of the Futurebuilders programme was outsourced to a new independent agency in 2008, the Adventure Capital Fund, which in turn established the Social Investment Business (SIB) (Alcock, 2010). The SIB became the main source of government investment for the infrastructure and development of the third sector through administering a range of programmes including the £100 million Social Enterprise Investment for social enterprises tendering to deliver health and social care services, the £70 million Communitybuilders fund to provide support for smaller voluntary sector organsiations. The SIB also hosted the £150 million ChangeUp funding programme to support infrastructure development organisations, such as national charities like NCVO and local Councils for Voluntary Services.

In 2006, the responsibility of ChangeUp was handed to a new government agency established by the OTS called Capacitybuilders, a name that reflected the ongoing commitment by the government to build up the capacity of individual organisations to deliver services as part of the wider market. The public investment for the voluntary sector outside of government investment also continued to grow throughout the Labour term. The introduction of the National Lottery programme in the early 1990s, distributed additional funding from the sale of national lottery tickets to charities through a number of Big Lottery programmes. With a much larger pool of resources to access funding from, the size of the voluntary sector expanded, as did the culture of contractualism in relation to this funding. For example, within just one portion of the voluntary sector, general charities, there was a 28% increase in income from 2000 to 2007, with approximately just under one third coming from statutory sources (Kane et al, 2010).

Nonetheless, many critics do not believe that Labour delivered on the promises it set out in the 'third way' or for the voluntary sector as a whole. For example, the emphasis on contracting bought to the fore a focus on the relationship between government and the voluntary sector. The implementation of the Compact, which was set to provide a framework for the relations, appeared to lack impetus at points. Established in 1998, it took until 2002 for a senior civil servant to assume responsibility for the Compact, thus demonstrating its lack of political priority. It then took until 2003 for the completion of underpinning codes, until 2006 for the appointment of a commissioner and until 2007, a full nine years after the initial Compact was launched, for the Commission for the Compact to be established, a bespoke agency, which tried to meet a number of targets already missed (Zimmeck, 2010). It took a total of ten years from the launch of the Compact for the first Local Compact Annual Conference to be held and it was not until 2009 that the final local Compact was signed, which was a full five years later than the target date. In her examination of the history of the Compact, Zimmeck (2010) argues that the government failed to recognise the size of the task before them and provided insufficient financial investment, lacked meaningful engagement and failed to 'establish the credibility of arrangements for evaluating and resolving problems' (Zimmeck, 2010: 127). Carrington (2002) agrees, suggesting that the government did not show 'visible and enthusiastic engagement' (p 5) with the Compact and therefore undermined its credibility. Undermining credibility further internal governmental decisions such as the government terminating the 'Campaigning Research Programme', 'without warning and without consultation, shortly after naming the grant winners', (Zimmeck, 2010: 127) fundamentally went against the principles of the Compact. Secure funding agreements, which lasted for a minimum of three years in term and delivered full cost recovery, were central themes to the Compact. However, in 2007 the Commission for the Compact identified that only 54% of government contracts met this target (Diamond, 2007: 7) and 68% of charities reported having funding agreements of less than a year (Charity Commission, 2007a: 14). Alongside this in 2006, only 12% of charities reported achieving full cost recovery across all of their services, while 43% said that they had not achieved full cost recovery in any of their services (Charity Commission, 2007a: 10).

In summary, Labour's commitment to the third sector, to the policy development of the 'Third Way' and to the promotion of the mixed welfare state as a way of achieving this brought the voluntary sector to the centre of public policy. However, underpinning this was an accountability driven discourse that focused on outputs and outcomes. The development of this focus on outcomes as a 'what works' approach gave charitable organisations the opportunity to start bidding and tendering for services previously delivered by the state (Alcock and Kendall, 2010) through commissioning processes (explored in further depth in Part III). Nonetheless, the policy for an increased involvement by the voluntary sector in service delivery coupled with a local governance agenda to evolve the role of the voluntary sector in promoting citizenship and civic engagement was firmly established (Alcock and Kendall, 2010). The significant financial investment in, and the infrastructure development of, the voluntary sector attempted to make a reality of Blair's vision statement in 1998, when promoting support for the voluntary sector: 'They [voluntary sector organisations] enable individuals to contribute to the development of their communities. By so doing they promote citizenship, help to re-establish a sense of community and make a crucial contribution to our aim of a just and inclusive society' (Home Office, 1998: 1).

Despite the outlined issues and criticisms, throughout the 13 years in which Labour were in power, the voluntary sector and the state enjoyed an unprecedented close relationship. As argued, on election, Labour fought hard to present the 'Third Way' as new ideology which distanced it from previous Labour governments and the previous Conservative administration. However, though it is likely, as Alcock (2011) identifies, 'history may judge the New Labour era to have been a high-water mark in partnership between the state and the sector' (p 179) the distance between the 'Third Way' and the 'Big Society' is not as great as it would first appear. Therefore, in 2010, when Labour lost the general election and the Conservative-led Coalition came into power what really changed for relationship between the state and the voluntary sector? We explore this in depth in Chapter 2.

Conclusion

In this chapter we have outlined how policy and the governance of interdisciplinary discourse latterly emerged and became a particular configuration of Blair's New Labour Modernisation agenda. The immediate background to this is illustrated by what was termed 'the new children's workforce' (Barker, 2009) whereby policy named a wide variety of careers and jobs from both statutory and voluntary services. The consequence (or enactment) of these policies involved changes in emphasis in the way accountability, participation and inclusion were managed. In theory, the aim of the Common Assessment Framework (CAF) was to provide an assessment tool that could be used by non-social work professional employees in education, children's social care, health and allied professions. The introduction of the Common Assessment Framework and the Every Child Matters agenda marked an intent by government to ensure that agencies worked together in meeting the needs of all children. Its emphasis was corporate responsibility for all children with the intention of safeguarding children and early intervention when necessary, rather than reacting with too little too late after neglect had taken place.

As we have explored in this chapter, Labour's initiatives, reforms, policies and services for children, young people and families centred on the concept of social exclusion (Artaraz et al, 2007).

There were several influential factors, which underpinned this, one of which was the ongoing and recognised poor performance by the UK in terms of Child Poverty in comparison to European counterparts. In 2007, the United Nations Children's Fund (UNICEF) published the much-debated report, Child Poverty in Perspective. This report suggested that children in the UK were among the unhappiest, most materially impoverished and suffering the poorest relationships within Europe. Having pledged in 2000 to eradicate child poverty by 2020 this was a difficult political blow for the Labour government, who had dedicated a significant amount of political attention to tackling social exclusion as a means of eradicating poverty. However, this ranking used data collected in 2000. An updated version of this research based predominantly on data collected 2009 to 2010 indicated an improved position with UK rising from 21st out of 21 in 2000/2001 to a mid-table position of 16th out of 29 in 2009/2010 (UNICEF, 2013).

With the continued rising concerns about poverty and the long-term impacts of social exclusion, the national government and local authorities sought to provide preventative interventions for children considered to be socially excluded, and thus likely to experience negative outcomes as an adult, to divert them instead onto an inclusive trajectory. As part of the response to this problem, Labour launched two central programmes, Sure Start and the National Children's Fund programme. The Sure Start programme was established in 1998 with the aim of 'giving children the best possible start in life' by increasing and improving childcare, early education and access to family support (Glass, 1999). Targeted at families with children aged 0 to 5 the programme particularly focused upon outreach and community development work. Initially planned as a ten-year programme of support through nationally-controlled Sure Start local programmes, in 2003 Labour outlined a longer-term intention to support the work, and in 2005 transferred control of the programme to local government, setting up Sure Start children's centres. This programme has continued to the present day, although it has not gone unscathed under the Coalition and Conservative reforms, with a number of councils announcing cuts to their Sure Start programmes in 2010/11 and over 1,000 closures of children's centres across the country.

Coupled with the Sure Start programme, was the National Children's Fund programme. Launched in 2000, this programme set out to tackle social exclusion and poverty among 5–13 year-olds. With a total of £960 million allocated between 2000 and 2008 this programme targeted the lower end of social exclusion, when children were identified as requiring intervention to prevent escalation of issues that did not require professional or institutionalised services. In this context, preventative services have been widely assumed to be an area best addressed by the voluntary sector, and therefore distribution of this budget targeted supporting voluntary sector providers in delivering these services (Artaraz et al, 2007; Morris et al, 2009). This assumption is thought to have been 'fed perhaps by the level of responsiveness and flexibility shown by the voluntary and community sector to venture in the "new frontier" of preventative services defined by the (then) current child welfare agenda' (Artaraz et al, 2007: 308). When the National Children's Fund programme came to an end in 2008, budgets were pooled within the local authorities and distributed against local priorities outlined in the local Children and Young People's Plan. Multi-agency working became a common phrase under Labour with the 'duty to cooperate' enshrined in the Children Act 2004 section 10, which saw the formation of Children's Trust Boards in all local authority areas and, in most areas, subsequent Local Children's Trusts Boards established under these to represent the local communities. Each Children's Trust Board had to produce and monitor a local Children and Young People's Plan. However, as we explore in subsequent chapters, this intensive focus on and funding for local support was short lived.

2

Contemporary preventative services, coalitions and the Conservatives

In this chapter we explore contemporary children's services, discussing how the persuasive logic of prevention has been adopted in more modern service delivery. Focusing specifically on the early 2010s, we map the shift from the Conservative flagship project of the Big Society, to the renewed localism project of the Civil Society Strategy. The links between the societal hardening of focus, from universal provision to the targeting of preventative services will be delineated, and the role of the voluntary sector in the delivery of these services will be discussed. The aim is to highlight the lived realities of service delivery for children, which will then be discussed over the remainder of this book.

The Big Society to civil society

The Big Society was promoted by the Conservative government as a solution to the financial crisis which had gripped the UK and much of Europe since 2008. In 2009, David Cameron initially outlined the Conservative's vision for the 'Big Society' in his Hugo Young Memorial Lecture, controversially presenting Labour as 'big government' but still following themes that resonated with the 'third way'. At that time, Cameron suggested: 'Because we believe that a strong society will solve our problems more effectively than big government has or ever will, we want the state to act as an instrument for helping to create a strong society … Our alternative to big government is the Big Society' (Cameron, 2009).

The concept of the Big Society remained confusing. It was an integral part of the Conservative/Liberal Democrats Coalition's plans, on their election in 2010, for public sector service provision retraction and emphasised the voluntary sector and 'civil society' delivering public services in a more cost-efficient manner during an economic downturn. For the Conservatives, the Big Society focused on providing answers to the central problems that they argued faced Britain under Labour rule. Citing the financial crisis, decreases in employment and increases in poverty, they argued that Britain was 'broken' financially, socially and politically (Evans, 2011). The concept of the Big Society suggested that by supporting civil action and community spirit, the Big Society could mend Britain socially. By finding cheaper alternatives in the delivery of services in the public sector and helping the unemployed back to work the Big Society could mend Britain financially. Finally, by empowering the voters to hold those in power to account, the Big Society could mend Britain politically (Evans, 2011).

The Coalition was keen to demonstrate that the Big Society was a shift away from the previous government's concept of the third sector. This was highlighted by a change in language, dropping the rather condescending term 'third sector' as Cameron (2009) referred to it and adopting an ideologically driven narrative that discussed the voluntary sector as the 'first sector' and more commonly 'civil society'. Following this the Office for Third Sector was quickly renamed the 'Office for Civil Society' (OCS). Though retained in the Cabinet Office its primary functions were to enable voluntary sector organisations to work with the state, allowing the free flow of resources to the sector and make the management of these organisations easier. Some new forms of funding emerged including the establishment of the Big Society Bank and Social Impact Bonds. However, the 2010 public spending review triggered a number of major spending cuts that would directly affect the voluntary sector. For example, the OCS had its budget cut by 60%, the loss of quangos such as Capacitybuilders and the Commission for Compact; horizontal funding programmes developed by Labour such as Futurebuilders, the Social Enterprise Investment fund and Change up came to an end and there was a significant cut in support for strategic infrastructure partners. Prior to feeling the impact of the public spending review, the voluntary sector had already experienced £118 million worth of cuts in funding from local authorities in England between May and September of 2010 alone, with many more following (Alcock et al, 2012). The voluntary sector was being simultaneously encouraged to tender to deliver services on behalf of local authorities and the government, while being warned about being too 'dependent' upon government funding and therefore at risk in an economic downturn (Evans, 2011). According to the NCVO Almanac (2014) between 2010/11 and 2011/12 the total funding allocated by government to the voluntary sector fell by 8.8% in real terms. This was a funding reduction of £1.3 billion, in which social services organisations, and education and training organisations saw the largest reductions of £361 million and £230 million respectively. Health organisations experienced a slightly smaller loss and only international organisations saw a slight overall increase.

Arguably used to differentiate the public spending cutbacks from those of the 1980s (Bach, 2012), the term 'Big Society' has appeared at times to attempt to become all-encompassing, to represent both public spending cuts and to commission ineffectively run public services out to voluntary sector providers and social enterprises. The rhetoric surrounding the Big Society has been used to 'soften' an otherwise harsh image of the Conservative party (Albrow, 2012), communicating to a wider audience and attempting to show an empathetic and understanding Conservative party. Within this, there was the suggestion of rebuilding civic duty and voluntary action to fill in any voids. However, there was no single definition or shared understanding of the term 'Big Society'. Indeed, the House of Commons Public Administration Select Committee (PASC, 2011) highlighted lack of understanding surrounding the concept of Big Society and furthermore drew attention to the potential negative impacts for the voluntary sector including loss of sector independence. Furthermore, the committee drew attention to the questionable nature of the voluntary sector being the 'cheaper' alternative (PASC, 2011). In contrast to this, due to the vagueness surrounding the Big Society, many commentators dismissed the concept as little other than a 'smokescreen' for continual and unrelenting cuts and privatisation of public services (Sage, 2012; Whitfield, 2012). Bach (2012) argues that the government has attempted to distance the concept of Big Society from numerous austerity measures since the comprehensive spending review in 2012. However, when almost three quarters of the reduction to the deficit were set to come from reductions in public spending it is difficult to separate the two. Though these austerity measures have had significant impact on the workforce and services of the public sector, our interest in the concept of Big Society turns to one of examining the impact on the voluntary sector.

During the May 2010 general elections, in the Conservatives' manifesto, the policy agenda of Big Society had three main themes, 'community empowerment', 'opening up public services' and 'social action'. These translated respectively into localism and decentralisation of power to local communities; public services reform where public services would be commissioned out to charities and private sector business; and programmes to engage individuals as active citizens within their communities, for example the National Citizen Service for 16-year-olds (Macmillan, 2013a). The concept of Big Society has however had a problematic start with what appear to be several re-launches (Macmillan, 2013b) and ongoing critical commentary and academic analysis, despite the decline of policy statements and speeches within which it features (Sage, 2012; Scott, 2011). However, it is possible to extract some of the government's intentions through these policy strands. First, the emphasis upon localism and decentralisation focused on the enhancement of the role of the local community. Bach argues that though localism is an 'innocuous term' the intent is 'to encourage competition and choice' (Bach, 2012: 404) at a local, service provision level. Not only is this opposed to the authority of locally elected local authorities, the Localism Bill (now the Localism Act) went further to suggest and encourage voluntary sector organisations and local communities to oppose and challenge existing service provision, and to tender to manage and deliver the services themselves. The government was explicit about this within the guidance on the Localism Bill which aims to 'identify and tackle public sector monopolies across the board ... all public services should be open to diverse provision' (HM Government, 2011: 9). The second policy strand focused upon the provision of public services delivered by a diverse range of organisations. In particular, social enterprises, mutuals, cooperatives and charities were encouraged to expand within this area. The 'Right to Provide' initiative which aims to 'unleash the power of employee ownership and control' had a slow take up (Bach, 2012). The third strand of the policy development couples the intent to increase volunteerism among individuals and communities, with the increasing role of the voluntary sector. The provision of funding was intended to help resolve the funding deficits due to the economic downturn and local authority cuts. Underpinning this, the Coalition aimed to train and up-skill 5000 'community organisers' to facilitate local community action to tackle local and larger social issues. The question arises, was this the Coalition's way of empowering communities, or abdicating responsibility? Critics argue (for example, Bach, 2012) that these three policy strands have been underpinned by few actual initiatives but rather have been used 'to weave together disparate policies and its imprecision may serve to disguise the extent of marketization and service withdrawal associated with the Coalition's public service agenda' (Bach, 2012: 404).

By 2012 the term 'Big Society' was fading fast from the public realm, more commonly replaced by terms such as 'civil society'. This was epitomised further by the publication of the government's Civil Society Strategy in 2018. With debates about Britain's withdrawal from the European Union in full swing and divisions within civil society on the rise, it is unsurprising that the government launched a strategy which called for unity and support among communities. The strategy itself was an important step, as it delivered a uniting thread across government departments about the importance of civil society in both tackling contemporary problems and developing innovative solutions. The central tenet of the strategy is that communities can be helped to thrive, through the strengthening of 'five foundations of social value', people, places, the social sector, the private sector and the public sector.

The first theme, people, seeks to encourage individuals to have more control over their futures and communities, and to support them in taking action on issues which they care about. This taps into established programmes such as the national *#iwill* campaign, which encourages young people to volunteer, and place-based social action programmes, which encourages local responses to local needs. Fundamentally, the government wants more people who use public services involved in running those services. The second theme, places, seeks to encourage communities to be responsible for where they live. As part of this the government launched a new 'Innovation in Democracy' programme, to encourage new ways of individuals being involved in decision making which affects them. The third theme, the social sector, focuses on ensuring that voluntary organisations have impact on and help shape policy. The fourth theme, the private sector, seeks to encourage businesses to be socially and environmentally responsible. Finally, the fifth theme, the public sector, outlines a commitment to more collaborative commissioning processes. While not entirely new, more a re-hash of previous promises, commitments and dedicated funding, the strategy distinctly builds on the ideology set out in the earlier Conservative plans, around the Big Society and localism. However, it is a vision of sorts, but without the detail of how longer-term issues around funding, commissioning and reducing public sector funds are to be addressed, and it is likely to face some of the very same criticisms levelled at the Big Society.

Conservatives, children and early intervention

In 2010 with the establishment of the Coalition government came a range of structural and policy changes for children's services. Arguing that the Children's Trust Boards (see chapter 1) were over prescriptive, statutory guidance on these boards was withdrawn in 2010, meaning that there was no longer a statutory requirement for local authorities to produce a Children and Young People's Plan (LGA, 2010). The requirement of a Children's Trust Board was then removed altogether. Further changes followed, including the withdrawal of the ContactPoint database in 2010, the national Children's Workforce Development Council was wound up in 2012 and Ofsted's powers and functions were reviewed. However, the Coalition made some concrete attempts in committing to meet the needs of what it defined as 'vulnerable' children and young people, promoting a mixed welfare economy of statutory, voluntary and private sector providers. In 2010 the Coalition government commissioned the high profile and influential Munro Report (Munro, 2011) which argued for early intervention 'to avoid costly interventions' (Munro, 2011: 22). Echoing Allen's (2011a) desire for 'evidence-based practice', Munro (2011) advocated for a more child centred approach to child protection and a focus on partnership working. Alongside this in 2012 the Institute for Public Policy Research published 'A long division: Closing the attainment gap in England's secondary schools' (Clifton and Cook, 2012). This paper argued heavily in favour of early intervention provision, suggesting that unless children started school on a 'level playing field', schools and academies could not close the attainment gaps between the rich and poor. This paper echoed Allen's (2011a) first Early Intervention publication in that it placed a heavy emphasis on 'school and life readiness'. In February 2013, the Department for Education and the Early Intervention Foundation consortium agreed funding and signed a contract to create a new and independent Early Intervention Foundation (EIF), which was launched in April 2013, and became an independent charity in July 2013. They applied the following definition to early intervention:

> Early Intervention is about addressing the root causes of social disadvantage, ensuring that everyone is able to realise their full potential by developing the range of skills we all need to thrive. It is about getting extra, effective and timely interventions to all babies, children and young people who need them, allowing them to flourish and preventing harmful and costly long-term consequences. (EIF, 2013)

This definition resonates strongly with Labour's definition of social exclusion, as do the solutions focusing on a model of social investment. However, this definition places greater emphasis upon early intervention in terms of both risk factors and age of children. The Munro Report (Munro, 2011), highlighted the term 'early help' as a positive replacement for the term 'early intervention'. Munro (2011) identified this as a term that suggested a working together of professional services and families, rather than professional services intervening and 'doing to' families as implied by early intervention. Considered as a more positive and progressive term than 'early intervention' (Frost et al, 2015), early help is defined as 'an ambiguous term, referring both to help in the early years of a child or young person's life and early in the emergence of any stage in their lives' (Munro, 2011: 69). What is important here is that Munro argued that early help was a societal 'moral imperative' (Munro, 2011) to minimise suffering and would help achieve cost savings by preventing problems rather than trying to reverse damage later on in individuals' lives. What is important is that the Munro Report reinforced the role of the voluntary sector, suggesting that engagement of families was central to their work.

In a period of economic decline, however, long-term preventative services moved down the list of priorities in favour of more targeted intervention. For example, through continued commitment to early intervention, Waldegrave (2013) highlighted the fact that children's centres, a statutory provision to provide universal and early support to families, experienced on average a 28% decrease in their funding between 2010 and 2012, with more significant cuts to follow. Indeed by 2018, over 1,000 children's centres had closed because of funding shortages.

Funding cuts inevitably result in fewer services and a more targeted approach being adopted (Waldegrave, 2013). The ideological notion that the voluntary sector will be able to attract other funding to achieve this then becomes increasingly important. To put this risk into perspective, in 2015 the National Children's Bureau reported an overall 55% reduction in early intervention funding under the Coalition government (2010–2015), which equates to cuts of £1.8 billion per year. By 2018, this funding slump had deepened, with figures from the National Audit Office showing a £763 million slump in funding for children and family support since the Coalition government was first elected in 2010, while funding for services for young people has fallen by £855 million. Alongside this, according to the Institute of Fiscal

Studies (IFS) (2018), since 2010 schools have experienced an 8% decline per pupil funding, coupled with rising costs.

The assumption that the voluntary and private sectors could replace this funding was crucial to the success of the Big Society and the subsequent Civil Society strategy. Indeed, despite widespread protest, the current Conservative government insisted that no more funding was available for children and education services. Therefore, the voluntary sector becomes a critical partner in its assumed ability to attract, recruit and retain volunteers over that of public and private sector organisations. Coote (2011) argues that this key premise, that voluntary organisations can replace paid labour with unpaid labour through voluntarism, is fundamentally flawed. Furthermore, the assumption that withdrawal of state funding from voluntary organisations will be replaced by philanthropy, donations and voluntarism action is unproven (Albrow, 2012). Additionally, this risks the exploitation of the fundamental concept of voluntary action which is the giving of one's skills, money and time as a gift and risked reinvigorating a postcode lottery, as areas within which people have the time and means to 'gift' do not correspond areas of 'need' (Evans, 2011).

The evolving discourse of prevention

Considering the challenges posed by the ongoing political shifts about who should support vulnerable groups in society, the discourse of prevention has also experienced changes. Though welcomed overall across children's services, Labour's recognition and definition of social exclusion and thus their concern with child poverty has been widely debated. Labour clearly located the concept of prevention within the context of social exclusion. With this came the conceptualisation of children deemed to be 'at risk' and factors associated with the 'at risk' child. Labour started from the premise of concern for all children and young people's wellbeing. The repeated emphasis within this framework was upon children who were considered to be particularly at risk of social exclusion and poor outcomes. Morris et al (2008) suggested 'these children are seen to present real challenges to the political aspirations for socially and economically viable citizens, and as such, additional interventions have been proposed as necessary to ensure that the investment in childhood does deliver later benefits' (p 30). This social investment model requires early intervention in order to prevent future burdens on the state constructs children as future 'investments'. Critics of this approach (for example, Prout, 2000; Lister, 2003) have suggested that the model adopted by Labour focused too much on a model of social investment, constructing children as an investment for our future. Rather than focusing upon tackling inequality and redistribution of wealth and opportunity, a social investment model focuses upon a political version of social inclusion and draws upon education as the means and vehicle into future employability. Such an approach not only suggests the perceived inter-changeability between social exclusion and poverty but also, as critics argue (for example, Fawcett et al, 2004), neglects the wellbeing of a child. Perversely, by targeting groups identified as at risk, children may suffer from stigmatisation that could heighten their risk of social exclusion in the future (Fawcett et al, 2004).

Interpretation of the discourse surrounding the issue of 'risk' presents several challenging concepts that are not helpful to the development of a child. Therefore, many academics and practitioners favour the concept of 'resilience' as a term that focuses more directly on the wellbeing of the child and the development of skills and attributes that help them cope with difficult circumstances. Broadly speaking, the concept of resilience focuses on an on-going process between the individual and the social context within which they exist (Howard et al, 1999). Defined by Fonagy et al (1994) as 'normal development under difficult circumstances' (p 233), resilience stresses the importance of the relationship between the child and their family, and the child's ability to engage with protective factors, with their family's support, to offset the risks. Throughout the Labour term there was a growing pool of evidence that suggested the importance of focusing upon the resilience of the community or family, as well as the individual (Mackey, 2003). For example, Gilligan (1999) highlighted the role of communities and peer groups in providing children with social support networks, helping to establish resilience factors. Therefore, Labour's focus on child welfare policy, social exclusion and resilience led to a framework of interventions that aimed to take a more holistic approach. Communities and service providers aimed to provide community-based interventions, which were integrated and involved children, young people and their families in a participative approach (Evans and Pinnock, 2007). The 'risk, resilience and protection-focused prevention paradigm' (France and Utting, 2005) therefore became a key feature of the national Children's Fund programme, although the long-term benefits of such interventions remain unclear (Evans et al, 2006; Frost et al, 2015).

The shift in the notion of prevention from the risk of being significantly harmed, to the risk of being socially excluded saw the rise of several new policy discourses. Prior to this prevention was more commonly used in the context of preventing harm within the fora of child protection. As Little et al (2003) identified, this more commonly referred to the avoidance of a child maltreatment. The launch of Every Child Matters (DfES, 2003) and the subsequent, Every Child Matters: Change for Children (DfES, 2004) saw a significant shift in the conceptualisation of 'at risk'. This new articulation of 'at risk' was more likely to focus upon children and young people experiencing poor outcomes through poor educational attainment, lower social participation, demonstrating poor health or anti-social behaviours (Morris et al, 2009). This suggests that the social construction of the term 'at risk' determines children as vulnerable or at risk whose circumstances are not in keeping with the dominant middle class in either culture, values, family, structures, language or appearance (Howard et al, 1999). Risk factors, however, continuously remain difficult to identify with little consensus about what measurements to use, and a continued lack of evidence about causal links between identified risk factors and the future outcomes of the child (Hansen and Plewis, 2004). The core focus of children within preventative type services prior to the Every Child Matters agenda tended to be, for example, those who were in the care system or considered disabled. The Every Child Matters agenda fundamentally changed the discourse of prevention to one that was concerned with the needs of all children, introducing a new conceptual framework for risk. For those working with children and young people this presented 'a series of tensions between historical responsibilities for children who may suffer significant harm, and new experiences for holistic responses to children and young people' (Morris et al, 2009: 33).

The construction of 'good' and 'bad' parenting within the prevention discourse is equally as important. With the introduction of initiatives such as Sure Start, which partly focused on parenting and thereby positively influencing children's trajectories from a young age, and the National Academy for Parenting Practitioners, highlighting the preference for shared and pooled knowledge about good parenting, there was a clear aim of establishing and enforcing a political version of good parenting norms and values. Gillies (2005) suggested that this removed the discussions of parenting away from societal cause, such as poverty or social injustice, and instead focused upon individual engagement. Gillies (2005) argues that this is a change in preventative discourse, seeing those 'at risk' as both perpetrators and victims of their own exclusion, further arguing that in the context of parenting and families the path to social inclusion reflects middle-class values and culture. As a result, those parents not demonstrating politically approved parenting approaches require 'parenting support' and new legal and punitive powers that aimed to 'punish' parents who failed to deliver to these standards. Walters and Woodward (2007) suggests that this shift in discourse has seen the 'needs' of parents of vulnerable children moved aside while their 'responsibilities' become the dominant feature. Morris et al's (2008) literature review of 'whole family approaches' which sought to help overcome or prevent social exclusion revealed an almost one-dimensional focus on parenting activities, mainly focused on the mother and her role in securing positive outcomes for her children. When translated at a policy level this focus reflects the political concern of social exclusion transferring through generations, with children replicating behaviours of their socially excluded parents.

As the Labour term evolved, the notion of targeting families and particularly those families considered to be most at risk of social exclusion increased (Morris and Barnes, 2008). The idea of the 'normal' family dominated the social policy discourse (France et al, 2010). The imagery of the hard working, socially participative and economically active family arguably reinforced and maintained marginalisation of those 'other' families who failed to conform (Morris et al, 2009). Though Labour heavily focused on these families, as Levitas (2005) noted, there was little data gathered from these families to support such assumptions. With families highlighted as a key concern in Every Child Matters and subsequent initiatives, there was a shift in focus to those families perceived as being the 'most disruptive'. This focus provided the backdrop for publications such as the 'Think Family' series from the SEU (Morris et al, 2008) and marked a shift in discourse from the more holistic approach outlined in Every Child Matters, to a vastly interventionist approach which required 'forceful sanctions' to ensure compliance and a return to social acceptability (Morris et al, 2009). Underpinned by the 'Respect' agenda highlighting the need for intensive family intervention programmes, there was a focus on tackling poor parenting and the provision of positive activities for vulnerable children and young people. Therefore, the trajectory of prevention discourse appeared to be moving away from holistic service provision for the wellbeing of children and towards providing 'treatment' for the socially unacceptable.

Within this discourse of prevention, under Labour there was a move away from the concept of social exclusion and addressing the consequences of the wider societal problem, towards that of addressing individual problematic families. This gave room for the Social Exclusion Task Force to drive forward the Family Pathfinder pilots (Cabinet Office, 2008), targeting these families through multi-agency responses, and thus a greater distinction between mainstream or universal services, and targeted services emerged. Some critics have argued that this shift in discourse poses a greater threat to these 'hard to reach families'. The lack of focus on the structural and cultural context surrounding these families has, some argue, led to 'defeated' families (Krumer-Nevo, 2003). Defeated families are those who have been marginalised by society due to economic, social and cultural forces and then let down by the services which have tried to serve them through intensive interventions which have only had partial impact, resulting in these families continuing to experience social and economic deprivation. In short, between 1997 and

2010, the policy discourse around prevention experienced a specific shift from the concepts of social exclusion and the need to promote social inclusion, to those of social investment and economic decision making, where decisions focused on the greatest investment would have the greatest impact. Though it is clear that the concept of social investment was entrenched in the preventative discourse of the 'third way' (Giddens, 1998) its significance and status only increased over Labour's time in power.

This concept of social investment was further developed by the Conservatives, based on the foundational ideas of Labour's 'third way', which advocated active citizenship and community participation within the concept of Cameron's 'Big Society'. The Big Society ideology was based upon the notion of communities and families taking responsibility for themselves, for the overall benefit of society. In his examination of the social investment model, Gray (2013) observes that while social inclusion, rather than exclusion, still exists as a concept within preventative services it has shifted away from the previous rhetoric of social and community participation to one of economic participation through the act of work, or seeking to work. Jenson (2010) suggested that the concept of social investment which was beginning to dominate prevention discourse saw a shift from the idea of 'protecting' families and children from harm, to making people more integrated within society and eliminate those who remain dependent upon welfare. This notion was heavily based upon the concept of establishing and increasing human and social capital enabling people to become fully integrated and contribute to society. As Gray states, 'founded on psychological research on human cognitive and personality development, social investment moves the focus of social policy away from remedial welfare to early childhood education and care' (2013: 2). Continuing in a similar rhetoric to where the Labour party left off, investing in children as future socioeconomic actors and investing in the concept of the good parent remained at the forefront of preventative policy discourse. In keeping with the previous Think Family agenda, the Troubled Families approach launched by the Conservatives in 2011 epitomised this social investment approach. Focusing multi-agency teams on the 400,000 most 'troubled' families in Britain, the project aims to 'turn around' these families in order to successfully integrate them into 'normal' society. The expectation was that for every £4,500 (one-off annual investment) spent on families, a saving of £15,000 per year would be achieved.

Allen (2011a; 2011b) highlighted a number of individual level initiatives, while providing the backdrop for the continued development of this preventative discourse. Whereas Labour heavily invested early on in the concept of social exclusion, the Coalition remained more concerned with the concept of early intervention as a vehicle of prevention. The wider approach to prevention within these reports heavily leans upon early engagement of children, at the earliest stage possible, in order to ensure that they are most likely to pursue positive trajectories. The motivations and methods of such an approach has, however, been heavily criticised by some. The emphasis on parenting is once again strongly significant. Placing early intervention central to the government rhetoric on children and families seemingly provided a smooth transition from the Labour Every Child Matters agenda. However, the wider idiom surrounding this, critics argued, created a fundamentally different discourse for prevention, which appeared to suggest 'contempt for poor and marginalised families' (Garrett, 2014: 83). The approach of Michael Gove, the Secretary of State for Education, 2010 to 2014, to early intervention and social work appears to shift to one of wanting to 'rescue' children from these poorly performing and socially marginalised parents. In a speech in 2012 he stated:

> In all too many cases when we decide to leave children in need with their biological parents we are leaving them to endure a life of soiled nappies and scummy baths, chaos and hunger, hopelessness and despair. These children need to be rescued, just as much as the victims of any other natural disaster. (Gove, 2012)

This additional shift in prevention discourse appears to some critics to further support the rise of the neoliberal ideology set out by Margret Thatcher in 1979 when she infamously stated, 'there is no such thing as society ... only the individual and his family'. The impact on social values that this had was significant. As Couldry (2011) suggests, the pursuit of independence, personal responsibility, self-interest and recognition of the importance and almost sanctity of the market became the commonly held beliefs for maximising the wellbeing of people. Examining the politicisation of relationships within the family sphere, Gillies (2014) argues that these neoliberal values 'permeated' through the Labour preventative discourse, setting aside the importance of relationship bonds, love and care in favour of technical approaches to the assessment of 'parenting skills'. The introduction of parenting orders in Labour's 1998 Crime and Punishment Disorder Act saw a clear step towards greater involvement of the state in family life, with an apparent assertion that some parents 'wilfully' neglected their responsibilities (Grover, 2008). This theme, Gillies argues, has continued into the current government and that this apparent concern for responsible parenting and the children's wellbeing and protection 'have been appropriated to justify a highly regulatory approach to family policy, eventually morphing into the distinct doctrine of "early intervention" under the auspices of the [then] current Conservative-led Coalition government' (Gillies, 2014: 205). This suggests a view of intervention being more about the individual, focusing on personal decisions rather than being the victim of structural inequalities. Gillies further develops this argument by suggesting that the prevention discourse, in continuing to move towards a neoliberal understanding of early intervention, is used as a 'political rallying point', targeting poor families to break a perceived cycle of deprivation, while in practice personalising and normalising inequality by making individual parents accountable, under the auspices of caring about children's wellbeing. As Gillies states: 'in cementing a broader shift away from state support towards a social investment model, the principle of early intervention marks an ideological convergence between traditional conservatism and economic liberalism, galvanising a cross-party political consensus in the process' (2014: 205). However, she further suggests that this doctrine is increasingly unstable, based on poor ideas, lack of evidence-based policy and the pursuit of ideological policy.

Reay (2012) argues that the cultural context surrounding parenting and child wellbeing increasingly embraces this individualistic and competitive neoliberal approach with 'good' parents being increasingly the 'good' consumer, evaluating services and products with rigour and pursuing all avenues to ensure that their child succeeds. This ideology of 'parentocracy' presented by Reay focuses on the perceived gold-standard of parenting which is largely child-centred, gender specific and heavily reliant upon mothers nurturing children's emotional wellbeing and self-confidence. Such an approach ensured class-specific approaches were 'held to account for the social and structural positions they reflect' (Gillies, 2014: 211). However, Gillies goes on to argue that most of the central claims that support the parent-centric approach dominating preventative discourse, remain unproven and undefined. This includes Alan Milburn over-claiming Blanden's (2006) research citing that 'parenting is four times more influential than socio-economic background', though regularly re-printed in the media and used to support policy decisions, the original evidence source does not actually suggest this link as starkly (Gillies, 2014). Feinstein's (2003) study included a secondary analysis of a cohort of people born in the 1970s and relayed interesting findings about the significance of class from an early age in determining outcomes for children. However, there was no identified link to the impact of parenting in this data. Perhaps most famously was Allen's (2011a) complete misrepresentation of longitudinal neuroscience studies, which he claimed demonstrated the huge and significant impact of neglect on a child's brain development. The study in fact was based upon extreme cases of neglect far beyond that of the reach of early intervention services. However, Allen visually and literally used this research to suggest significant links between 'poor' parenting and a child's physical development in *Early intervention: The next steps* (2011a), and was subsequently accused as using a 'scientific vehicle for public relations campaign to promote early childhood programs more for rhetorical, than scientific reasons' (Bruer, 2011: 2). However, this research continued to be widely cited in the media though the premise was proved flawed. Furthermore, the continuation of a 'scientific' approach to early intervention continues to be part of the early intervention discourse, for example as Allen states: 'Too few of the Early Intervention Programmes currently being tried in the UK have been rigorously evaluated, making it difficult for the public sector and impossible for the private sector to invest with any confidence' (2011a: 68).

Thus, there has been a focus on randomised controlled trials to 'prove' the impact of certain interventions and to demonstrate a causal link between intervention programmes and outcomes. However, critics of this approach argue that the social world is more complex and not appropriate for such measurements, especially as changes and 'good' outcomes remain problematic and debatable (Frost et al, 2015) – for example, how does one define 'good' parenting?

The voluntary sector's role in preventative services for children and families

Suggested as naturally having sympathies with children and families defined as 'in need' or 'at risk' (Morris et al, 2009), the voluntary sector is automatically set from a mission and moral viewpoint to want to respond to these welfare issues (Billis, 2001). However, theories and research around the voluntary sector's role in the provision of prevention services for children varies between the recognition of them being well placed in order to engender trust and community engagement, to the voluntary sector as an agency of social control and coercion.

Labour's policy for transforming the delivery of the public services throughout the late 1990s and 2000s increased the involvement and prominence of the voluntary sector. The consequence of this transformation was a rapid and considerable expansion in the number of services and goods purchased or commissioned from the voluntary sector, resituating the relationship between the state and the voluntary sector. As Blake et al (2006) identified 'the relationship becomes characterised by the prescription and targets set by central government departments' (Blake et al, 2006: 26). There are concerns that this relationship leads voluntary sector organisations to being resource led rather than mission or needs led, with organisations compromising values in order to win contracts. Nevertheless, the voluntary sector has historically had a significant role in the wellbeing of children since the Victorian era, for example, with charities such as Banardos, which was founded in 1867 after an outbreak of cholera killed 3,000 people, leaving thousands of children homeless and orphaned (Morris et al, 2009). Labour's commitment to increase this significance of the voluntary sector within child welfare services saw voluntary sector organisations increasing their contribution to statutory children's services on a variety of different levels. This included the direct delivery of services to children and their families, advocating on behalf of and supporting work with children, and facilitating participation with children and their families in consultation processes (Kellett, 2011).

As previously mentioned, the Children's Fund programme, launched in 2000, was one of the key Labour initiatives which widely promoted partnership working with the voluntary sector, and 'created a test ground between the voluntary sector as well as the statutory sector to provide preventative services to overcome the effects of poverty and disadvantage' (Artaraz et al, 2007: 307–308). Ring-fencing a large proportion of the funding to commission services from voluntary sector organisations, there was an entrenched assumption that locally placed voluntary sector organisations would be best suited to deliver these types of services at a community-based level. While there is evidence that the voluntary sector can offer a more accessible service to children and families through engendering more trust than state interventions (Artaraz and Thurston, 2005) research into this area is limited. Undertaking a critical analysis of the 'child rescue' paradigm in the context of voluntary sector delivery of preventative services, Artaraz et al (2007) found that there exists the assumption that voluntary sector organisations are the sole service providers of prevention services. However, they go on to argue that this was a misconception, 'resulting from the perception of the flexibility, capacity and fluidity of the sector to 'venture into new frontiers' (p 308).

Therefore, the state hopes to capture this uniqueness through partnership and multi-agency working. However, their examination of the evaluation of the National Children's Fund programme revealed that this is not necessarily the case and remains more of an expectation than a reality (Morris and Barnes, 2008). The evaluation of the Children's Fund programme identified that while families found the services delivered by the voluntary sector to be accessible, parents were concerned about lack of ongoing support and there was little evidence of multi-agency working. This suggested that the 'relationship between risk and protective factor and long-term outcomes for children remains unclear' (Evans et al, 2006). Evans and Pinnock's (2007) research also suggested voluntary sector organisations delivering community-based interventions were more likely to adopt 'single-dimensional' approaches and often neglected to engage holistically with children's family or work with other professionals to address wider needs and concerns. This led to projects tackling behaviours, attitudes and capabilities in individual children rather than adopting a holistic, community-based approach to build more supportive social environments. This single-dimensional approach was also highlighted by Middleton's (1999) study, within which she carried out a series of semi-structured interviews with voluntary sector organisations providing preventative services for children with disabilities. Middleton argued that the rise of the contract culture, partnered with the targeting of services was reinforcing the separation of minority groups from wider social groups and was thus viewed as reinforcing social exclusion rather than tackling it. Furthermore, Evans and Pinnock (2007) argue that the often short-term nature and inconsistency of funding can lead to mistrust in sustainability and engagement. Morris et al's (2009) study examining the National Evaluation of the Children's Fund supports Evan et al's research (2006), suggesting that though policy shifts have required local authorities to commit to greater integrated working and joining up of services, the voluntary sector's role in the delivery of these preventative services has been somewhat inconsistent:

> At times, the history and experience of the voluntary and community sector in developing and delivering prevention has been recognised and valued. But other developments have – on occasion almost simultaneously – rendered the third sector vulnerable

and dependant on the goodwill and accessibility of local mainstream providers. While the voluntary sector can argue a long history in seeking to meet the needs of children and families at risk of social exclusion, its capacity to influence and inform statutory providers has waxed and waned. (Morris et al, 2009: 132)

Therefore, the preventative landscape of service provision is heavily dominated by the voluntary sector under both Labour and Conservatives. However, there is a concern that though assumed to be better placed to respond to need, voluntary sector organisations are less likely to follow a systematic approach to provision which can result in services that are disconnected from one another and fragmented (Artaraz et al, 2007; Frost et al, 2015). Contaldo (2007), writing on behalf of HM Treasury, argued that the state encourages commissioning from the voluntary sector as it recognises that there are certain characteristics which enable it to be more effective in service provision, including being closer to communities, increased flexibility in delivery and the capability to rapidly react to the needs of beneficiaries. However, Contaldo also points out that even with this paradigm, there are effective and ineffective organisations, warning that voluntary sector organisations are not the best placed providers simply due to their structure, but nevertheless strongly encouraged the commissioning of services from effective 'third sector' providers. There is evidence to support this notion that the voluntary sector is often able to offer a more accessible service to children and families through engendering more trust than do state interventions (Artaraz and Thurston, 2005). Indeed, successive governments appear to rely on this concept of engendering trust as the voluntary sector becomes central to and increasingly involved in initiatives around early intervention, parenting and families, and can be argued as a method of social control. Donzelot's (1980) study of the 'policing of families' in the nineteenth century, provides us with valuable insights into the role of voluntary sector organisations in preventative services. Describing a phase of philanthropy that was influenced heavily by the desire for social control, philanthropic organisations were authorised by public authorities to provide preventative services, which were supported by the criminal justice system. Donzelot suggested that this relationship between the family and philanthropic organisations was significant for the 'moralisation' of children and their 'normalisation'. The moralisation strategy was used for the 'deserving' poor whose situation was beyond their control, these families were offered material and financial assistance to encourage them to 'overcome their moral failures'. The normalisation strategy was aimed at embedding certain norms via education, health and legislative means to bring about changes in their lifestyles. Coercive strategies would be used if the normalisation or moralisation strategies failed. Critics argue preventative early intervention services targeting parenting encompass this model with voluntary sector bodies delivering this form of social control under the direction of statutory services. These parents are identified as a risk to the wider community and thus offered therapeutic support in terms of training, education and support to become 'good' parents (normalisation and moralisation strategies), if not successful they are then subject to the punitive punishments of the state such as parenting orders (Dean, 2010). Dean suggests that the 'third sector employ technologies of agency to transform "at-risk" and "high-risk" groups into active citizens' (Dean, 2010: 199). This notion of 'a priori trust' (Anheier and Kendall, 2002) can be especially important in terms of prevention services where state intervention, for example social services, can be limiting and viewed with suspicion and mistrust. Conversely, Frost et al (2015) recognised the potential benefits brought forward by the voluntary sector delivering early interventions services. However, they argue that the lack of consistency about the definition of early intervention has resulted in individual interpretation of service needs by statutory and voluntary sector providers. Consequently, there are a wide range of diverse and inconsistent services delivered, often based on limited evidence which results in gaps in provision for the most marginalised groups (Frost et al, 2015).

Conclusion

There is a strong paradox between the persuasive logic, which supports early intervention and prevention, versus the enactment and mobilisation of these concepts into preventative services for children. Underpinned by ideological concepts such as social exclusion, early intervention and identification of risk factors for problem families (France et al, 2010), preventative discourse has become a widely debated topic. The voluntary sector has been pulled to the centre of this debate as a deliverer of early intervention and prevention services. The increasing emphasis on prevention represents a growing move towards children and young people being viewed as an investment by the state, emphasising the longer-term economic and social outcomes for children (Fawcett et al, 2004). The concept of the 'social investment state' (Giddens, 1998; Lister, 2003) has been explored by various academics in terms how it could be applied to children and childhood. Through this concept, children could be understood as investments for the future, and therefore by developing holistic, yet targeted, strategies in alliance with parents this investment could be maximised. This analysis and understanding formed much of the thinking for the policy backdrop of Labour's 'Every Child Matters' Green Paper and for general approaches to children within social policy discourse. Furthermore, though there exists a political and social assumption that the voluntary sector will be at the forefront of tackling social exclusion and providing preventative services for children and young people, how this translates into practice remains contested and highly politicised, especially at a local level.

Following this, Conservative approaches continue to reflect a neoliberal assumption that poor families naturally want to 'improve' their position in line with values specified by others. Those who do not are deemed as 'troubled families'. This, coupled with a rise in the policing of parenting with an increasing number of parents facing Parenting Orders (introduced under Labour) and record numbers of parents facing fines and jail due to their child or children truanting, reflects an increasing punitive and ideologically fuelled discourse taking over, disguised in the context of prevention. In the climate of austerity, preventative discourse has moved to a neoliberal stance, blaming parents for issues within society rather than looking at the social backdrop. This is a distinctively different path to the concept of social exclusion that dominated preventative policy during the late 1990s and early 2000s.

There is an assumption that 'preventative' work with children and young people remains a dominant and important factor in supporting them to achieve their full potential and that the voluntary sector has an important role to play in this (Frost et al, 2015). As discussed, the concept of prevention has experienced an increasing hardening towards vulnerable children and families, especially parenting. This is coupled with a shifting paradigm in terms of prevention, which has witnessed an increasing effort to quantify and objectify risk factors under a 'scientific discourse' approach (France et al, 2010) and has created mechanisms in which certain children, young people and their families are specifically targeted with particular services (we expand on this in Chapter 3).

This paradigm of quantifiable, measurable outputs and outcomes has translated directly into the commissioning of preventative services for children and young people (explored further in Part III). With an increasingly outcome-based focus which relies on quantified information as measurements of success, voluntary sector organisations delivering commissioned services are forced to become targeted and specific about whom they support. This shifts beneficiary engagement from stakeholders who actively seek support, to those who are problematised and targeted through a risk factor, diagnostic system. As such, services are designed around this conceptualisation of 'problem families' who are both the cause of anti-social type behaviours and the place where these problems can be solved (Parr, 2009). Engaging charitable organisations in this agenda through the commissioning process continues this ideological positioning beyond statutory services, citing the source of social problems with individual problem families, rather than societal system itself. Thus, when we combine this shifting context of prevention with the developing commissioning discourse, which equally seeks to achieve these targeted services, the voluntary sector is left in a potentially difficult juxtaposition. Does it pursue a social justice discourse within which it seeks to address larger inequalities within societies, does it conform to a politically positioned discourse based upon risk factors and increasingly targeted services, or can voluntary sector organisations adopt a dual approach and operate within both discourses simultaneously?

PART II

On the frontline of early intervention

3

The policy and service delivery field of early intervention services

> In all honesty I am not sure what early intervention means any more, I change my definition of what it is depending on what meeting I am in. If I am with the local authority then broadly I am talking about Tier 3, intensive support services, if I'm in a team meeting at work, early intervention means helping whenever a child needs help. (CEO, medium children's charity)

Introduction

In this chapter we start by discussing what we mean by early intervention, and continue to go on to discuss how charities implement this in practice. Early intervention means both identifying and providing support to children and young people who are at risk of poor social, educational or physical outcomes. The concept is simple, tackle problems at the earliest opportunity to prevent them from escalating. This does not mean however that early intervention is always about the early years; rather, it is about recognising that problems can arise at any point in a child or young person's life and tackling them early helps prevent the problems from getting worse.

This, of course, all sounds great: the provision of early help to tackle problems head-on. However, according to the Early Intervention Foundation (2018), major issues are both persisting and getting worse. For example, they state that four million children were living in poverty in 2018, with the Institute for Fiscal Studies predicting that this would rise to five million by 2020 (Cribb et al, 2018); one third of children are overweight or obese; increasing numbers of children are experiencing mental health problems and youth violence is a pressing concern. A House of Commons report (Powell, 2019) highlighted the ongoing shift in support away from early intervention into costly late intervention services. Their survey across directors of children's services revealed that 89% found it increasingly challenging to fulfil their statutory duties. Indeed, in a report published to celebrate their 150th year, Action for Children (2019) highlight how across those 150 years, while there have been marked improvements in children's services, they also note that in the past decade, particularly since the financial crash in 2008, children's lives have seemingly got worse. Alongside noting increases in child poverty, there are more children than ever subject to a child protection plan and increasing numbers of children going into care. While children's mental health problems grow, services shrink, and many children are left without support. In short, a lack of focus on early intervention and funds being increasingly directed towards late intervention has resulted in numerous problems which mean that many children's lives are getting worse.

The shifting paradigm of prevention

Within the discourse of prevention there has emerged a narrower debate in terms of how early intervention and preventative services are enacted in a service provision sense. As discussed in Chapter 2, the discourse of early intervention has survived successive governments under the assumption that it will work in tackling multiple and overlapping needs of children, and indeed is credited as the mechanism for breaking the causal chains of disadvantage (Axford and Berry, 2017; EIF, 2018). As such, within this discourse the notion has developed that we can scientifically identify risk factors associated with particular groups in society and therefore provide support before problems escalate (France et al, 2010).

Hardiker et al (1989; 1991) set out an argument which suggested differential understanding of the welfare state based upon the conceptualisation of the role of the state. For a welfare state that accepts inequality as a potential driver for a free market, welfare support is provided as the last option for families struggling in that system; therefore, early intervention services would be highly targeted and restricted in eligibility, seeking to reduce the individual difficulties which families experience (Morris and Barnes, 2008). However, welfare state models, which seek to address widescale inequalities through state provision, would view preventative services as open access, within which such provision seeks to support wider social change (Morris and Barnes, 2008). Hardiker et al argued that central to understanding how to target preventative work was the theoretical conceptualisation of the welfare state and values: 'Our hypothesis is that it is consideration of the value base underlying the intervention which helps towards greater conceptual clarity about preventative work' (Hardiker et al, 1989: 355).

Hardiker et al's work has been widely adopted by policymakers but has suffered something of a dilution in terms of the preventative activity being linked to the theoretical analysis of the welfare state, and as such much of the context and objectives of prevention were also diluted: 'As a result, the focus of policy and practice analysis became the type of service and intensity of the problem, rather than exploring assumptions about the rationale for provision' (Morris and Barnes, 2008: 1198).

This discourse, however, has fuelled debate surrounding accepted 'tiers' of intervention and potentially seeks a redefinition of what is meant by the term 'prevention'. Hardiker et al (1989; 1991) first developed the concept of the four tiers of intervention; primary, secondary, tertiary and quaternary (see Figure 3.1). They sought to separate out those children, young people and their families who required time-limited support, from those who were at risk of separation. Therefore, within this four-tiered framework, the primary tier (Tier 1) constituted universal service delivery, which was accessible for all children and young people. The secondary tier (Tier 2) would be defined as 'early identification of comparatively mild problems with a hopeful outcome' and the tertiary tier (Tier 3) constitutes 'more serious problems involving risk, in which amelioration and containment might be all that could be achieved' (p 347). This tier became the level at which children and young people were considered to be at risk of needing to be taken into social care. Quaternary (Tier 4) refers to this support as at a higher intensity, and often considered as institutionalised services.

Figure 3.1: Tiers of intervention

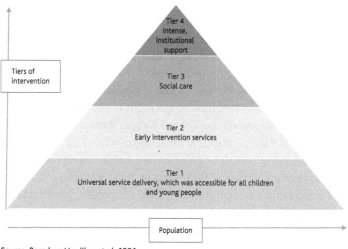

Source: Based on Hardiker et al, 1991

The push to identify the risk factors associated with these tiers of intervention has been problematic (Pithouse, 2008). As such, this has led to an interesting paradox within which prevention discourse has a persuasive, scientific logic, however in practice is difficult to enact. Indeed, the identification of these risk factors can be connected to the previously discussed Sure Start and Children's Fund programmes (see Chapter 2). Sure Start was established based on research which suggested that early intervention would help reduce risks of costlier issues in the future (Pugh, 2007), and the Children's Fund was established to tackle the risk factors associated with social exclusion (Morris and Barnes, 2008). Consolidating this approach further, the UK spending review of 2002 (HM Treasury, 2002) recommended that prevention became more centralised within social welfare agencies. Supported by the development of the Every Child Matters agenda, preventative-type work became the focus of all agencies delivering services to children and young people. Within this policy shift, identification and management of risk factors became fundamental to the delivery of these services. To support this, strategies and mechanisms were created to not only identify, but also to track those children and young people identified as at risk (Parton, 2008).

The concept of identification of risk factors within preventative discourse has had its advantages in terms of centralising the concept of preventative work within children's services, and given it a sense of renewed focus in terms of how we support vulnerable children and young people (France et al, 2010). However, although it is commonly accepted as a 'good thing' to tackle problems early, the central purpose, as identified by Pithouse, is not entirely altruistic or focused on children and young people:

> it is also part of an organizational and strategic discourse wherein it is believed that delivering particular services with particular recipients at particular times will ultimately optimize medium- to long-term outcomes for service users and, by extension, we the citizenry will be less exposed to the higher risks (and costs) of problems becoming more entrenched by inaction. (2008: 1537)

Therefore, by using particular risk factors as identification for future problems the idea is that the right services will be put in place to prevent the escalation of these issues. This, however, is not always the case. For example, it is estimated that almost three quarters of children and young people with severe mental health needs do not get the support they need at an early enough stage. However, this does not mean to suggest that using risk factors is not a helpful or useful approach, as research shows (Allcock, 2019) by targeting problems early we reduce the likelihood of increased social problems later in a child's life. Indeed, there are a number of persuasive arguments which support using the identification of risk factors to intervene early, the challenge presents itself in the 'fundamental difficulties in identifying who does what, when, with whom, and ensuring that this happens' (Pithouse, 2008: 1528). Furthermore, there is a danger within this to categorise 'problem' families away from the wider picture of entrenched social problems, such as poverty, employment market issues and social inequalities. As such, this shift in the paradigm of prevention services legitimatised a political discussion concerning the 'problem families' and situated that narrative in the demonisation of a minority of individuals 'who disrupt the quality of life of whole communities and make the lives of residents around them miserable' (Respect Taskforce, 2006: 21). Such an approach echoes Hardiker et al's (1991) concern regarding the welfare state, which accepts inequalities as part of the free market rather than a tool to help overcome wider social inequalities. For example, there is an underpinning causal relationship suggested between risk factors and future outcomes for children, for which there is little supporting research-based evidence (France et al, 2010). This quantified and scientific approach to working with children not only suggests the ability to predict what the life course of the child would be without intervention, it also assumes what it should be and assumes the focus and purpose of the early intervention (France et al, 2010).

Critics argue that such an approach separates the child from the social, economic and political context within which they operate (Prout, 2000) and when translating into service provision the tiers of services approach was not fit for purpose (for example in terms of the Children's Fund Programme [Morris and Barnes, 2008]). Many are highly critical of this risk factors approach to preventative services suggesting that 'such a view fails to take into account the widespread ambiguity over values and norms and the complexity of how social problems might emerge' (France et al, 2010: 1197). Thus, we are left with many continuing to argue that early intervention needs to be a central and integrated part of tackling wider social concerns, rather than enacted as a time limited intervention to apparently solve the identified problem.

In more recent years, there has been an increasing move from terminology of early intervention to early help. Early help, is a Conservative government approach to early intervention, seeking to promote the welfare of children as soon as problems emerge. However, this is still problematic as preventative services, a persistent part of early intervention, are considered to be more proactive than reactive. Equally, the concept of early help, supporting issues as soon as they emerge, supports an approach which is reactive to social issues, rather than questioning underpinning causes. According to *Working together* guidance, effective early help relies upon multi-agency working to identify children and families who need support, support assessment processes and provide targeted early help services. Indeed, local authorities, under section 10 of the Children Act 2004, have a responsibility to promote inter-agency cooperation to improve the welfare of all children. Section 10 of the Children Act 2004 requires each local authority to make arrangements to promote cooperation between the authority, partners, organisations and services working with children in the local authority's area. Thus, from a policy perspective the relationship between the voluntary sector and local authority is an important one.

Statutory guidance

Under the 1989 Children Act, 'every local authority shall take reasonable steps to identify the extent to which there are children in need within their area', as well as to publish information about the services it provides to children in need (and other groups) and to 'take such steps as are reasonably practicable to ensure that those who might benefit from the services receive the information relevant to them'.

This statutory duty remains, although there have been several changes in policy over the past decade, many in response to public outcry. In 2008, following the tragic death of 1-year-old Peter Connelly, Lord Laming carried out a damning review of social services. His progress report, published in 2009, suggested a total of 58 recommendations for child protection reforms (Laming, 2009). As discussed in Chapter 1, when the Conservative led coalition came to power in 2010, the then new Secretary of State for Education, Michael Gove, commissioned Professor Eileen Munro to conduct an independent review of child protection in England. At the same time the Minister for Children and Families, Tim Loughton, announced that Local Safeguarding Boards in England should publish the overview report and executive summary of all case reviews initiated on or after 10 June 2010. Professor Munro's report *A child-centred system* (2011) set out recommendations to 'help to reform the child protection system from being over-bureaucratised and concerned with compliance to one that keeps a focus on children, checking whether they are being effectively helped, and adapting when problems are identified'. Around the same time, the UK was reeling from the rising number of sexual abuse allegations against Jimmy Saville and others. As a result, operation Yew Tree was set up to investigate in 2012. Following this the independent review into child sexual exploitation in Rochdale examined the council's response to issues around child sexual exploitation. The Children's and Families Act was given royal assent in 2014, offering greater protection to vulnerable children. This was followed by the Children and Social Work Act in 2017, which gave specific rights, protections and provisions to children in care and care leavers. Throughout this period of time, overarching guidance has attempted to encourage inter-agency and partnership working.

The government has published a series of versions of *Working together to safeguard children*, which is statutory guidance to all local authorities and others such as schools. The document states that 'anyone who has concerns about a child's welfare should make a referral to local authority children's social care and should do so immediately if there is a concern that the child is suffering significant harm or is likely to do so'. *Working together to safeguard children* was first published in 2006: 'A guide to inter-agency working to safeguard and promote the welfare of children' is the government's statutory guidance for all organisations and agencies who work with, or carry out work related to children. In 2010 this was superseded by a later version which expanded the focus on interagency working and took into account the recommendations of Lord Laming's 2009 progress report, *The protection of children in England* which suggested that it was imperative that frontline professionals focused on child centred services. In 2013, responding to rising multiple concerns another new version of *Working together to safeguard children* was published in England, informed by the Munro review. This was then updated again in 2015. Following the Independent Inquiry into Child Sexual Abuse in England and Wales officially launched to consider the growing evidence of institutional failures to protect children from child sexual abuse. In 2018 the latest iteration of *Working together to safeguard children* (HM Government, 2018a) was then published for England. The guidance sets out protocols for inter-agency working and for promoting the welfare of children from all backgrounds, in all settings.

Established to ensure that support is provided for all children in need, the guidance itself lacks clear definition about what constitutes a child in need. The term 'child in need' is a statutory term as set out in the Children Act 1989. According to this act any child can be considered as a child in need, even if they are living with their family. It is the role of a local authority's children's services department to assess and provide services in respect of children in need. Section 17 of the 1989 Act defines a child in need as follows:

a) he is unlikely to achieve or maintain, or to have the opportunity of achieving or maintaining, a reasonable standard of health or development without the provision for him of services by a local authority;
b) his health or development is likely to be significantly impaired, or further impaired, without the provision for him of such services;
c) he is disabled where 'family' in relation to such a child includes 'any person who has parental responsibility for the child and any other person with whom he has been living'.

A number of terms used in section 17 are clarified within the act, for example 'development' means physical, intellectual, emotional, social or behavioural development; 'disabled' means if he is blind, deaf or dumb or suffers from mental health issue of any kind or is substantially and permanently disabled by illness, injury or congenital deformity or such other disability as may be prescribed; and 'health' means physical or mental health.

While this guidance exists, it is down to the safeguarding partners, the local authority, the local clinical commissioning group and chief officer of police to define the thresholds of what constitutes a child in need. Together this group is responsible for agreeing the different levels for different types of assessments and the services to be commissioned and delivered. The safeguarding partners are expected to publish a 'threshold' document, which indicates the level of need for when a child should be referred to the local authority's social care. Whether the child is in need or not is then down to the discretion of the local authority, drawing on recommendations from social workers and practitioners.

Working together to safeguard children: early help

The 2017 Children and Social Work Act sets out how agencies must work together by placing new duties on the police, clinical commissioning groups and the local authority to make arrangements to work together and with other partners locally to safeguard and promote the welfare of all children in their area. However, this policy is pre-dated by numerous attempts (some successful, some not) of working together.

Here we set out a summary of chapter 1 of *Working together to safeguard children* (DfE, 2018). Much of this section is almost quoted verbatim, or very close to the wording used in the original guidance, to ensure that meaning is not lost in translation. This guidance highlights the importance of early intervention, under the title of early help. Here all organisations are offered guidance on identifying children and families who would benefit from early help, accessing help and services and information sharing with other organisations/agencies (HM Government, 2018a).

Based on the latest iteration of this guidance all local organisations and agencies should have in place effective ways to identify emerging problems and potential unmet needs of individual children and families. Local authorities should work with organisations, including voluntary sector organisations, and agencies to develop joined-up early help services based on a clear understanding of local needs. This requires all practitioners, including those in universal services and those providing services to adults with children, to understand their role in identifying emerging problems and to share information with other practitioners to support early identification and assessment.

The guidance prioritises multi-agency working, ensuring that practitioners working across universal and targeted service, come together to develop collective understanding of local needs. Practitioners are expected to be able to identify neglect, and to share that information appropriately to provide children with child-centred support. There is an expectation that all practitioners will engage in ongoing training to develop their skills and knowledge.

The *Working together* document sets out guidance for effective assessment of the need for early help. There is a clear recognition in the guidance that children and families may need support from a wide range of local organisations and agencies. Inter-agency assessments should be completed where a child and family would benefit from coordinated support from more than one organisation or agency (for example, education, health, housing, police). The guidance states that early help assessments should be evidence-based, be clear about the action to be taken and services to be provided. A lead practitioner should undertake the assessment, provide help to the child and family, act as an advocate on their behalf and coordinate the delivery of support services. A GP, family support worker, school nurse, teacher, health visitor and/or special educational needs coordinator could undertake the lead practitioner role. Decisions about who should be the lead practitioner should be taken on a case-by-case basis and should be informed by the views of the child and family.

The guidance states that for an early help assessment to be effective it should be undertaken with the agreement of the child and their parents or carers, involving the child and family as well as all the practitioners who are working with them. It should take account of the child's wishes and feelings wherever possible, their age, family circumstances and the wider community context in which they are living. Practitioners should be able to discuss concerns they may have about a child and family with a social worker in the local authority. Local authority children's social care should set out the process for how this will happen (DFE, 2018: 14).

Working together in practice

As the rest of this book outlines, working together in practice is very different to how it is set out in the document outlined above. Working together has become an important part of the narrative surrounding statutory early help, education, social care and children's charities. However, inconsistencies about what this guidance means in practice has led to stark differences between support available for children, leading to a postcode lottery of service provision. This was particularly highlighted in the Ofsted report, *Early help: whose responsibility?* published in 2015. In 2015 Ofsted carried out an inspection across 12 local authorities examining 56 early help cases. In over a third of these cases they found that children could have been supported earlier, and in over half, poor early help assessment meant that the child was not receiving adequate support. Poor training of early help workers and partner agencies (such as schools and voluntary sector organisations) and a lack of coherent joined-up working was blamed. In many cases professionals had not engaged the child and relied solely on information from the parents, and two thirds of the case plans which had been put in place were ineffective.

Inspectors found that most of the support plans did not take into account the children's individual circumstances when deciding on action, lacked clear objectives and were not regularly reviewed. Furthermore, inspectors found that when reviews took place, they focused on the actions taken rather than outcomes and impact for the child. As a result, inspectors suggested that there were multiple serious weaknesses in how cases were managed, and in some cases no formal management existed at all. Worryingly, inspectors found that local safeguarding children boards (LSCBs) were not monitoring the management and oversight of early help practice. In addition, local authorities and partners were not evaluating early help work, with audits overly focusing on compliance with process, rather than improving children's lives. Further concerns were raised about a lack of monitoring about what help children were receiving and when, alongside ongoing concerns about practitioners' access to appropriate training.

Finally, the inspectors found that there was significant variation in how local authorities and partners shared accountability and coordinated early help services. The report highlighted that the, then most current, guidance was unclear about the roles and responsibilities of various partners and how they should be involved in early help services. In conclusion, the report highlighted that local authorities continue to fail to learn from past mistakes and serious case reviews. Early help services continue to require significant work to ensure that they improve.

Such findings are echoed and expanded on throughout this book, for example as one children's charity manager summarises here, the relationship remains complicated:

> I'm a manager of a family intervention service, we are a commissioned service by the local authority, even though we're in the voluntary sector. The structure of early help and preventative services in the local authority at the moment is that they have unit leads across the county, each county has so many units and each unit has a unit lead and early help workers and then obviously, they go out and work with the families. So they work mainly, if we're talking about a tiered level of service, so you've got a universal service at Tier 1, you've got Tier 2 which is targeted support, Tier 3 which is an intensive intervention of early help, which is where we are at Tier 3 and Tier 2 and then you've got Tier 4 which is statutory service, social care. So early help and preventative services will do the majority of work at Tier 3 but we do also take Tier 2 targeted work. So as a commissioned service, I'm commissioned to do exactly the same as early help, but we are on a different database to Early Help which in my mind is a safeguarding nightmare if OFSTED came to visit because you've got all of that information that's shared in the local authority and yet they then put that information onto a different database and give it to us, and when we think about the Munro Report and the fact that actually one should always be on the same database, that for me is a huge risk for me, for the information sharing in my families. (Early Intervention Manager, medium children's charity)

Of particular interest here is the definition of early help as a Tier 3 service, which as discussed traditionally deals with more formal social care, suggesting a raising of thresholds for support. We discuss this further in Chapter 6.

The role of the voluntary sector?

While early help is used as an umbrella term to cover the statutory duties towards children under early intervention, early intervention itself is a much more generic term which goes beyond the bounds of early help provision. For example, in terms of voluntary sector organisations involved in this research, some are commissioned to formally deliver early help services in line with the local authority, while others deliver services outside of this arrangement which still fall under the remit of early intervention – however, all of those included have received grant funding from the local authority, under early intervention programmes, prior to the more formal shift to 'commissioned services'.

Children's charities perform either, or both, direct service delivery, and/or advocacy and campaigning for children. On a national scale we see these roles undertaken by some of the significant major players in the sector, such as Barnardo's, Action for Children, Children's Society, National Children's Bureau, NSPCC and Save the Children UK. Each of these organisations both actively deliver services and are involved in campaigning, to different degrees, for services for children. Other organisations such as Children England work hard to campaign and bring the sector together and have been central to many key debates promoting rights for children. The Early Intervention Foundation, as another charitable organisation, seeks to promote 'evidence-based' good practice for early intervention, however this has not been without some significant criticism (for example see Edwards et al, 2016).

Beneath these major 'players' in the field of early intervention exist a multitude of micro, small, medium and large organisations. They are extremely diverse in their missions and approaches, but they are all connected by a shared desire to improve outcomes for children and their families at the earliest opportunity possible. Such organisations include, for example, The Lucy Faithfull Foundation, which aims to prevent the sexual abuse of children and young people by working with protective adults, those affected by abuse and those perpetrating it, including young people with harmful sexual behaviour; Storybook Dads, who help children connect and reconnect with an imprisoned parent through storytelling; the Children's Respite Trust who provide care and support for families of disabled children. These are just a few of the smaller charities and voluntary sector organisations that operate in communities and neighbourhoods throughout the UK, providing vital services for children and young people to help prevent them reaching crisis point.

On the frontline

The children's charities which contributed to this research all sit on the frontline of early intervention services, they varied from micro to major in size, some aligning themselves with the state, some purposefully distancing themselves. They included organisations employing a range of senior professional practitioners, to grass-root volunteer organisations trying to support their local community. They deliver services ranging from youth work, to mental health support, to supporting victims of domestic abuse, and many more in between. They deliver services to children in schools, to families at home and within the community. They are connected by their shared passion, but also their increasing competition for a diminishing pool of resources within a single geographic area.

In order to understand the diverse nature of this field, a few of those organisations included in this book here highlight their work. For example, some organisations work within a specific issue area such as domestic abuse:

> We provide a refuge service for women and children and deliver a county wide independent domestic abuse advisors service which is a high-risk service for those in the community and we are the lead agency for that in the local domestic abuse consortium. We also provide a children and young people's team, which includes services commissioned and our own funded services ... over the past five years we've increased our focus in children and young people in

the community, early intervention and prevention as that is a need people are recognising over the last few years. (CEO, medium children's charity)

We offer accommodation for women and children who have suffered domestic abuse. We work in schools about prevention of abusive relationships. We work with umm young girls, well that's part of the consortium that we are part of, to prevent, well the whole idea was to prevent teenage pregnancy umm but it is about actually preventing abusive relationships and trying to get young people to think things through. We also offer a young person's accommodation, that's 16 to 21. (CEO, small children's charity)

Others defined themselves more as youth work organisations, offering a wider range of services:

So under early intervention and prevention we deliver things like parenting programmes, our young healthy minds which is emotional health and wellbeing service, we do some play work, we do some low level engagement, and I would say although we describe it internally differently I would describe the youth work, youth service commissioned stuff, as early intervention as far as I am concerned. (Early Intervention Manager, large children's charity)

We are a youth club, delivering youth work. We have a very holistic, overall approach. We are more like a one stop shop, it is more than the young people paying the 50p to access the youth club, but those nights are still some of the most important that we have. We deliver dance, art, drama and sports. This is a kids-led club, they choose, design and manage what we deliver. In doing that we support them with their school work, family issues, drug issues, relationships … We don't have any commissioned

money, it would stop us doing what we do!
(CEO, small children's charity)

Others, however, used specific sports or activities to engage vulnerable children and young people in positive activities:

All our programmes are based on music, dance and creative arts. We are in one of the most deprived areas in the country, the children here often struggle with aspirations and attainment at school. We counter that by offering an alternative space to thrive. We encourage young singers and writers and have a band factory for young bands. We work with babies on an eight-week programme to aid early years development and parental bonding. We train members of the community to run it as well. In doing this we also run one stop projects, where the young people we work with can access support on their health, emotional needs in a really informal way – like we have a drug advisor and a mental health person on site. (CEO, small children's charity)

At the same time, some of the charities involved offered a range of services which they highlighted as early intervention:

We provide an emotional health and wellbeing service for young people which is part of a consortium, which is a different way of working. We have family mediation which is again working county wide, and we also offer supported accommodation for young people, and we have a rural youth service. (CEO, medium children's charity)

Conclusion

This chapter has sought to outline the realities of early intervention policy and begins to look at the lived experience of delivering services on the frontline. What is evident is that practice in children's social care and early intervention is struggling to keep up with the demands and the diversity of demands placed upon services. Voluntary sector and statutory services are facing increasing cuts as thresholds for defining a 'child in need' increasingly shift up. Children's outcomes and the services available to them are widely varied depending on the type of support they require and where they live.

In the next chapter we explore this specifically from the point of view of schools, examining how they are coping with delivering early intervention in increasingly challenging times.

4

State education: the relationships between schools and charity?

> Schools are increasingly having to behave and think like charities. The funding simply isn't there to support our most vulnerable children, and the support services around us have been demolished – we now act as a charity to protect our children. (Headteacher)

Introduction

Education is a core service which provides the grounding, qualification and socialisation for children and young people, which is likely to have an impact on them for the rest of their lives (Biesta, 2013). As a primary tool for increasing social equality, achieving aspirations and supporting children and young people to become active, pro-social citizens, it is unsurprising that this is an area of interest for many philanthropists, charities and voluntary sector organisations. Similarly, as schools face increasing fiscal, performance, recruitment and retention pressures, we see them increasingly turning to voluntary action – that is fundraising and volunteers – to counter resource pressures.

This chapter explores this core concept, the relationship between education and charity. Focusing particularly on primary education which concentrates on 4–11 year-olds, we investigate how charities shape and support education, and indeed how schools engage in voluntary action to support their day to day delivery. We consider the implications of this work and what this means for the charitable sector and early intervention. In this chapter we deliberately avoid the topic of independent schools and charitable status. This is not to suggest that this topic does not warrant research; it does in fact deserve significant attention from policymakers, practitioners and academics, but it simply is not the topic up for debate within this chapter.

We first explore the marketisation of education (that is the exposure of education to market forces) tracking the policy history and, most recently, funding reforms, which have meant that schools increasingly have to squeeze budgets and find new ways to increase their resources. We view what this voluntary action in primary education looks like through two lenses: first, how charity shapes education, and second, how schools are fundraising and encouraging volunteering in schools. We finally conclude with what this means for schools, and what is most important, what this means for the children they seek to serve.

Policy context

Education policy in England is creating testing times for schools. In 2019, there are 32,113 schools in England. Of these, 20,925 are primary schools and 4,168 are secondary schools. There are 2,381 independent schools, 1,256 special schools and 351 pupil referral units. Faced with decreasing budgets per pupil, increasing numbers of children with additional needs, a teacher recruitment and retention crisis, and bewildering performance pressures, schools are struggling almost across the board. Here we take a moment to consider the policy backdrop that creates these challenging times for schools. According to Ball and Youdell (2008) there is 'a growing tendency among governments world-wide to introduce forms of privatisation into public education and to move to privatise sections of public education' (p 8). Is this an entirely new situation, or has this been brewing for some time?

A brief background to education policy in England

Education for all, free at point of access, is a relatively new phenomenon in England. Up until the end of the nineteenth century, education was primarily an exclusive luxury, reserved for the middle and upper classes. Primary education was introduced nationally with the introduction of the Elementary Education Act of 1870, made compulsory in 1880 and made free 1891. Just over a decade later, the Balfour Act (also known as the Education Act 1902) saw the introduction of a national secondary education.

It was the end of the Second World War, under the 1944 Butler Act (also known as the Education Act 1944), when we arguably saw the greatest shifts in the system across England and Wales. Universal primary and secondary education was mandated in law, and the addition of further education created a tripartite system. Nonetheless, while the Butler Act resulted in increased social equality in education, demand quickly outstripped capacity and some children, particularly among the most disadvantaged, continued to not receive an education.

Crucially, towards the end of the 1970s and into the 1980s, the Thatcher-led Conservative government progressively marketised the education system, including giving more power to parents, reducing the control of local educational authorities. The 1988 Education Reform Act created the first single national curriculum for all compulsory schools, defining four stages of compulsory education based on age groups (5–7, 8–11, 12–14, 15–16). While the election of New Labour in 1997 in many ways continued the marketisation of education, prioritising parental choice and involvement throughout their term, they received criticism for further exacerbating inequalities. The comprehensive approach to education established in the 1988 Act, was gradually dismantled, with schools becoming increasingly differentiated, and individually selective. Towards the end of the New Labour term, educational reform focused upon increasing freedom for teachers, increasing the school leaving age and the diversity of the types of state schools.

Current education policy

Under current education structures a wide variety of state-funded schools exist, which are each differentiated by their governance and reporting structures. For example:

- community schools, are managed by local authorities and are not influenced by business or religious groups;
- academies, are run by independent governing bodies and can follow a different curriculum;
- foundation schools, have more control over their organisation and curriculum;
- grammar schools, which select their pupils through entry examinations and are run by councils, foundations, or trusts;
- faith schools, which are connected to a specific religion, can be of different types of school, but must follow the national curriculum except in the area of religious studies.

The introduction of academies perhaps marked one of the most fundamental changes in education policy in the past two decades. Introduced in the Learning and Skills Act 2000, the percentage of schools which actually converted to academy status remained low until the election of the Conservative-led coalition government in 2010. The Academies Act 2010 aimed to significantly increase the number of academies, enabling all maintained schools to convert to academy status and new academies to be created via the Free School Programme. Although free schools are government-funded, they have greater autonomy, do not have to follow the national curriculum, can independently set their pay and conditions for staff and can alter the length of the school day and term time. While the government backed down on its initial assertion that it would force all schools to become academies, by February 2018, 72% of secondary schools and 27% of primary schools in England are academies (as of 2019), of which 7% were free schools.

Subsequent education policies pursued since 2010, included significant and continued budget cuts, intensified focus on testing and monitoring and the abolishment of bureaucratic bodies such as the Curriculum Development Agency. Increasingly schools are expected to manage and raise their own funds, as state funding reduces. This was perhaps best epitomised by guidance published by the Department of Education, *Supporting excellent school resource management* (2018), which aimed to make 'every pound count and getting the best value from all of their [schools] resources' (p 3).

A variety of wider policy initiatives – such as Big Society, localism and the Civil Society Strategy – have placed community partnerships and voluntary action on the political agenda, alongside the ongoing reforms to the education policy in England. Driven by a neoliberal ideology, education policy has undergone a series of sweeping changes and disjointed reforms producing a particular version of a 'good school' which rewards children and their schools who perform well in tests while potentially excluding those who do not. This underlying ideology of public policy in England in recent years supports the notion that children will attain greater achievements if state schools face more competition and have greater autonomy (Adonis, 2012). The DfE white paper in 2010 helped create this new policy landscape, with the encouragement, as discussed, for all schools to become academies; new providers expected to set up free schools; reduction in guidance from central government and creation of a funding premium to follow disadvantaged pupils. This approach shifted responsibility for 'closing the gap' between advantaged and disadvantaged children away from central government onto our local schools (DFE, 2010).

Challenges facing education

Funding woes

It is difficult to get to the bottom of the funding crisis in education. For several years schools have been campaigning about the fact that they do not have enough funding, while the Department for Education continuously repeats the claim that they are funding education more than ever before. In fact, both claims are true, if not rather misleading on the part of the Department for Education.

Between 2008 and 2018, there was a rise of 8% in the number of pupils in primary and secondary schools, increasing from 7.4 million to just under 8 million. This was coupled with increased running costs for schools on the goods and services they produce, as well as increasing staff costs. Responding to the Department for Education claims, in July 2018, the well reputed Institute of Fiscal Studies reported that between 2009/

10 and 2017/18 school funding per pupil in England fell by about 8% in real terms. So, while school funding is at a record high, so are the pressures on that funding. The reality is that when school leaders look at their bottom line, they have less money to spend per pupil.

In 2018, a new national funding formula for schools in England came into force replacing the 152 different local authority funding formulae with one single formula. Such was the scale of the plans that the Institute for Fiscal Studies described them as, 'the most ambitious reform to the school funding system for over 25 years'. However, this formula did not come with additional funding, instead just different criteria were being used to redistribute the current funding. So, when, Damian Hinds, Secretary of State for Education, responded to a question in parliament in 2018 stating that 'in real terms funding per pupil is increasing across the system', the UK statistics authority disagreed, and quickly forced an amendment to the parliamentary record (Norgrave, 2018).

Schools and unions have been campaigning against the enforcement of the new system, arguing that cuts to some schools' budgets are not the solution when school budgets are in crisis. A survey of 1,500 headteachers in 2019 by the lobbying campaign group *Worth Less?* found 90% of schools are having to use part of the 'pupil premium' allocated for disadvantaged pupils to fund core budgets, 80% are cutting numbers of teaching assistants and support staff, and 60% are removing teaching posts to balance budgets.

Implementing this reform at a time when there is already considerable pressure on school budgets was inevitably difficult. While the desire to make school funding more equitable across the country is laudable, the new formula leaves the majority of schools even worse off than previously. In this context, it is not surprising that schools are placing more emphasis on charitable and voluntary action as a means of boosting school budgets and providing additional resources. The capacity of schools to do more non-core work is decreasing, while, as we discuss elsewhere in this book, the need for that work is increasing and community-based organisations are struggling to meet that need.

Recruitment and retention struggles

In December 2018, for the sixth year running, the annual teacher-trainee census showed that the government has missed its targets for recruitment to secondary school subjects (DfE, 2018). While this problem affects secondary schools much more than it does primary schools, the number of individuals training to become primary school teachers is falling, especially among men. In addition, over a third of teachers leave the profession within five years of qualifying, with a survey by the National Education Union in 2017 finding that excessive, unmanageable workloads, inflexible curriculums and impossible performance measures are at the forefront of reasons given (NEU, 2018).

Achievement and attainment gaps

Successive governments have sought to improve social mobility in England so that children and young people, whatever their background, can succeed. However, the achievement gaps – where certain groups of children are not doing as well others – continues to be a policy issue. Despite all efforts, narrowing these gaps has proved problematic. The gaps relate to socioeconomic, cultural and geographic factors. While the school system has long been considered a vital tool to support equality of opportunity and to secure better outcomes for disadvantaged children, progress is slow. The Education Policy Institute (Andrews et al, 2017), for example, estimated that at current rates it would take more than 50 years to close the gap between disadvantaged pupils and their better-off peers.

Schools face huge pressures to 'improve': to improve their pupil outcomes, to improve qualifications achieved, to improve attendance and to improve wellbeing. Rather than getting extra support to achieve this, however, schools must do this with fewer resources, less staff and less support. Poor test results for pupils trigger an Ofsted inspection and league tables form the new measure of quality, as schools constantly battle increasing critical scrutiny. The changing school system, increasing marketisation and narrowing of curriculum freedom means that schools are facing some unprecedented challenges. Furthermore, the cuts to community support services, early intervention budgets and family support services, discussed elsewhere in this book, deal schools a double blow, as they are left at the forefront of supporting children, with diminishing resources and capacity. It is therefore unsurprising that schools, who are centrally tasked with improving social equality, turn to voluntary action, charities and philanthropy for help, and that in turn parents, communities, charities and philanthropists are keen and often very willing to help; however, this is not without its problems (as we discuss later).

Schools and charities working in partnership for public good

Now we have established why schools are increasingly turning to voluntary action and charities to support delivery of education, we now turn our attention to how, starting with schools and charities working in partnership for public good.

Education and charity have been inextricably linked since the start of formal education. The Kings School in Canterbury, Kent, for example, claims to be one of the oldest charities in England, tracing its roots back to 597 (Breeze et al, 2015). Charities have been supporting and working in schools for a long time, to achieve joint benefits for the children and communities they serve. However, given the policy backdrop and challenges facing education and early intervention support services, as already discussed, the interaction between charities and schools is changing, altering both the role and nature of the relationships. In this section we explore ways in which charities and philanthropists work with schools, from helping to shape education to providing support services, and the policy and practice which underpins this activity.

Shaping education

Charities have an important role in campaigning, advocating and championing support for vulnerable and disadvantaged children. We know that education in England continues to perpetuate inequality. Simply put, children eligible for free school meals are less likely to get good GCSEs and go on to higher education.

Indeed, over a third of children entitled to free school meals leave primary school without meeting the expected levels for reading, writing and maths. Charities work at a practical level, and a systematic level, to try and address these inequalities, for example:

- *The Sutton Trust* systematically works to challenge inequalities in education. Their mission, as outlined on their website (2019), to 'work to raise aspirations of young people from low- and middle-income backgrounds and to increase their chances of accessing top universities and the professions. We do this by delivering programmes, evidence-based research, and influencing public policy'. A major part of their work includes the Education Endowment Fund, which was set up by the Sutton Trust, Impetus PEF and the Department for Education, to specifically focus on improving the outcomes for the most disadvantaged pupils.
- *Future First*, is a charity supported by high profile funders such as Garfield Weston, Esmee Fairbairn and the Pears foundation, established to support state schools and colleges to build, engage and activate their alumni communities in order to raise aspirations and equip students from disadvantaged background to do well. With an income of just over £1.5 million in 2017/18, they claim to have created the momentum behind a cultural change that has seen the numbers of schools engaging alumni effectively shift from 1% to approximately 25% of all schools.
- *Teach First*, a charity established in 2002 with strong political support, with a turnover of over £16 million (in 2016/17) and a string of wealthy and high profile backers, seeks to directly target social inequalities in education by training and supporting high quality teachers who are placed in primary and secondary schools in disadvantaged areas. Not without controversy, it has received criticism for presenting itself 'as an idealistic and exceptional external force taking action on a broken state, relationships and the redundant knowledge of professionals' (Ellis et al, 2016: 75). However independent evidence does suggest that it has had some positive impact in the schools within which it works (Allen and Allnutt, 2017).

Nevertheless, evidence on the systematic changes produced are sketchy at best. There is some limited evidence which suggests the attainment gap is closing, but progress is slow, with an estimation of 50–70 years work before the gap is lost at current rates of improvement. The *Fair Education Alliance* (2018) who campaign to reduce social inequality found that large gaps between the performance of students from low income backgrounds and their wealthier peers remained. In addition, the rate of school exclusions in England continues to rise 'at an alarming rate', with students on free school meals four times as likely to be excluded than their peers.

Children's charities supporting education

Relationships between schools, charities and socially orientated businesses can be beneficial not only for children within the school, but also the wider community and beyond. There are a variety of different relationships held by schools which can have an impact on both their philanthropic income and volunteers; these include corporate partners, individual philanthropists and third sector organisations.

Research suggests that just over one fifth of primary school's report having a formal partnership with an individual charity (Body et al, 2017). Often this requires a school 'buying in' the support; for example, buying into reading schemes, emotional wellbeing support and extra-curricular activities. At other times this involves a school and charity working together to raise funds to address a local community need, for example, as one charity leader illustrated:

> We worked with this one school who had some massive issues. They had a transient school population, and over 30% of the pupils changed each year as families moved in and out of the area. Though they had some extra funding to help with this, the biggest issue was among the parents and out in the community. Community disputes and arguments tumbled off the streets into the playground, impacting on children's learning and the school couldn't do a

lot about it. We worked with them to tackle this. As a charity we could apply for funds that they couldn't and were able to deliver a whole suite of support which focused on bringing the community and school together. (CEO, medium children's charity)

Indeed, schools welcome partnerships with charities, viewing them as particularly advantageous to their most vulnerable pupils in a time of decreased assistance from community support services. However, in the face of diminishing early intervention services, schools are confronted with dealing with an increasing number of complex issues which span beyond the realms of education. For example, the following primary school, situated in an area of economic deprivation with a higher than average number of children on free school meals, recognised that a particular group of children were coming to school hungry every day and more were being affected by 'holiday hunger', where children have less food available to them through the holidays. In response, the parent council of the school worked with a local foodbank to help counter these pressures on the children within their community.

> Once the level of understanding about need was in place, and the parent council understood the severity of hunger that many of our local families face, we decided to launch three schemes within the school. This would include: holiday hunger club, emergency breakfast scheme and myself being trained, to be able to issue food bank vouchers. Currently, we have at least six children a day, who come to school hungry and many families struggling to make ends meet with regards to feeding themselves and their children. The need was evident for us all to see, and we have taken it upon ourselves as a group, to support these families as best as we can. I feel a level of responsibility to the families and children within the school. With finances being stretched within both families and education, it was evident to me that the grand scale of the potential situation would mean that we needed

the support of a charity, such as the food bank, to guide us in this process. Ultimately, if we do not set up a holiday hunger scheme, these children will not receive a hot meal during school holidays and if we do not have a supply of breakfast food for the children in school, they will remain hungry and their education will suffer. The knock-on effects of benefit waiting times and school budgets, mean that voluntary groups such as our own parent council, are trying to fill the food crisis gap for children. (Chair Parent Council, Primary School)

Working Together policy in schools

Schools' duties under Early Help are clear. The Early Help offer was recommended by the Munro Review in 2011 – she called for a duty on local authorities to provide Early Help services. Ministers did not adopt this recommendation as they felt the existing duty to cooperate as set out in Sections 10 and 11 of the Children Act 2004 to be sufficient.

Since the report, however, revised government guidance has clearly stated how schools should be using Early Help. This is tackled most recently in the revised Keeping Children Safe in Education statutory guidance document, published in 2019, where it is stated that:

- All staff should be prepared to identify children who may benefit from early help. Early help means providing support as soon as a problem emerges at any point in a child's life, from the foundation years through to the teenage years (p 6).
- All staff should be aware of their local early help process and understand their role in it (p 8).
- Staff may be required to support other agencies and professionals in an early help assessment, in some cases acting as the lead practitioner. Any such cases should be kept under constant review and consideration given to a referral to children's social care for assessment for statutory services, if the

child's situation does not appear to be improving or is getting worse. (DfE, 2019: 12)

Working Together in practice in schools

Children's charities and schools identify particular tensions between early intervention services, which fall broadly under the category of social care, and education. As some schools receive devolved budgets and act more autonomously from the local authority, for example academies, they are entitled to less support paid for via commissioned services, therefore creating barriers of support between early intervention and needs to be 'schools'. For example, as one CEO articulates:

I think interestingly an issue is the relationship between education and social care as well. Because we used to have a really strong link with social services and education when we were working with young people and doing mediation for example, we would do a lot work in the school and meetings in the school and have joint meetings with social services, schools, families and I think that worked really well. We had school clinics so we would see young people in school as well for a one to one, now that was when we were working at a district based level and most district and social services managers supported that, you got a few who were a bit funny and saying I'm not paying you to go into a school, they should be paying. And then it really got to this point where people said well if education have got like that they can pay for their own service and I'm not paying for that, and this complete internal divide in the local authority seemed to happen and all those school clinics were stopped 'cause we weren't allowed to do them anymore and they were such a valuable way of working. It didn't matter how much we tried to persuade people that actually these were good and yes we were going into the school building and that is where that young person is, at least they are in school that day for a start and also we used to bring the parents in too for meetings, and often parents didn't have a good relationship with school, often 'cause they didn't as kids, and so that relationship building worked really well but it was then very [much] seen as a well that's a school service so we are not paying for that, so that all finished, so education and social services seem to be at loggerheads which doesn't help anyone. (CEO, medium children's charity)

This example of a divide between education and social care is not an isolated case. Increasingly schools have been removed from many commissioned services, based on an expectation that schools are well positioned to directly 'spot purchase' support from charities and support organisations instead. Thus, many children's charities see schools as commissioning organisations and have adapted their business models to accommodate this:

I mean it is quite tricky for us because our second biggest commissioners are now schools, and schools spot purchase, so they don't commission in the same way as the local authority they just purchase services and they will just say right I want to buy someone for just two days a week for the rest of the year and that is how they go about it and it is a very different experience. It makes planning difficult but it also makes working in partnership with the school tricky, you see they become our customer. We supply a service, it isn't always the service they need though. If we had a more holistic partnership where we, the school and the commissioners all worked together we could provide a much better joined-up service which actually supported the whole family. (Early Intervention Manager, large children's charity)

While another commented:

Our business model has shifted, we are now selling and competing against others, absolutely, and compared to where we started [2008] and the amount of revenue we brought in from schools, it's a different world. Apart from the contracts we have from the local authority that it is our biggest income, financial money that comes in from schools. (CEO, medium children's charities)

As a result, children's charities and schools identify increased barriers to working in partnership with one another and furthermore in engaging support from Early Help. For example, as one Deputy Headteacher commented:

I have given up with Early Help, we have referred one too many cases where they simply say 'nope, doesn't meet the threshold', they only speak to the parents, not to us, not to the children – if a child needs support I know it has to be our job to supply it. So my staff have become housing advisers, psychiatrists, counsellors and therapists … As if we didn't have enough to do to just keep up with teaching demands. (Deputy Headteacher, Primary School)

Schools feel increasingly marginalised in Early Help processes, with less access to support services. Indeed, schools and children's charities provided multiple accounts where commissioned services were actively prevented from working in schools, while charities increasingly must charge schools for services. As schools deal with increasingly complex cases turned down by the state's Early Help support, they are left to either manage more vulnerable pupils on their own or seek alternative income to support these children. As one children's charity summarises:

Because the local authority is now saying they cannot cope so anything that's a targeted support is now going to go back to schools and organisations. Schools are up in arms, because before they could in the past access all this targeted support, so they used to have CAF, used to have all these great people doing great work in schools, we stopped it, the local authority then said 'Hand it all over to us because we've got all this Early Help and preventative services workers', so the last three years, that's happened, Early Help has taken all of the schools' referrals. Schools have now reduced all their capacity to manage it because of austerity and cuts, they've got nobody in schools and now the local authority has said to them, 'actually, we can't cope either, you're now having it all back.' (Early Intervention Manager, medium children's charity)

Bolstering budgets: voluntary action in primary schools[1]

From here on, this chapter discusses and recaps research completed by this books author Alison Body and her colleague Eddy Hogg, exploring the nature of voluntary action in primary education (see Body and Hogg, 2018, Body et al, 2017 and Body, 2017). For hundreds of years, philanthropists, charities and local communities have worked together to help establish schools and provide education, however this was patchy and mainly privileged the already privileged. As we discuss earlier on in this chapter, it is only over the last century or so that we have seen decisive movement by the state to take responsibility for our children's education, partly in an effort to reduce social inequality. The government now assumes responsibility for the majority of primary education.

Even within the state-run system, charity in the form of voluntary action – the giving of time and/or money – has had a long history in the education of our children, bringing a wide range of positive benefits to schools, children, staff, the local community and volunteers alike.

> Where state schools are concerned, however, community participation in service provision significantly pre-dates the Big Society. Ever since the influential Plowden report stressed the value of parental involvement in schools, interested parents have participated in parent teacher associations (PTAs) or their equivalents, in fundraising ventures or by helping as volunteers, either in the classroom or by becoming governors. (Morris, 2011)

This actively enables schools to draw upon a wide range of additional skills and resources, can strengthen a school community and engage children in philanthropic activity from an early age. Schools continuously highlight how much they value the commitment, passion, skills and expertise brought into their community by volunteers, and recognise the advantages of fundraising in terms of community engagement, fostering philanthropic activity in children and providing additional income for the school. With an increasing range of literature, workshops and consultancy support available for schools, we recognise this as a growing market.

Unsurprisingly, voluntary action in education tends to be viewed as a positive and good thing and is increasingly encouraged within policy and practice. Volunteering and fundraising in primary schools is indeed becoming progressively central to school activities, with many primary schools keenly seeking to strategically engage and develop this area of activity. Schools increasingly purposefully foster the engagement of volunteers to help increase teacher capacity, support children through one-to-one activities and provide additional resources for both core and extra-curricular activities. Furthermore, schools highlight increasing focus on their fundraising activities to help support depleting budgets and growing demands (Body and Hogg, 2018).

Research here in the UK and abroad highlights that this activity is not without its problems. Reich's work into distribution of donated income across schools in California in the United States highlights the increasing reliance of public policy on philanthropy and evidences increasing inequality between schools as a result (Reich, 2018). Indeed, in the US, many schools or districts have professional fundraising functions which raise funds to support the school or schools. It is up to the school or district to decide whether these philanthropic donations can be spent on core academic activities or whether they can only be spent on extracurricular activities. Either way, this gives donors leverage over what the school is offering – if they do not like what the money is spent on, they can simply stop donating. The research also evidences that parents and others who donate to schools do so because they want to do the best by their children and to support local public services. Research into this topic looks at this issue from a UK perspective and shows that schools in more wealthy areas can raise substantially more than poorer areas (Body et al, 2017; Body and Hogg, 2018). The result of this is that schools in more socioeconomically advantaged areas will have more per head to spend on their pupils than schools in less socioeconomically advantaged areas (Body et al, 2017; Body and Hogg, 2018).

Schools behaving like charities

Schools are being forced to think and do things differently. There are fewer services available for schools to access to support their children, and they, as the service at the forefront of children's lives are left holding the tab. As discussed previously we see schools supporting children in their community suffering impacts from food poverty to homelessness, domestic abuse to parental mental health, alongside a number of other support services:

> If you have a child in need it is less easy to access local authority services because they just don't exist anymore in a way that they did, however people need to think differently, schools need to think differently about how you get those services, so there is a greater emphasis on schools thinking in the environment we work in, to buy in services that best meet the needs of their population. (CEO, medium children's charity)

It is unsurprising to note that in this environment schools are increasingly turning to voluntary action to bolster ever-reducing school budgets. Research by Body and Hogg (2018) revealed that the number of schools who say that they feel pressured to increase fundraised income rose from 66% to 94% between 2016 and 2018, and the proportion of schools who said that fundraising was a core strategic focus within their business planning processes more than doubled, rising from 29% in 2016 to 60% in 2018. This has significant impacts for schools, as less time is spent on focusing on high quality education for children, and more time spent balancing budgets. Primary headteachers suggested that on average they spent around 10–15% of their time each week exploring fundraising initiatives, with some headteachers reporting that this activity took up to 50% of their time.

It's about survival, and that's problematic

What becomes increasingly concerning about the role of voluntary action in education, is the that schools are ever-more reliant on this activity to support their core statutory provision. While many schools raise significant ideological challenges relating to engaging in voluntary action (Body et al, 2017), 94% of schools now identified voluntary action as a mechanism with which to respond to budgetary challenges (Body and Hogg, 2018). This has resulted in some worrying trends. As Body and Hogg (2018) identify, the percentage of schools who now say that they are at least partly reliant on voluntary action to deliver core, statutory education provision increased from 28% to 43% between 2016 and 2018, while 75% schools claimed in 2018 to be reliant on fundraised income to deliver general school activities, compared to 52% two years previously. Furthermore, over a third of primary schools surveyed reported that they have reduced their support staff and sought to replace them with volunteers, identifying this as a massive 'cost saving' for the school. At the heart of this issue, schools are becoming reliant on voluntary action to deliver core statutory services. Some schools are very successful in engaging voluntary action, although this success is not evenly distributed between schools.

How do schools fundraise?

Like most charities, primary schools fundraise in a range of different ways to secure additional resources (Body, 2017). School fairs, non-school uniform days, competitions and raffles remain the most popular fundraising mechanisms for schools. Nonetheless research suggests that more schools are relying on asking for donations directly from parents, the local community and businesses. The charity Parentkind suggest that over 40% of parents have been directly asked to contribute towards a school fund, and in March 2019, 7,000 headteachers wrote to parents asking them to lobby their MPs about school funding cuts as some schools seek drastic measure to counter budget cuts. As Figure 4.1 shows, while the days of school fairs, non-school uniform days and raffles still dominate fundraising efforts, increasingly schools are turning towards more strategic efforts to raise funds such as corporate sponsorship, asking parents for donations and approaching charitable trusts, all of which are growing in popularity.

In schools fundraising happens in two ways, directly through activities or requests made by the school, or through the school's parent–teacher association (PTA) or its equivalent. Most primary schools in England have a PTA. While best known for their fundraising efforts, the central aim of a PTA is to encourage closer links between home and school, through the collective engagement of parents and staff. The division of fundraising efforts in schools is very much dependent upon the individual school, however we do note that with areas of disadvantage the school is more likely to lead on fundraising, while in wealthier areas, the PTA is more likely to lead (for example, see Figure 4.2).

Schools' success in engaging voluntary action

With the intensified focus on fundraising activities and volunteer support in schools, quantitative data shows sharp increases in both

Figure 4.1: How schools raise funds

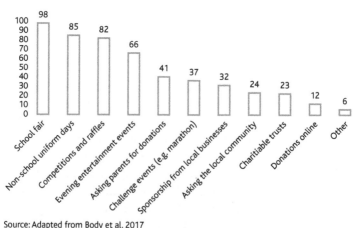

Source: Adapted from Body et al, 2017

fundraised income and volunteer activity in primary schools. In 2016, around 10% of schools secured more than £10,000 per year of fundraised income, by 2018, this figure had quadrupled to over 40%. Between 2016 and 2018, there was an overall 24% increase in the amount which schools were raising per pupil directly through donations to the school, increasing from £41 per pupil, per year, to £51. In addition, where schools had a PTA, we witnessed a 25% increase in the amount PTAs were raising per pupil per year on the school's behalf, increasing from £36 per pupil, per year, to £45 (Body and Hogg, 2018).

A similar pattern can be seen in research on volunteer support in schools. Excluding the role of the governor in the analysis, research suggests the average amount of time volunteers give, when calculated as a per child, per week amount, increased from an average of 12.5 minutes in 2016, to 21 minutes per pupil, per week in 2018. This is unsurprising when we compare it to the 2018 research in which 63% of schools stated that they increased their strategic focus on engaging and using volunteers over the past year, and 70% claimed to have increased the volunteer support which their school receives (Body and Hogg, 2018).

Is this success evenly distributed?

What Body and Hogg's (2018) research consistently highlights is that success in fundraising and volunteer engagement varies greatly across schools and is significantly affected by wider socioeconomic factors. Direct donations to schools along with that of their relative PTA's income, philanthropic income for schools in 2016/17 ranged from £1 to just over £170,000, equating to a range between £0 and £594 per pupil, per year of additional income. For the schools most successful in securing this additional income, this resulted in an 11% increase in the schools' budget (Body and Hogg, 2018). Figure 4.2 shows the relationship between school income and indices of multiple deprivation. Three important factors emerge from this data. First, the trendline demonstrates a clear link between an area's relative wealth, and the total amount of fundraised income which schools receive. Second, for schools within areas considered to

Figure 4.2: Average amount raised per school, versus index of multiple deprivation data

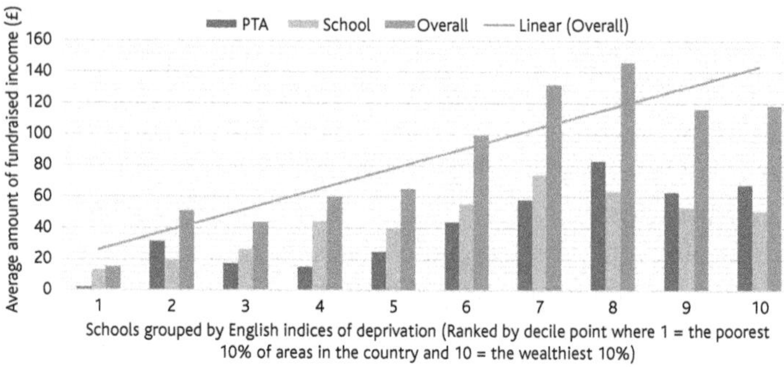

Source: Body and Hogg, 2018

be more deprived, fundraising income is generally dominated by donations directly to the schools, whereas for schools in wealthier areas PTA income plays a more equal, or even larger, role. Third, while there is a link between area wealth and overall fundraised income achieved by a school, this does not fully account for widening gaps in fundraised income by schools.

As with donations of money, volunteer time is not evenly distributed, which provides the second factor which increases inequality. Again, using indices of multiple deprivation, Figure 4.3 shows a clear relationship between how deprived an area a school is in and how much volunteer time it receives. The differences are stark. In the poorest 10% of areas, schools receive just 10 minutes of volunteer time per pupil per week, compared to 51 minutes in the wealthiest 10% of areas. Indeed, in the poorer half of areas, the average number of minutes is less than half of what it is in the wealthier half.

Volunteer skills?

Schools highlighted differences in the skills that their pool of volunteers could bring. For example, a school leader from a school in a wealthy area highlighted how they were achieving significant cost savings by reducing support staff time and replacing this with volunteers who were established child support professionals. On the other hand, leaders at a school in an area of significant deprivation highlighted how they

Figure 4.3: Average amount of volunteer time per pupil per week, versus index of multiple deprivation data

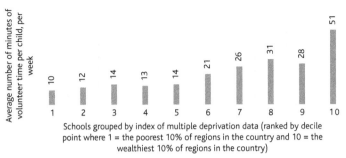

Schools grouped by index of multiple deprivation data (ranked by decile point where 1 = the poorest 10% of regions in the country and 10 = the wealthiest 10% of regions in the country)

Source: Body and Hogg, 2018

struggled to get parents to engage in the school more generally, and that a high proportion of their parents did not speak fluent English. Therefore, their 'friend's association' focused solely on engaging parents in the school community, and volunteering and fundraising was viewed as 'a step too far' (Head-teacher).

The breakaway schools

Finally, there is an increasingly disproportionate amount of total fundraised income which is harnessed by the top 10% of fundraising primary schools, and particularly by the top 1%. While the average school, taking into account both funds donated directly to schools and PTA income, fundraised approximately £19,883 in 2016/17, equating to £94 per pupil – in terms of distribution less than a third of the schools made this or above. A large proportion of fundraised income is concentrated in a few schools – the top 10% accounted for 25% of all the donated income, and the top 1% of schools account for 10% of all the donated income. If we translate this into figures, in 2016/17 the top 1% of the schools, by fundraised income per pupil, collectively raised £476,784, this compares to a total of fundraised income of £875 for the bottom 1%. In terms of the amount raised per pupil, this means the top 1% of fundraising schools bring in £563 of additional income per child through donations, versus the bottom 1% who secure £0.33 per child, per year of additional income.

A marketised education system

The education mantras of successive governments has been focused on raising standards in our schools. Indeed, schools are held publicly accountable for the test scores of their 11 and 16 year-olds, with multiple tools created to compare and cross reference schools against one another based on this matrix. It is commonplace for media outlets to publish the top 100 worst schools or similar, with little discussion about the narrative or real meaning behind these statistics. The result has been an education system within which teachers teach a rigid curriculum, with regular testing making judgements about both children's learning and teachers' teaching. Education has become skewed towards testing, which has restricted the breadth of education and understates the breadth of other work that a school does. Is a school's job simply to achieve qualifications? Biesta (2013) would argue otherwise, highlighting the role of education in the socialisation of our children and the importance of wider holistic learning. Instead, children are at risk of becoming a liability to a school's performance matrix.

There is an absolute buy-in from the UK government that improving test scores means progress, and the way to achieve this is to create and sustain a diverse education market. Charities, alongside private providers, form a crucial part of that education market. Under New Labour this market was managed, which sought centralised control of national strategies to drive up standards. The more recent Conservative drive has seen an alternative market ideology driven by freedom for actors to drive up test scores, while the state remains in control of key policies. Effectively the state devolves responsibility to schools but holds fast to key drivers of an exam-based education, resulting in a narrowing of learning. For example, a school in England can only achieve an outstanding Ofsted grading if it achieves the correct level of progress in children's assessments. This test-driven culture dominates much of school life, continuing a neoliberal theme driven by free market and economic principles. The evidence and research suggests that in terms of inequalities these strategies are simply not working, with many practitioners highlighting a concern that we are turning children off education. As charities increasingly become part of this marketised education system, as laudable as their efforts are, we must ask whether they merely end up reproducing the inequalities entrenched in the education system.

Conclusion

Education policy has been on a specific path focused on increased marketisation and competition. Driven by a neoliberal ideology, UK education policy has undergone a series of sweeping changes and disjointed reforms producing a particular version of a 'good school' which rewards children and their schools who perform well in tests while potentially excluding those who do not. As a result, 2018/19 has been a point to mark in education history, as we witness an unprecedented grass-roots uprising of headteachers campaigning against school budget cuts. Teaching union members, parents and staff have taken part in various protests about the fiscal challenges over the past few years. However, headteachers marching on Downing Street (28 September 2018) and 7,000 headteachers writing to parents pleading them to lobby their local MPs about funding cuts in education (8 March 2019) is very different. It is action made up of those people who run the schools – who set the budgets and who feel that they no longer have any place to turn.

The Department for Education claim that they are funding education more than ever before, although this is instantly disputed by the Institute of Fiscal Studies' report which pointed to an overall cut in real terms of 8% for schools (IFS, 2018). At the same time schools are being asked to spread their income further, as community support services previously funded by the government are cut and schools take on increasing devolved responsibility for their everyday running costs.

Grass-root campaign groups such as Worth Less?, School Cuts and Fair Funding for All Schools draw together parents, teachers, headteachers and communities in highlighting these growing budgetary challenges. As a result, schools are taking drastic action with far-reaching consequences, reducing staffing, increasing class sizes, severely reducing pastoral and mental health support and even cutting down the length of time they are open or the number of days they open for. They simply cannot manage on the financial resources they are currently allocated, without making some difficult decisions. Now there is no room for further cuts, headteachers reluctantly turn to voluntary action to both bolster funds and campaign against government funding of education.

As schools turn to their communities in this way, however, we see huge disparities in the success they experience. Despite their best efforts, some schools start from a position of significant disadvantage with the pool of their potential resources being drastically smaller than those schools in wealthier areas. This resulted in schools in wealthier areas attracting almost £600 per pupil per year in fundraised income compared to 12p per pupil per year in poorer areas.

Nonetheless, we should not blame or criticise any individual school for taking forward this action. Schools are doing all they can to continue to deliver the best education they can for children, this is a political issue about how this government values education. Within this we see the issue of early intervention services and school's relationships with charities and indeed the state. Commissioned services appear to be creating further barriers between other services and education, as disputes over who pays rise and charities adopt more customer/provider relationships with schools. As schools take responsibility for food poverty, housing advice and early intervention support, it appears that services that are both universal and targeted are becoming more disparate and delivered on a shoe-string rather than the collaborative, working together promoted by policy.

Note

[1] Pages 96–106 recap research completed and written with Eddy Hogg, University of Kent. This is published in the report by Body and Hogg (2018) *A bridge too far? The increasing role of voluntary action in primary education*, University of Kent. I am grateful for Dr. Hogg's permission to republish the research here.

PART III

The lived realities
of commissioning children's early
intervention services

5

Commissioning children's services: challenges, contestation and crisis

There is what commissioning is supposed to be, the story I am supposed to tell, and what commissioning is in reality … They're two very different things. (Commissioner)

Introduction

A quick internet search of the word 'commissioning', and you are immediately inundated with countless 'how-to' toolkits and a plethora of guidance about how it is supposed to work in practice and what it is supposed to achieve. However, the lived realities of commissioning have received less academic attention. What are commissioners' and voluntary sector providers' everyday lived experiences of commissioning? Is it the seamless, logical process we are led to believe in the literature, or as some other commentators have suggested, is it a messier and more complex process?

Defined as 'a cycle of assessing the needs of people in an area, designing and then securing an appropriate service' (Cabinet Office, 2006), commissioning remains one of the most contentious issues for modern day children's charities. Early intervention and preventative services for children sit central to this debate – these statutory services at the heart of local government are often commissioned out to voluntary sector organisations for delivery, and form the very focus of this book. Over the following three chapters we explore the relationship between the voluntary sector and the state in detail, drawing on both voices from the voluntary sector and commissioners themselves.

The central argument to this section is that commissioning in its current form as a competitive market process is largely failing vulnerable children, it threatens the very survival of local voluntary sector organisations seeking to support children and young people, and, rightly so, is coming under increasing scrutiny. High profile cases such as the demise of the charity Kids Company, led by the charismatic Camila Batmanghelidjh, have brought the relationship between the state and sector to the fore of public and academic debate. In the simplest terms it raises the question of how should the state and children's charities work together to ensure the best possible outcomes for children. In this chapter we begin to unpick some of that debate, examining what has happened over the past decade, charities experiences and how we may potentially move forwards. Drawing on the voices of children's charity leaders, and commissioners themselves, we argue that commissioning in children's services, in its current form, is a failed project, which lets down children and young people.

Policy context: competitive commissioning, a better approach to service delivery?

Commissioning has its roots in the discourse of new public management (NPM). NPM is an approach to running public sector services widely adopted in government, public service institutions and agencies, locally and nationally. Developed in the 1980s, NPM was a distinct move to make public services more business-like. Based on private sector models, emphasis is placed on efficiency and a customer service approach. Citizens are viewed as customers, and the professionals and public servants are viewed as the managers. Services are delivered within a framework of performance management targets.

As part of this discourse, the concept of commissioning emerged prominently in the UK in the early 1980s. The development of the dialogue around the purchaser–provider split, market testing and the mixed welfare economy was accompanied with the launch of compulsory competitive tendering (CCT). Introduced by the Conservative government in the 1980s, CCT is a requirement for public sector organisations to allow private sector firms to bid for the delivery of services (such as catering, cleaning, security and transport) in competition with any internal provision by the organisation itself. The policy intention was to drive forwards a 'market relationship' within the public sector, based on an assumption that this would reduce costs and increase efficiencies. The reality is, that this led to tenders being won by organisations who could deliver cheaply, with quality of service provision coming in second to price in the competitive process. While CCT was relaxed by the Labour government on their election in 1997, the practice remained, and the transfer of public sector service delivery to voluntary sector and private providers has persisted.

The rise of commissioning of children's services

In the context of children's services, this sustained push towards commissioning was epitomised through focus on 'joint, strategic and effective commissioning' in the Every Child Matters White Paper and the Children's Act 2004. Building on this, the 2006 Joint Planning and Commissioning Framework for Children, Young People and Maternity Services sought to deliver holistic, local services to meet local need. This emphasis on multi-agency working became commonplace under Labour with the 'duty to cooperate' enshrined in the Children Act 2004 section 10, which saw the formation of Children's Trust Boards in all local authority areas. Subsequent Local Children's Trusts Boards were established under these to represent smaller local communities. Each Children's Trust Board had to produce and monitor a local Children and Young People's Plan, which was used to advise commissioning priorities and decisions.

The emphasis on commissioning in children's services was further strengthened by the launch of the Commissioning Support Programme in 2008. This programme aimed to work with local children's services, specifically Children's Trust Boards, to help them use their resources to improve outcomes for children and families, 'efficiently, equitably and sustainably'. There was a simple, arguably unsubstantiated, assumption which underpinned this programme: better commissioning would result in better outcomes for children.

2008 onwards

In 2010, the election of the Conservative Coalition government saw significant changes for the public sector and children's services. The statutory requirement for children's trusts was removed, followed by a shift to a more localised approach to identifying local needs and funding. Coupled with severe fiscal pressures, commissioning increasingly became about cost saving. There was an intensified commitment to use commissioning as a mechanism to reform and reshape the landscape of public services (Rees, 2014).

Following the economic crisis in 2008/9 the Conservative Coalition government, abandoned the statutory requirement for Children's Trusts and the Every Child Matters agenda. In its place it established an independent review of the policy field of child protection/prevention. As previously discussed, the Munro Report recommendations focused on multi-agency working. However, with the government openly focusing on the 'reduction of public finance debt', funding for early intervention services were cut by almost one quarter in their first year in office, with the funding for the voluntary sector in this field particularly affected (Gill et al, 2011). Simultaneously a new approach to preventative policy was adopted which abandoned 'supporting families', and emphasised 'rescuing children from chaotic, neglectful and abusive homes' (Parton and Williams, 2017). This resulted in a wave of commissioning of children's services which focused on highly prescriptive, targeted, short-term interventions, which were in contrast to the longer term, relationship-based approaches adopted by most voluntary sector organisations within this field (Gill et al, 2011).

In the backdrop to all of this, children's services in the UK are in the storm of a funding crisis, from social care to education, austerity bites from all angles. Since 2008 the economic crisis has resulted in a 'doing more for less' culture. The term 'efficiency savings', has become a euphemism for funding cuts, coupled with the term 'innovation' as a way of doing more for less. At the forefront of this, councils in the most disadvantaged areas carry the burden of the most significant funding cuts (Tinson et al, 2018).

The challenges of commissioning

Unsurprisingly there are ongoing concerns about voluntary sector organisations who are increasingly reliant upon the state for a large proportion, if not the majority, of their income (for example see Milbourne and Murray, 2014). Critics argue that by forming a close relationship with the state and securing most funds from state sources, voluntary organisations face the risk of losing their independence (Independence Panel, 2015). Furthermore, the development of these relationships results in voluntary organisations being increasingly reliant upon the availability and continuity of government funding streams and therefore vulnerable to the inevitable changes in government policy and priorities. Within such relationships, these organisations are pushed to 'improve', to continuously demonstrate accountability and performance to both service users and the government, which can often be at odds with one another and poses a risk of losing sight of their original purpose. This brings to the fore concerns about marketisation of the voluntary sector and welfare reform, with a growing emphasis placed on commissioning for outcomes and efficiency savings (Milbourne and Murray, 2017).

Partly due to the previously discussed evolving ideological frameworks and the economic climate, children's charities deliver increased amounts of public sector children and family support services. However, due to the economic downturn and austerity since 2008, the resources to support the voluntary sector delivering these services have not been as forthcoming as they were previously, both in terms of funding available and infrastructure support. Therefore, we are witnessing a significant period of change for the voluntary sector, dominated by shifting government policy, which stresses the need for localism and a mixed welfare economy, alongside a rapidly changing economic climate. Some commentators welcome this activity, suggesting that it will improve relations between state and the voluntary sector (Buckingham, 2011), while others remain concerned (Milbourne and Murray, 2014).

British literature (for example Milbourne and Murray, 2017; Rees and Mullins, 2016), suggests that a range of political, ideological, policy and economic ingredients come together to generate both barriers to, and opportunities for, productive commissioning relationships. Most noticeably since 2008, public budget attrition and the intensification of organising ideas derived from NPM broadly stressing competition, choice and the importation of techniques from business, have all had to be taken as 'givens' in the new landscape (Hood, 1995). Furthermore, the research stresses that such pressures can result in voluntary sector organisations struggling to sustain their independent identities, potentially becoming supplicants to the 'marketised state' with whom they have become entangled; or perhaps seeking to opt out, distancing themselves from such processes, but as a result potentially foregoing chances to achieve valued social outcomes (Body and Kendall, 2020).

There have been multiple rationales presented for commissioning from a focus on increasing choice, devolving decision making to local areas, increasing public services efficiency while making them more accountable, transparent and opening services to a wider set of providers (HM Government, 2011). Further rationales have included increasing value for money, encouraging increased joint working and information sharing, as well as creating shared and pooled budgets (Rees et al, 2017). Nonetheless, many still have reservations about how best to commission services and who might provide them, with directors of children's services, for example, expressing concerns about accountability and quality assurance. Commissioning is a contested concept, open to interpretation, which has been summarised by various actors in different ways (Bovaird et al, 2012; Dickinson, 2014; Rees et al, 2017). The widely accepted idea of the commissioning 'cycle' approach has been broadly adopted across government (Bovaird et al, 2012). Nevertheless, there is considerable variation in how this process has been adopted in practice, leading to confusion in both theory and practice (Macmillan, 2013a; Miller and Rees, 2014; Rees et al, 2017), alongside differential emphasis applied to the different parts of this cycle (Rees, 2014). While the term 'commissioning' has been adopted widely in discourse, establishing a single definition remains problematic. Indeed, Checkland et al (2012) comment that 'commissioners and providers struggled with the more fundamental ideas underpinning commissioning, suggesting that shared understanding is far from the norm' (p 540).

The lived realities of commissioning

Central to this book are the lived experiences of 100 voices of individuals affected by commissioning arrangements. In this section we begin to draw together these voices to present some of the challenges that face those engaged in commissioning of children's services.

Definition issues

While having a shared passion about 'getting it right' and a sense of moral duty towards children, there is a distinct lack of consistency in how commissioners themselves perceive commissioning and the role of the commissioner. This is significant in the commissioning process, as it results in substantial differentiations in how commissioning is carried out in different service fields and indeed in different localities. Most notably voluntary sector organisations who work across policy areas, such as children and adult services and/or geographical areas, experience very different approaches to commissioning.

What's more, commissioners view their roles very differently. Definition of the role tends to fall under one of three orientations. For example, some commissioners frame their role in terms of procurement and efficiency saving:

> We spend the council's money, we justify what we spend it on, and prove that it was spent accurately and appropriately ... And right now that driving priority is cost savings. (Commissioner)

While this is the least likely primary framing of the role, accounting for just one fifth of how the commissioners defined it, all the commissioners acknowledged increasing financial pressures as a driver for commissioning. Under this understanding of commissioning, commissioners view commissioning primarily as a cost saving process, with value for money being a prominent part of the competitive process. Their role in that process is one of preserving the most cost-effective services for children. Under this conceptualisation of commissioning, market engagement on consultative activities with wider stakeholders was very minimal.

Alternatively, and perhaps a more popular orientation of commissioning, just over half of the commissioners frame their role in terms of service provision:

> My role, as I see it, is to, well basically ensure we provide the right services to stop children going into care. The right services in the right places. (Commissioner)

In this definition of commissioning, the commissioner is more likely to see themselves as the expert in the field, tasked with choosing who should deliver services. Service design is more likely to take place within the commissioning organisation, with some, though limited, and largely formal consultative activities. However, contract management, including the monitoring and quality assurance processes is seen as paramount within the relationship.

The remaining commissioners see themselves as the coordinator of a process:

> Commissioners coordinate the commissioning process, we do not necessarily need to be experts of the topic, that is why we consult, we bring together the right experts at the right points, and that should include the voluntary sector, but lots of others as well. (Commissioner)

Under this less common understanding of commissioning the commissioner is more likely to view voluntary sector organisations as equal partners, with whom they work in close partnership with, in order to achieve service provision for children. These commissioners are likely to view their voluntary sector partners as experts in their field and often seek to involve them in the full commissioning cycle, formally and informally.

Part of the disparity in commissioning can therefore be explained by the different approaches adopted by these individual commissioners. For example, from the very outset, when we consider how commissioners view the partnership between the public sector and the voluntary sector, views vary. Tensions emerge between those who see children's charities as independent, equal partners, and those who view those same providers as an 'extension of [the] public sector workforce' (Commissioner). This results in fundamental variations about how relationships between the voluntary sector and state are managed, with some relationships informed by principles of co-production, and others managed through a bureaucratic, administrative process driven approach – an approach which currently dominates practice (this is further expanded in Chapters 6 and 7).

Dominance of process-driven commissioning approaches

Crouch (2011) argues convincingly that it is not commissioning per se which causes contestation between state and voluntary sector organisations, but rather how the process is carried out. There is significant tension between two types of commissioning approaches: 'process driven' commissioning and 'relational driven' commissioning.

Process driven commissioning is a commissioning process which broadly focuses primarily on the administrational, financial and monitoring aspects of the commissioning process, and is constructed on a restrictive, overly bureaucratic, transactional logic. This is in keeping with Martikke and Moxham's (2010) suggestion that over-bureaucratisation of commissioning processes, lack of engagement with voluntary sector organisations and limited flexibility mean that potential benefits of commissioning such as voluntary sector providers engendering trust and beneficiary centred approaches are not fully achieved. For example:

> I think we were afraid to talk to providers, we followed the letter of the law and the process. We were kept a very close eye on by procurement, they

monitored everything, it was all by the book ... You don't get sued that way. (Commissioner)

In contrast, though less common, voluntary sector providers also identify 'relational driven' commissioning approaches which focus more on a child/young person-centred approach, defined by co-production and partnership. For example.

Before we got the contract they spoke to us and others about what the service was, then once we got it we agreed with them some sensible outcomes and outputs. It's not always that way mind you. (CEO, medium children's charity)

This dichotomy in approaches is not an either/or option, but rather a continuum of practice depending on the context of the commissioning process. Across the experiences we reflect on in this book, there is little evidence of any clear consistency in commissioning processes, nor was an 'ideal' model in commissioning 'discovered' during the research process for this book. Instead, there exists a wide variety in commissioning approaches, which vary across commissioners, commissioning organisations, and even within commissioning teams. Nevertheless, practices tending towards the process driven end of the spectrum dominate commissioning approaches. For example, as one provider comments on the commissioning of early intervention services:

They don't know better than us in terms of what children need, and that would be my message, why don't you use the expertise that we have and tap into that and work creatively to do something really amazing rather than assuming you know best and putting closed down targeted services that offer no scope for creativity. (CEO, large children's charity)

These process driven approaches were perceived to result in a polarisation of commissioner and provider relationships. Providers associate the more process focused commissioning with adversarial relationships, restrictive contracts and punitive approaches to monitoring and evaluation, which often fail to really capture the true nature of what providers felt that they had to offer.

This is problematic. For example, where issues arise in the contracts or service delivery, children's charities felt unable to discuss the best ways to manage and respond, restricting their ability to provide innovative, creative or alternative responses. The process driven commissioning relationships left children's charities feeling 'powerless' (CEO, medium children's charity), 'helpless' (CEO, small children's charity) and 'vulnerable' (CEO, large children's charity). As a result, where these charities felt this approach dominated, they actively sought ways to distance their relationship from the commissioning organisation and were reluctant to engage in any further commissioning processes:

> It's about money, tick boxes and jumping through ridiculous hoops that help no-one, so we've moved our position and now the substantial amount of our funding comes from other sources, this gives us some sort of leverage in being able to bring some more of that funding in and you are not completely reliant on the local authority so you can challenge. My board's vision and our strategic plan is to be totally independent from the local authority. You know because the hassles we get at times, are not worth it and it can be very stressful. (CEO, medium children's charity)

This perception of an unequal relationship is not unique, and shared by many of the children's charities featured in this book:

> There is an imbalance in what the local authority can potentially get away with and what we can. So for example in procurement they changed the timeframes all the time, they change the date that things have to be in all the time, but if we did that it would be 'No' you've got to keep to our timeframes. So there is not an equity in the way that kind of thing works. (CEO, large children's charity)

The more process driven commissioning approaches dominate current commissioning practices. We followed over 80 commissioning processes, within which four out of five adopted a more process driven commissioning approach, which favoured contracting and procurement processes over collaborative commissioning. However, there is an alternative in the more relational commissioning processes, within which providers work in partnership with the commissioner. In such relationships, providers are enabled to negotiate around the service need, facilitating a higher level of cooperation and innovation to shared problem solving. However, within the experiences shared for this book, this more cooperative, collaborative relationship is often reliant upon a single relationship between two individuals. Nonetheless, such an approach sought to create space wherein commissioners and providers could really work together and exercise their professional skills, judgement and expertise. For example, a CEO of a medium children's charity commented:

> On one of our services we were able to go back to the commissioner to say this isn't working and together we negotiated the service model and expected outcomes. The service was much better after that.

While another commented:

> At the moment, we have XXX as our commissioner and she is amazing, she is one of the best commissioning managers we have ever had and she takes time to understand what is happening in the service and making some allowances for when there have been difficulties that haven't been our responsibility ... And she will take that and she will take our messages up to people further up who need to know that. So if you have got people who you have got the relationship with you feel like you are a little bit more on a par. (CEO, large children's charity)

Within this context of more relational commissioning, the role of the individual commissioner is important. Whereas more process driven commissioning is associated with the financial procurement elements of commissioning, relational driven commissioning appeared more in line with the role of the commissioner as a coordinator of the process, set to bring together actors to find a combined solution. However, providers more frequently expressed concern about the more process driven, economic rationales dominating commissioning, for example:

> I think price is still a massive issue, and I understand that, but I do think that sometimes it clouds everything, it's just … well I could sit here for hours and write the most amazing bid in the whole world but if I am £1 over per hour from the other person it was pointless, and a lot of it just comes down to money and it is a guessing game cause it's like this is the contract price but obviously we don't want to pay that so come in below it, well how far below it? How much do we shave off, how much do we say well we are going to make a loss but the organisation is going to cover it. You know you can't do that on every contract you going to tender for. Mediation service, we really wanted mediation, so we are making a loss on it, but it is something we desperately wanted to be delivering and the trustees were prepared to make that loss. If you don't come in below you're not even in the race so if we don't have contracts going forwards when all the tenders come out we're in a much weaker position so it is really important that the contracts we've got at the moment are running well, delivering the right outcomes, we can evidence everything, so when we come to tender later on in the year, we are in a strong position as other organisations. (CEO, medium children's charity)

Another commented:

> I think it [the future] depends a little bit on how commissioning pans out and how much the local

authority are prepared to listen to the voluntary sector in what they see as the need, as opposed to what the local authority think they need. I think things are driven by different forces, the local authority is driven by Ofsted, and national government targets and things like that whereas voluntary sector are often more driven by what they see on the ground at that particular time and the two don't always match up so you know. (Business Manager, medium children's charity)

Over-formalisation of relationships

A risk adverse culture dominates commissioning organisations. Described as a 'culture of fear' (Commissioner) due to job insecurities, austerity and political pressures, commissioners are often prevented from actively engaging providers both indirectly and directly, and instead resort to more formal and prescriptive modes of engagement:

> I don't actually believe commissioners have to be experts within their field but they have to be taking advice from experts in their field and that is the difference. Where it is working well they are either experts in their field or they are taking advice from experts in their field, where it is not working so well, the people commissioning assume they are experts and they are not and that is really problematic for us as a sector ... Sadly it is becoming more commonplace, there is a growing gap between us and the commissioners. (Business Manager, medium children's charity)

Multiple and ongoing restructures within the public sector have left commissioners concerned about 'rocking the boat' or challenging internal processes, due to fear of reprisal from management. This is coupled with a fragmented approach to commissioning; varying across individuals, departments, organisations and localities which, as discussed earlier, creates confusion within commissioning processes, as one commissioner comments:

> Sometimes I feel we sort of make it up as we go along … And no-one wants to be the person who says 'what are we actually doing?'. We had a consultant come in once and try to tell us how to commission and it was nothing like what we did before she came or is it now after! (Commissioner)

As such, those in the role of commissioning reported frequently feeling 'exposed' (Commissioner) and 'vulnerable' (Commissioner).

More directly, children's charities are experiencing a significant decline in infrastructure support, networking opportunities and representative involvement in decision-making groups, needs analysis and service design processes. For example, one small charity reported that up until 2011 they had sat on five local decision making and networking boards for children's services, by 2018 they attended none of these as all of these groups had ceased to exist. Furthermore, a commissioner comments:

> The mantra used to be ask the voluntary sector, make sure they are represented, and we'd wheel in the same two or three people – that doesn't really happen now. We have to be very careful about how we engage with 'the market'. (Commissioner)

As suggested by this quote, justified in terms of avoiding unfair advantage in competitive processes, commissioners actively disassociate with the wider market, unless in formal 'market engagement' events. Indeed, children's charities and commissioners equally recognise that there is little representation of the voluntary sector on decision making groups, and when there is, 'it is not a true voice of the sector' (CEO, medium children's charity). Often one or two individuals from the larger, commissioned charities represent the wider sector, with little evidence of impact and with no 'authority' by the rest of the children's charitable sector to do so.

In particular, the majority of the children's charities felt that there was a lack of consultation with the charitable sector during the needs analysis or service design phase. For example, one stated:

> Decisions are made in isolation from us, we deliver the service day to day and know what works and what doesn't but get no say. They recently restructured a service and we just sat back and thought how fundamentally flawed it was – and we know that because that's the model we tried once and it failed. But you can't tell them that, nope you can't tell them that. (CEO, medium children's charity)

While another suggested:

> The voluntary sector has been cut out of the planning process almost entirely, but I think this is purposeful. It puts the sector in its place as a provider and the local authority as the customer. So organisations now make sure they are pleasing the customer and not their beneficiary. There is something deeply unsettling about that shift. (CEO, large children's charity)

Indeed, majority of the charities felt that they were actively 'pushed out' of having a voice, regardless of size:

> Yes, there's been, over the last two years, a total disengagement from the sector. I personally think as an organisation [the local authority] it is more detached as there is a push to not work in partnership but to work in contractual relationships … There has been an agenda driven by the local authority without any reference to the outside world over the last two years, and that has damaged relationships. So actually very often I will think to act politically, to voice my opinion, and then think there is no point as they are on their own pathway and they are not going to be diverted and they

are not going to be listening to any other voices.
(CEO, major children's charity)

Several of the commissioning organisations involved in this book, however, had faced high profile, costly, legal challenges with regards to children's services, which is likely to have created increased caution. Therefore, depending on the team involved, the relational aspects of their role could be considered highly problematic.

The formalisation of the commissioner–provider relationship also affected the contract management process. Contract management is the process by which commissioners use performance monitoring and evaluation to assess the success of the contract and delivery as per the service specification. During contract management processes, children's charities identify several often absurd, irrelevant and inappropriate demands placed upon them; this could be being asked to provide data and information which is of no relevance to the contract they are delivering (for example, the smoking status of parents). Indeed, drawing on the voices from children's charities, contract management remains one of the biggest areas of contention among those engaged in delivering statutory services under contract (such findings are consistent with others, for example Cairns (2009) and Martikke and Moxham (2010)). Closely related to the commissioning approaches discussed previously, and from the point of view of both providers and commissioners, a good commissioner–provider relationship is essential, although unfortunately, this appears to be rarely achieved.

For instance, monitoring requirements regularly change and, from the children's charities perspectives did not demonstrate what the charities felt that they are really achieving with beneficiaries. For instance, one charity leader commented:

> Between 2012 and 2014 the monitoring forms were changed five times without any prior warning to us it was just dropped into the inbox saying this quarter we will be monitoring this, I'd say you can't do that, it was awful. (CEO, medium children's charity)

This was a common complaint from children's charities. Monitoring requirements were regularly changed often resulting in charities having to heavily invest in administrative support to gather that data retrospectively. As well as being practically problematic many children's charities felt such a focus on form filling and data collection alienated the very children and families whom they were aiming to support.

While quantitative key performance indicators are commonplace in the for-profit sector, many of the children's charities argue that the translation of these into the non-profit sector loses sight of the added social value which charities seek to achieve, and instead creates barriers to achieving real outcomes:

> Commissioned services are just focused on hitting targets not on telling the truth. There is no place in commissioned services for them to say well we didn't make our targets so we will do x, y or z in place. No one says can we help you, what should we do – they don't ask us – they tell us what to do and then add these targets to it. The attitude is you have that money, you hit that target otherwise we will take money off you. So the commissioned services actually lie to say they've met those targets, they're forced to bend the figures to make it look good. I would put it down to the people who commission the work. They get all these applications in and they go for figures rather than quality, so the service has to then lie 'cause they can't deliver. It's all for show and no real work is happening to change children's lives, everyone just pats each other on the back for making the figures look good. (Service Lead, small children's charity)

As a result, we suggest that contract management and monitoring requirements often undermine service improvement within charities.

Inconsistent across commissioners and commissioning organisations, contract management processes appear highly dependent on the individual(s) or team of commissioners.

Children's charities raised issues around 'adversarial' and 'difficult' contract management relationships, where it was felt that the needs of the beneficiaries were not a priority and the skills and knowledge of voluntary organisation were not considered in addressing any issues. As such, many organisations have lost confidence in the commissioner–provider relationship and often do not feel respected for their skills or knowledge base. For example, one business manager in a children's charity talked about feeling bullied and attacked in monitoring meetings if they did not respond to questions as the commissioner required, comparing themselves to a 'naughty child' (Business Manager, medium children's charity). Whereas another commented that they felt their 'views were invisible and dismissed' (Early Intervention Worker, medium children's charity) without consideration. This was a trend across the children's charities involved in this book. Overall children's charities consistently feel under-engaged in the commissioning process, and largely excluded from needs assessment and design of services (Martikke and Moxham, 2010).

Size matters

Research consistently highlights that small- and medium-sized charities (those under £1 million turnover) have experienced higher income volatility than larger charities (Lloyds Bank Foundation, 2016; Mohan et al, 2016; Rees and Mullins, 2017). For instance, over half of the small and medium charities have experienced a rise or fall in income of over 20% and experienced disproportionate government funding cuts when compared to larger charities.

As detailed in the appendix to this book, we tracked the financial information of 231 children's charities, working within the field of children's early intervention services, all operating in a single geographical area. In 2008, each of the 231 organisations in the initial sample were in receipt of some form of support from statutory services, with 87% in the form of grant funding and infrastructure support, and 13% receiving infrastructure support and/or advice.

To gain an overview of the direction of financial travel of these charities the financial trajectory of these organisations was tracked. This data was based upon their real budget as reported in their financial accounts for the respective years. Table 5.1 details the direction of financial travel, based on monetary income, between 2008/09 and 2013/14. Initial size classification was based on the organisational size according to their 2008 accounts.

It is interesting to note that though there is a fairly even spread of the children's charities who have increased, decreased or ceased over the period of time, this is not evenly represented across organisational size with charities under £100,000 turnover per annum appearing particularly vulnerable. However, it is difficult to compare these figures to national trends given the specific nature, both in terms of period explored and specific focus on the area of children's preventative services. Nonetheless, the data published in the prominent *Civil Society Almanac* by the National Council of Voluntary Organisations (NCVO, 2015) supports these trends, identifying that small- and medium-sized organisations have been most affected by government spending cuts, with those under £1 million turnover experiencing a 34–38% decrease in funding. Furthermore, it suggests that these trends in income are reflected in staffing levels with large and major charities experiencing increases in staffing, whereas small and micro charities experienced significant drops in staffing levels over the same period.

While we can suggest that commissioning and public sector cuts have had a significant impact, it is important to note that they certainly are not the only factors at play. For example, other notable factors include welfare reforms, austerity and changes in

Table 5.1: Changes in children's charities income by size 2008–2014 (%)

Size*	Increased	Decreased	Ceased	Merged	Of overall sample
Micro	5.1	35.9	56.4	2.6	16.9
Small	18.7	26.7	49.3	5.3	32.5
Medium	46.5	33.8	16.9	2.8	30.7
Large	67.9	25.0	0.0	7.1	12.1
Major	55.6	38.9	5.6	0.0	7.8
Of overall sample	33.8	31.2	31.2	3.9	100.0

Note: *Micro < £10,000, Small £10,001–£100,000, Medium £100,001–£1 million, Large £1 million–£10 million, Major >£10 million philanthropic giving. Mohan et al (2016) suggest that in addition to size of charities, the strongest predictors of concern regarding financial changes, relates to being based in areas of disadvantage and the age of the charity, with charities in areas of deprivation and newer charities (those established after 1997) experiencing the greatest concerns regarding resources.

A lack of support for smaller charities to participate in commissioning processes has, however, led to a perception of commissioning processes being 'geared for a national, corporate entity' (CEO, small children's charity), a viewpoint which is shared across the children's charities:

> The concept of commissioned services is not supporting or helping smaller charities. Totally the opposite it is watching them collapse! Larger companies and charities are dominating the commissioned bids which leaves the smaller charities no option but to fade away into the unknown – it's carnage. (CEO, large children's charity)

Nevertheless, those children's charities successful in securing tenders, and heavily reliant on contracted income expressed an acceptance of this approach and identified it as part of the 'rules of the game' (CEO, medium children's charity). As such, they are potentially complicit in the process and frame this as legitimate action:

> I don't think it is an equitable process, but I think it probably is fair, and by that I mean I don't think everybody has equal access, if I am honest, that is equal access to the contracts ... for example, you have to show two years of bank accounts, and cover a certain area, so that rules out some of the organisations who have just started or are smaller. If you have just started that puts you in a very compromising position, but if you can't evidence you are experienced, are you really able to deliver? It is laborious and if you haven't got the money to pay someone to do it, or the time to do it, let alone having the skills you are

unlikely to be successful, and that is not about the quality of your work; that is about your ability to bid write. So I suppose that is what I mean, I think that is fair, we are all in that position, we all need to know whether we can bid write or not. Is it equitable? Small organisations are disadvantaged by the current rigour of the process, but that also means maybe they are not placed to deliver if they are not stable, or large enough to be resilient to market forces around them. (CEO, large children's charity)

Notably, this view of inequitable access was consistent among the large and major charities:

I think the process was ethically completely wrong and the commissioners completely missed the point in terms of the community budgets that they set and the fact the larger players who were more successful at tendering were able to apply for that and cleaned it up, and just added that to the portfolio of what they doing already and actually contradicted the ethos behind what that budget was supposed to be doing and that was completely wrong, but equally we are part of that. (CEO, major children's charity)

Nonetheless, though laudable that these larger and more advantageously positioned children's charities note these inequalities, it is also important to note that none of the charities who were successful in the commissioning processes, who engaged in the research for this book, sought to challenge this inequality in access, and arguably by participating within these processes simply reinforce and consent to this system.

Micro-, small- and some medium-sized children's charities lack the capacity and geographical breadth to tender for the majority of the contracts – this is a prominent issue in children's charities of up to £500,000 turnover per annum. Children's charities which delivered on a district or local level were the most significantly disadvantaged as many contracts are either advertised as countywide or divided into parcels which are out of reach of local organisations. This meant that if smaller organisations wished to compete, they either tried to expand quickly and justify coverage across a wider area or join a consortium or partnership. This left small- and some medium-sized charities in a dilemma of 'survival versus mission' (CEO, small children's charity). For example, as one medium charity commented:

> I feel that us smaller charities have been let down by many other services [charities] and from the likes of XXX [name of a larger charity]. When all those people were saying well this is how it should be, we need to have local provision by local people, and now they are on the other side, they are getting the money, the tune has changed and it seems to me they are there just to pick up a pay-cheque – they've sold out ... And I can't sign up to that, I can't put us into bed with them when they've sold out. (CEO, medium children's charity)

Bureaucratic procurement processes

Developing tenders is a time-consuming task, overly cumbersome, bureaucratic and administrative. Small- and medium-sized organisations particularly feel the disadvantage (Cairns et al, 2005). Larger charities are better equipped to tackle these bureaucratic processes, often with an individual or team of dedicated fundraisers, business managers or employed consultants to do the work. In contrast, CEOs of smaller children's charities report spending up to 60 hours per tender, completing the paper work. In terms of time, this draws them away from their day-to-day work within their charity, where they are often involved in frontline delivery, as well as organisational management. The overly burdensome processes did not only affect the small charities, however, as this CEO of a medium-sized charity reports:

> I logged my hours, just to get us onto the commissioning portal and when it was all downloaded it was a 48 hour piece of work, if

> I had been a smaller charity, I'd have had to put out
> a sign, closed for a week and a half. (CEO, medium
> children's charity)

These bureaucratic processes do not just have implications on time and resources for smaller organisations, but also on individuals' emotions, motivations and, at times, their personal wellbeing. Simply put, people working in and leading children's charities are angry and increasingly disenfranchised by these processes. For example, a CEO of a locally based project supporting local vulnerable families since 1990 expressed the following about the move from grants to commissioning:

> And then there was this really quick transition from
> local grants and it was reined into the central local
> authority, and then they said well we won't do that
> anymore we will just see who we want to commission
> and the way they went about it and the business portal
> you went through, and register and go through a
> formal commissioning process for the framework, and
> I got really fired up – I tried on one major one and
> I thought what the heck? It was geared for a large,
> corporate, professional organisations and there was
> no way a small little project like mine could even
> access what was being asked for on the portal, so we
> couldn't even get to the end of that as we could not
> meet the criteria. If you have a national charity who
> have a commissioning team, they are geared up for
> that, and that is what really wound me up, the way
> we were treated as a project, we had served them well
> for years and after all that time we were just being
> thrown out. There were no other funding routes or
> access routes offered – and I think the biggest and
> most upsetting thing was, we had had this ongoing
> good working relationship with local managers, who
> had some autonomy and knew us – and then it went
> from that to a group of commissioners centrally, who
> didn't know the area, who didn't know the local
> need, who didn't know us – they just didn't know

us, they didn't know the local skills, the knowledge
we had, the relationships we had locally – they didn't
know about our working relationships with the local
people, they weren't interested and it was all done
through that damn portal … A lot of projects just
went under – a lot have gone from around here.
(CEO, small children's charity)

These charities consistently share concern about commissioning
simply securing the 'best bid writers and lowest cost, rather than
the right organisation to deliver the service' (CEO, medium
children's charity). The fear of the longer-term impact,
potential loss of specialisms and established experience, is
explored later in this book, but here the feelings of powerless
and inaccessibility are clear. This was not a view that was
limited to charities, but one shared as a common theme by
commissioners as well:

Commissioning is set up to tick boxes on price
favouring low cost, and it discriminates against small
local charities because it wants countywide provision
and accepts unproven promises over experience and
proven worth from previous service evaluations.
(Commissioner)

Another bone of contention for charities consists of the ability,
or lack thereof, to negotiate and challenge contracts. Children's
charities who engaged in the contracting processes, identified
circumstances within which they felt they should challenge the
commissioning organisation, or seek to renegotiate contract
expectations, but felt unable to do so. This particularly affected
the small and medium children's charities who lacked additional
resources to form legal challenges. Therefore, challenging
contract management rarely appeared to be a reality, with
charities identifying fear of punitive repercussions or damaging
reputation as the primary reason. For example, one medium
children's charity felt that they had been asked to accommodate
additional beneficiaries outside of the original contract with
no increase in funding. They felt that this was 'in breach of

contract ... but it was politically unwise to challenge' (CEO, medium children's charity), as they were in process of tendering for another contract and felt that a challenge would negatively affect their chances of securing that tender. Further examination of the relationship between commissioners and charities also revealed a sense of powerlessness, especially from smaller- and medium-sized organisations engaged in contract delivery. One charity reflects on their experience of feeling that a contractual change partway through the contract was illegal and ultimately damaging for beneficiaries:

> But the ultimate feeling was even if we are right, it wasn't fair, who wants to take the local authority to court. We certainly don't have those resources to challenge them in court, we've never had to do that and never would want to, but you are left with an absolute sense of powerlessness because ultimately it is our staff and young people who bare the brunt of that change. (CEO, medium children's charity)

Challenges in working together

Children's charities identify that collaborative working between charities has reduced over the past decade. This is not a sweeping statement which can apply to all charities and charity types (see Chapter 6), however if we focus upon those contracted to work in partnership with the state we begin to unpick two barriers which can prevent partnership working between charities; competition and perceived predatory behaviours.

Competition

Children's charities, working within the field of early intervention services, are more likely to see other children's charities as competitors rather than collaborators with whom to cooperate. Centred on the concept of competition, understood as 'when different groups vie for advantage' (Fligstein and McAdam, 2012: 14), children's charities recognise an ongoing and increasing competition for resources, resulting in a reduction in cooperative action. In these terms, cooperation is understood as a 'combination of shared interests and common collective identity' (Fligstein and McAdam, 2012: 15). For example, as one CEO commentated as a reflection on the impact of commissioning:

> I feel there is a disconnect among voluntary organisations, there is a sense of territorialism which has been growing there for years and I think it gets more difficult the harder resources are to come by, certainly from a funding point of view. You would think a consortium going would be the way forwards but a lot aren't even up for that, they are just drawing back, going well we are doing ok thanks, or no this is our area don't get involved. It is very, this is our patch and that is prevalent, well even more so now. (CEO, small children's charity)

While another, when asked if commissioning had increased partnership working, stated:

> No, it [partnership working] has decreased, absolutely. It is a negative thing, but there is a worry about competition. (CEO, medium children's charity)

Such concerns raised several potential tensions among the children's charities. The majority of frontline workers report a recognition of an ongoing and rising turbulence in how children's charities relate to one another, a negative impact they relate to commissioning. This results in a polarisation of some charities and the creation of heightened tension alongside decreasing cooperative communication. For example:

> I thought we'd come together when a tender came out, as we all wanted the same thing from it. But actually, it wasn't the case, everyone was very closed really, to be honest. I've noticed a few years ago people were working in their silos and they didn't dare talk to each other as they were worried somebody might pinch some work off them … I've

noticed more so in the last 18 months people have gone back to their 'I need to keep this contract and I'm not going to talk to anybody cause I've got to make sure nobody takes what's ours' stance. So, the process doesn't necessarily allow opportunities for organisations to really talk openly about what they are doing and have that openness. (CEO, medium children's charity)

Nonetheless, examples of formal partnership working, such as sub-contracting, mergers and consortium working, are evident in commissioning processes. Indeed, the National Council for Voluntary Organisations' *Navigating change* report (Crees et al, 2016) identifies a rise in these formal relationships over recent years. However, our discussions with charities also reveals a difference between charities who form formal partnerships because of a tender opportunity with little previous working relationships, and those who have enjoyed a historic working relationship. For example:

We came together to form a consortium to bid for the local authority contracts. And there were two reasons we did that, one we all more or less think the same things, and that is why it has worked well us coming together, and we've known each other for a long, long time, it wasn't just done because this is what we need to be doing, it was done because actually we want to do this. We all think the same and certainly what was happening within the refuge movement locally and nationally, was larger organisations were coming in and taking over the running and yes they can offer it as a cheaper service, and yes the frontline worker may be enthusiastic and very for it, but it didn't come out of the women's movement, and that's where we were coming from so it was a slightly different ethos. (CEO, small children's charity)

In this and other similar examples, children's charities with a shared historic relationship and similar ethos often shared skills and led on themes across the partnership. For example, another partnership of three providers formed teams across a geographic area to deal with different elements of a commissioned contract. None of these charities had capacity to deliver the tender individually, but together they were more able. As a result, they shared resources, line management and support services for staff outside of their individual charities. These forms of partnership are potentially more robust in responding to any problems that may arise, with charities having a stronger commitment to retaining relationships above competition.

In contrast, charities with no historic relationship coming together to secure commissioned contracts were more likely to each deliver segments of a service in isolation, and at times with little awareness of what each other was doing. For example, a consortium of charities secured a tender to deliver an emotional wellbeing service across a single local authority area. Each charity was tasked to deliver in their own geographic area, often using different models of delivery, with one 'lead' charity taking overall responsibility for the contract and financial management. The charities involved in this project felt it was 'unequal', 'unfair' and that the lead charity was 'in it for profit, contributing little while everyone did the work.' As such another member of this consortium commented 'we should not have got into this with them, our values and priorities are just too different' (CEO, medium children's charity). Each of the charities involved in this consortium reported that they would be unlikely to seek a partnership with the consortium beyond the life-time of the project.

Notably, commissioners assume that larger organisations will form partnerships with small local organisations. However, this is not often a reality. Based on the voices who have contributed to this book, charities are most likely to form partnerships with those who resemble themselves in size, scope and mission. For example, of the 40 charities we spoke to, 16 were currently involved in some form of a formal, contractual partnership with another charity (30 had been involved in at least one formal partnership within the past three years), all of these were medium to major charities, only three of these partnerships involved a small charity.

Children's charities largely see this increase in competition as a deliberate move by commissioning organisations to focus their relationships on particular parts of the market, suggesting that 'they only want to have to deal with a couple of major players and leave the rest of the sector to fight it out' (CEO, medium children's charity).

Predatory behaviours

The increasing marketisation of the voluntary sector and charities, coupled with the promotion of large professional third sector organisations under Labour (1997–2010), and up-scaled contracts through the Conservative Coalition (2010–2015) government into the current Conservative government (2015–), has seen an upsurge in the perception of predatory behaviours among children's charities.

> We felt very resentful to people coming in and taking work which we have been doing for years.
> (CEO, small children's charity)

Commissioning continuously favours large organisations over smaller (Milligan and Fyfe, 2005; Munoz, 2009). Consistent across the leaders of children's charities and commissioners interviewed, the 'predatory' behaviours of larger, and often perceived 'less ethical' (CEO, Small Children's Charities) charities are on the rise.

Poor commissioning practices were perceived to result in small and medium organisations being marginalised in local communities, driving out highly skilled local organisations, with established relationships and connections, and replacing them with large scale services, parachuted into a local area. This resulted in perceptions of unfair and unjust treatment of smaller charities:

> I am upset about commissioned services solely on the basis that I've certainly seen local organisations disappear and I've seen new ones form that I just will not accept are doing the job the old one was

doing 'cause I can clearly see that the young people are not accessing those services. (CEO, medium children's charity)

In these terms predatory behaviours are understood as a broader act within which some children's charities used mechanisms perceived as less legitimate by other actors within the field to gain advantage. For example, a CEO of a medium-sized charity viewed another similar-sized charity as 'going after every contract they can, regardless of whether they can deliver on it – they are just good bid writers and have the members' [local authority elected members] ear' (CEO, medium children's charity). Another defined 'predators' as 'those organisations who are just interested in chasing the money, so under-price a smaller group to win the contract even though they know others would be better at delivering that service' (CEO, small children's charity).

However, the legitimacy of these identified predatory behaviours is perceived differently by different actors. Commissioners appeared to recognise this perception of predatory behaviour as a 'necessary evil' (Commissioner) of the commissioning and tendering process, and some commissioners suggested that it resulted in the best provider being commissioned. Nonetheless, small charities which struggled to engage with the commissioning processes felt that it was against the ethos of 'charity', with several suggesting that it was both harmful to beneficiaries and betrayed voluntary sector values. For example, one charity leader commented:

> Commissioning brings out the worst in people, once it felt we were all in this together for the sake of children and communities. Now it feels like everyone out for themselves … It's not really what we're supposed to be about. (CEO, small children's charity)

The perception of predatory behaviours reduces partnership working, as smaller charities view larger counterparts as a threat to their survival. For example, a CEO of a small children's charity felt concerned when it came to competing with others for funding:

But funding is tricky, at the moment we are doing different services than these big players, but it is always keeping my eye on them, they are a threat. But there are other organisations that are a threat to me, [charity a] are a threat to me, because they are venturing into different things and they don't seem to look to whether it is already happening before they get funding … so that worries me a bit, that they are a bit of a loose cannon, there are quite few. [Charity b] are also a threat. They keep stepping outside of their remit into mine, it is very much 'Get out of my field', yeah because I literally could lose funding and bits of my organisation will close and I can't get funding 'cause you over there have got it [gestures to others in distance] and do you know how to serve this local community, no you don't. (CEO, medium children's charity)

Nonetheless this activity is legitimised by the larger children's charities working within the field of early intervention services, who saw the threat of predatory behaviour as problematic but also legitimate and acceptable:

Where we were in a position to apply, we did, and were successful and we won't apologise for that but we will feel sorry the rest of the sector who really deserve to have a better, a more advantageous approach to that budget, because it was reduced and it was … well if I take a step back from my role and the organisation and just purely give it an ethics view those smaller organisations have a greater impact for a smaller budget, that is where that money should have gone. (CEO, major children's charity)

Yet, what is also notable, is that all children's charities, regardless of their size, consistently highlighted a fear of larger organisations parachuting in and 'taking' their work, and furthermore the very real threat (and reality) of private organisations coming in to deliver welfare-based services. For example, one major children's charity leader commented:

> As the welfare state diminishes, there is space to compete for contracts currently, what will change that game completely is if we have external players come into our market place and that is always there as a threat. It hasn't yet been realised, it is the speck on the horizon that we've all sort of known is there but the minute Serco, Tribal, Babocks, Capita go 'that contract is worth our while' and move in and will take it on a loss leader basis to get a foothold in the local authority, and we are then very conscious that is some of the challenges we face in other areas as well, in that the people in these national or private groups, we understand that they will take it on as a loss leader. (CEO, major children's charity)

There is however a narrative of legitimisation of this parachuting-in behaviour among the large and major children's charities, legitimised through a diversifying to survive-type discourse:

> I am sure they (small charities) could find us predatory, 'cause we can find it predatory for example if some organisation suddenly turned up and started delivering all of our services and we would feel that is was inappropriate 'cause their local knowledge wasn't as good as ours and all those things those very small organisations can feel. I mean we are a funny size organisation, we are somewhere between those very grassroots organisations and those bigger regional based organisations, we are mid ground, and yes I can see how some other organisations can find that threatening. But I would ask would they find that threatening if it was another small organisation, very probably, if another small organisation moves into your local area and starts delivering services you have traditionally been delivering it is threatening,

but I don't think that is necessarily about size. (CEO, large children's charity)

Conclusion

Commissioning remains a dominating force in the definition of the relationship between the state and the voluntary sector (Rees, 2014). Nevertheless, the current, multiple and inconsistent models of commissioning evident even within the single field of activity of children's preventative services are not yet realising the perceived benefits of commissioning outlined in the multiple policy-based documents which have been adopted by commissioning bodies.

This chapter demonstrates some significant risks and pressures brought on by commissioning that can lead to negative consequences for some (but not all) children's charities. Too often commissioning is conflated with procurement, focusing on price over quality of service. Children's charities and commissioners each suggest that a more relationally driven model of commissioning, based on partnership brings benefits above those of more process-focused approaches, as it creates a permissive space which allows actors to draw on a range of professional skills, expertise and judgements to co-construct services. However, political pressures, risk adversity and a lack of cooperation among actors means that these relational processes are less frequently realised.

Furthermore, restrictive tendering and contract management processes threaten the perceived potential benefits of commissioning by preventing innovative, creative and beneficiary centred responses. As a result, we suggest that predefined service specifications, which do not take into account specialist knowledge from children's charities delivering in these areas, are leading to a potential loss of specialist skills and cooperation among actors (Moriarty and Manthrope, 2014) in supporting vulnerable children.

Moreover, for children's charities there is a real threat of mission drift (Cunningham, 2008), heightened concern about competitiveness and increased concern about voluntary sector independence, autonomy and critical voice. Therefore, in this book we call for a re-definition of the relationship between commissioning organisations, as state actors, and the voluntary sector. The current dominating hierarchical nature of this relationship potentially threatens to undermine the perceived benefits of commissioning and further increase instability within fields of activity.

Children's charities and commissioners clearly understand that finances are depleting, however rather than consistently working cooperatively together with one another to explore alternative ways to meet the needs of beneficiaries, the contestation within some of the relationships threatens to stifle innovative responses on all fronts. The current, varying practices of tendering processes and contract management further contradict this, with risks of mission drift, skill loss, funding inconsistencies and instabilities placed upon the voluntary sector. Equally, there is a recognition that the voluntary sector is not a passive recipient within this relationship. In order to redefine this relationship, charities have to alter their positioning and help redress issues around representation, managing relationships and addressing need. Increasing investment and support of infrastructure services for the voluntary sector could help address this. However, any redefinition of the relationship between state and voluntary sector actors relies on a focus on open, transparent communication and cooperation in solving local issues, openly involving all interested parties to contribute to the identification of needs and solutions.

Commissioning has not achieved a fully diverse model of services being delivered outside of the public sector and increasing choice as some advocates of commissioning would like (for example, Blatchford and Gash, 2012; Sturgess et al, 2011). Nor has it led to full marketisation and privatisation of services and complete loss of independence of voluntary sector organisations as critics suggest (for example, Benson, 2015; Davies, 2008). Instead commissioning appears to have left us with a somewhat messier, complex and contested space which is highly relational, political and often ambiguous. In terms of early intervention and preventative children's services this has led to a confused and often defensive voluntary sector with individual children's charities struggling to define or identify their position or role within this field of activity, as we explore in the next chapter.

6

The changing role of children's charities delivering early intervention services

> Early intervention is no longer about helping the postnatally weepy mother – we don't have time for that, because there is another one over there who is threatening to put a pillow over her baby's head – and that is what we now call 'early' intervention … we have become firefighters, nothing more.
> (Charity Worker, medium children's charity)

Introduction

We have thus far discussed how commissioning may be perceived as a failed project, and some of the challenges for both children's charities and commissioners in navigating the ever-changing landscape. Let's now move on to explore the impact of commissioning and policy changes on early intervention and preventative services for children, delivered by the charitable sector.

As we have discussed, the definition of early intervention and preventative services is highly contested and politicised within policy and commissioning processes. This reflects an ongoing debate regarding the shifting paradigm of prevention. Indeed, providers debate and disagree about exactly what early intervention and preventative services should look like, and indeed who should deliver them. However, the one thing they disagree less about is a shared understanding that commissioning arrangements negatively affect the delivery of early intervention services for children and young people.

As the commissioning narrative has matured, there has been an overall disengagement between the providers and the state. As the state seeks to redefine preventative services, it has been simultaneously disengaging with children's charities as partners (see Chapter 5). In reality, this has meant a cessation of partnership meetings and lack of engagement from local authorities and associated commissioning organisations in terms of service design and needs analysis.

As the charitable sector is increasingly exposed to intensifying marketisation, polarisation of relationships increases. Indeed, the tendency towards this polarisation of relationships is significant in terms of the discussion concerning redefinition of preventative services, highlighting the apparent lack of voice and agency of children's charities in terms of defining this area of activity. Conversely, however, children's charities are increasingly picking up this work and delivering on this agenda.

Policy overview: the relationship between the charitable sector and the state

Practitioners, academics and policymakers have had a long-term interest regarding the ongoing interplay between the government and the voluntary sector. Writing in the earlier stages of the Labour government Harris (2001) suggested that voluntary sector organisations were increasingly resembling governmental organisations, and 'are in effect "incorporated" into the public or business sectors through combined effect of competition for funding, tight contracts and close and detailed monitoring' (Harris, 2001: 215). Arguably, this view is precisely the outcome intended by the then Labour government moving towards a 'mixed economy of welfare with non-governmental organisations delivering services on behalf of the state and according to policies developed by politicians and government officials' (Harris, 2001: 215). Frumkin (2002) continued the theme of 'incorporation' through his study in which he recognises the four central functions of the voluntary sector as: service provision, social entrepreneurship, community and political engagement and the facilitator for operationalising individual's values. Frumkin argued that by balancing these four values and not allowing one to outcast another, voluntary sector organisations should thrive and attract sustainable financial investment. Presenting a bottom-up analysis of the loss of autonomy through contractualism, Frumkin argues that it is not the process of procurement, tendering and contracting with government that causes a loss of autonomy, but it is the competition with profit making businesses wherein the problem lies. The consequence of this competition, can lead to increasing professionalisation of charities as they deal with a larger variety of income streams. Not only does this result in 'mission drift' but also leads to the voluntary organisations becoming 'vendors' for the government, as the government's means of production (Frumkin, 2002). Fyfe (2005) suggested that this places the voluntary sector in a quandary. On one hand, if it delivers local 'neighbourhood-based services', it is therefore unable to contribute to a larger scale service delivery as per state requirements. On the other hand, to deliver such requirements would necessitate the restructuring and professionalisation of the voluntary sector which can lead to a division between volunteers, paid staff and beneficiaries of the organisations as a hierarchal structure is created mirroring that of state organisations.

Despite the concerns expressed, the prominence of commissioning has risen dramatically in public and social policy (Rees, 2014). However, as we identify in Chapter 5, commissioning itself was not a 'new' phenomena, originating from the 1980s push for compulsory competitive tendering (Entwhistle and Martin, 2005) and a continued shift in thinking by public sector bodies in how they accounted for and engaged in outsourcing services, alongside an increased focus on reducing public spending (Bartlett, 2009). Cunningham and James (2017) identified this rapid increase in outsourcing of statutory services to the voluntary sector under Labour 1997–2010 through grants and commissioning. This 'hyperactive' (Kendall, 2009) rise in contractualism and professionalism, resulted in many voluntary sector organisations entering into contracts and commissioning agreements for the first time. However, Evans (2011) argues that contracting and commissioning public sector responsibilities out to the voluntary sector is not 'transferring' public sector services authority to the civil society but 'merely the arrangement of alternative delivery agencies for services that public bodies remain accountable for' (p 166), this does not alter the power of 'big government' just simply makes it less visible.

There is an assumption that parts of the voluntary sector are expected to participate within the politics of policy formation, although it is rarely given the means (human resources, capacity, and so on) to do so. This therefore leads to smaller, more service based organisations being marginalised in such processes (Blake et al, 2006). Billis (2001) argued that there do exist some opportunities for the voluntary sector to participate in the political field of social policymaking, including careful selection of policy participation and the identifying and addressing of particular problems which receive individual high profile political focus. Additionally, infrastructure development organisations suggest that this relationship between the state and the voluntary sector decreases the local organisations' ability to exert political influence as they are competitively and directly involved in a purchaser–provider relationship, negating an ability to have an impact on resource allocation and commissioning priorities. The development of the 2013/14 lobbying bill, now enshrined as an act, popularly termed as the 'gagging bill', curbs the campaigning rights of charities 12 months before a general election potentially threatening their political voice (Independence Panel, 2015).

It is important to acknowledge that while the state provides a large amount of the funding reported by the voluntary sector, this is not the only source of income. For example, in 2015/16, of the £47.8 billion income for the sector, £22.3 billion came from individuals (donations, legacies, fees for services and individual fundraising), while £15.3 billion was income from government (grants, contracts and fees). The remaining amount came from voluntary sector grants and private sector donations, with the national lottery contributing £0.7 billion to the sector income (NCVO, 2018).

The argument for independence of the charitable sector

There is a growing body of academics, organisations and individuals campaigning for the independence of the voluntary sector. Throughout Labour's term in office the voice of concern grew, resulting in organised movements by the sector including the National Coalition for Independent Action (NCIA) and the publication of a series of assessments about voluntary sector independence from the 'Independence Panel'. Here we briefly explore the voices of dissent and understanding surrounding voluntary sector independence.

Established and funded by the Baring Foundation, the Panel on the Independence of the Voluntary Sector aimed 'to ensure that independence is seen as a top priority by the voluntary sector and those with whom it works and to make recommendations to ensure that it is not lost' (Independence Panel, 2015). The Independence Panel consisted of prominent, high profile members from across the voluntary sector community, including Sir Roger Singleton (Chair of National Council of Voluntary Child Care Organisations and Independent Safeguarding Authority, as well as a former Chief Executive of Barnados), Emiritus Professor Nicholas Deakin CBE from Birmingham University (Chair of the 1996 Deakin Commission) and Julia Unwin (Chief Executive of Joseph Rowntree Foundation). Commonly known as the Baring Commission, the panel began a series of annual benchmarking reports starting from a baseline assessment in 2012. The panels' second and third assessment in 2013 and 2014 respectively concluded that 'the independence of the voluntary sector is being undervalued and is under serious threat' (Independence Panel, 2015: 6). The report highlighted the importance of independence, stating: 'Voluntary sector organisations are widely valued and trusted because of their independence. Independence gives people confidence that charities and other voluntary organisations are pursuing a mission that is not state sponsored or driven by private gain but is furthering the public good' (Independence Panel, 2015: 6).

Crucially the Baring Commission argues that threats to the independence of the voluntary sector result in a loss of the independent voice in the policy framework which represents the most disadvantaged and deprived areas in the country. The threats to independence due to an ever-growing reliance by voluntary sector organisations upon the state, are presented under six main themes: loss of the sector's voice, loss of independence, lack of consultation, unsupportive statutory funding arrangements, ineffective safeguards and regulations protecting the sector and threats to independent governance (Independence Panel, 2015). The final report in 2015 suggested that instead of seeing improvements in any of these areas; none of the areas had shown any improvement and instead four of the six areas had worsened (Independence Panel, 2015).

The Baring Commission concentrated not only on the damaging impacts of the state–voluntary sector relations but also on the missed opportunities for these sectors to work together effectively. Furthermore, the reports draws attention to the tensions between the voluntary sector as a service provider and as an advocate for beneficiaries: 'The voluntary sector is being increasingly characterised as a service deliverer – valued as a contractor for public services at low cost, applauded as an agent for alleviating social problems, but attacked when it raises its voice in dissent or argues for change' (Independence Panel, 2015: 11).

Such concerns have not been helped by the comments of politicians such as Brett Newmark MP. The then new minister for charities, controversially remarked that 'the important thing charities should be doing is sticking to their knitting and doing the best they can to promote their agenda, which should be about helping others' (Fearn, 2014).

The Baring Commission is certainly not the only voice of discontent in the sector. In 2008, Andy Benson launched the National Coalition for Independent Action (NCIA) as a voice of dissent against what he termed as the sector becoming 'enslaved to the objectives of the state'. Funded by the Tudor Trust, an independent charitable trust, the NCIA defines itself as 'an alliance of individuals and organisations who believe that we need to unite in independent voluntary and community action' with two linked campaign areas –speaking out against privatisation and working with commissioners to promote other ways of commissioning. They promoted public activism and speaking out against social injustice. A growing number of voluntary sector practitioners, researchers, academics and scholars alike supported the NCIA. Though they state they are not a political lobbying group, a political bias against the coupling of the state and voluntary sector is clear throughout the work and the growing support they received. A number of academic and practitioner-led research papers have been produced, illustrating the strength and direction of the movement for voluntary sector independence. For example, Aiken's (2014) study for NCIA of small (under £100,000 turnover) and micro (under

£10,000 turnover) community support groups concluded that government spending cuts had affected them most significantly and the current commissioning arrangements resulted in very little of the government money reaching these organisations, with the largest 1.2% of charities taking over 69% of all the charitable income in 2013. Ryan (2014) argues that only 'mega charities are in any position to enter and hold their own in this increasingly marketized landscape' (2014: 23) and the outsourcing of services is simply badly disguised privatisation. Benson (2014) argues for a fundamental shift in how the voluntary sector is viewed in terms of its role in the community, and argues for the return to the grants-based system, rejecting current commissioning and procurement processes as too commercialised and reflecting private sector values. Milbourne and Murray (2014) present the argument, through case study analysis, that larger charities are seen as predatory within the sector at the cost of smaller charities, and though some demonstrate ethical practices in terms of the sector as a whole, the overwhelming feeling is one of private market competition. Rochester's (2014) study argued that the expansion of a workplace model approach for service delivery organisations, promoted through commissioning and contracting arrangements, is threatening the roles of volunteering and the work of smaller voluntary organisations. He concludes that 'the dominant paradigm threatens the untamed and often maverick expression of free will that defines the authentic spirit of the volunteering impulse, and can serve to separate and distance the work of voluntary sector organisations from those volunteers and voluntary groups that occupy the world of activism' (Rochester, 2014: 15). The NCIA ended in 2016, but not before raising a debate with Labour MPs and peers at the Commons in 2015. Benson's (2015) statement to MPs called for 'a chance to press our case for radical voluntary action. This, we hope, is a chance to tell Labour MPs and Peers what has been happening to voluntary groups and what needs to happen to put things right' (Benson, 2015). The debate sought to bring to the fore what NCIA representatives referred to as the 'catastrophic' impacts of the attempts of co-option of the voluntary sector into the public and private sectors and the impact this was having on voluntary action (Benson, 2015).

Debates surrounding the concepts which underpinned the Big Society continued upon the election of the Conservative party in 2015, which saw a continuation and strengthening of the neoliberal driven ideology, these debates have continued into the localism agenda and more recently the launch of the Civil Society Strategy in 2018. The strategy adopted by the Conservative government pivots on an increased role of the voluntary sector while seeking to demonstrate a commitment to the welfare state. In driving forward an austerity agenda there has been continued pressure to reduce public spending, while attempting to maintain electorate support, hence spending cuts have been concentrated on defined areas of activity. While the localism agenda suggests that the voluntary sector is best placed to deliver on social welfare, critics argue that this is not a redistribution of wealth but instead a shift in responsibility for providing a fair society: 'In the small society the poor and miserable are provided for by a welfare state. In the Big Society they are free to fend for themselves as self-responsible entrepreneurs of poverty' (Bonefield, 2015: 428).

Indeed, significant concerns regarding the independence of the voluntary sector in terms of voice, purpose and action remain. The Civil Exchange (2016) published its fifth annual assessment of the state of health of the voluntary sector in 2016. Entitled *Independence in question*, the report warns that independence in the voluntary sector is at a five-year low, leaving the voluntary sector at a significant risk of loss of autonomy and calling for unification of the voluntary sector to help avoid further threats. The 'no advocacy' rules which were introduced in February 2016 prevent voluntary sector organisations from campaigning and acting in roles of advocacy in all taxpayer funded grants and contracts. Such a clause inhibits the voice of voluntary sector organisations in the design of services to support society.

A complex picture

When considering the relationship between the state and voluntary sector through the lens of both Labour and Conservative ideologies we face a difficult scenario. Voluntary sector organisations are expected and encouraged to take on the delivery of public sector services, throughout the majority of the Labour term this was a relatively comfortable position as funding increased and was largely sustained. However, as Britain entered into the economic downturn this position became highly volatile and increasingly unstable. Charities have had to face difficult decisions about whether to alter what they do in order to continue to find income or alter how they work in order to stay committed to their central mission. Arguably in most cases there is likely to have been some sort of trade-off to one degree or another. The vanguard policy of the Big Society, for public sector employees to 'roll out' areas of the public sector as community mutual or social enterprises, highlights this risk. By becoming 'independent' organisations outside of the public sector they become vulnerable to further public spending cuts and an increasingly open market place where they could lose contracts to the private sector, and other voluntary sector organisations with increased scales of economies, thus offering a 'cheaper alternative' and more experienced and sophisticated tendering arrangements (Evans, 2011). Localism potentially signals a retraction of the welfare state, with the role of charities providing infrastructure much as they did pre-welfare state. However, the process that has been witnessed over this time has seen charities in the 1930s call for more state action; to a rethinking of the role of the voluntary sector in the 1970s; to an embracing of a voluntary sector and state relationship in the 1990s and 2000s; to one of both embracing, and dissent and rebellion against these relationships with the rise in prominence of commissioning and contractualism.

At the centre of this debate is the policy agenda and implementation of commissioning. Though often framed as a new process forced upon the voluntary sector, the discourse of commissioning started in the labour 'partnership' narrative following a continuum through the Coalition government (Painter, 2013) and into the current Conservative government. Essentially the concept and importance of the commissioning agenda has been an established part of the 'political narrative' (Rees, 2014: 59). Critically assessing commissioning as a policy agenda, it can be seen as an attempt to redesign the very essence of how public services are delivered (Rees, 2014). However, the multi-tiered and complex nature of political decision-making and responsibilities in the UK, results in a multifaceted picture within which policymaking at central government level can be interpreted differently at the local level, thus resulting in huge diversity among those implementing commissioning processes (Bovaird et al, 2012). Benson (2010) for example argues that public sector organisations are using commissioning as a tool of control over voluntary sector organisations, threatening their independence and mission. In contrast, Crouch (2011) asserts that it is the quality of commissioning processes that matter, and commissioning itself is not the central issue.

Therefore, when considering commissioning and the voluntary sector we are left with a somewhat complex and contested picture. As we have seen, there is an inclination for academics and practitioners to interpret commissioning with a sense of foreboding and doom. However, there are counter arguments which suggest that commissioning has the potential to offer a more collaborative approach and indeed offers the potential for voluntary sector organisations to gain an advantage in terms of recognition and driving forwards the delivery of social welfare outcomes (Miller, 2013; Rees, 2014). Such disparity in opinions, within the backdrop of an evolving and continuing developing policy agenda, gives rise to ongoing debate that requires further investigation. Coupled with this there is a lack of research detailing the actual impact felt by charities, from their perspectives, during the transition from Labour, to the Coalition, to the Conservative governments, and the 'Big Society' concept and how this has affected organisations. This brings us back to the central idea of this book, a specific focus on how children's charities have coped and responded during this decade of change.

Fluctuating thresholds: what is early intervention?

Here we discuss the factors which children's charities feel compromise their independence and autonomy. The tension surrounding the definition of early intervention reflects the problematic task facing services in terms of balancing their independence versus contractual obligations. As Hardiker et al

(1991) point out, how early intervention is defined by the state heavily influences the type of services delivered. When drawing analysis from this perspective it is interesting, though perhaps unsurprising, to note that overall children's charities demonstrating traits that are more conformist in their approach to sector–state relationships highlighted the need for early intervention to target particular 'problem' families. In contrast, children's charities who were demonstrating more dissenting traits, openly criticising the state's approach to early intervention, were more likely to be more fluid in their definition and reflect preventative services as needing to be open access or free to all at the point of need.

As such, the central understanding of preventative services is a cause of tension among frontline staff. Nevertheless, across the children's charities, there is shared consensus that tiers for intervention and support had notably shifted over the past decade (2008–2018). Children's charities feel this shift no longer reflected early intervention and preventative services as they understood the term, instead aligning it more with 'child in need' where children are considered to have 'more serious problems involving risk, in which amelioration and containment might be all that could be achieved' (Hardiker, 1991: 347). For example:

> Oh the thresholds have definitely gone up. We've seen that as a gradual creep with the crisis at Tier 3 [targeted] and Tier 4 [specialist] level services, the threshold for Tier 2 [early intervention] seems to be, you know, rising and rising so actually universal service is almost now what we would have called early intervention services. So actually all we're doing is just ratcheting up as we can afford to see less and less people as time goes on and budgets diminish. (CEO, major children's charity)

Another CEO described the shift as akin to 'moving the fence':

> I always use this cliff top metaphor. The families in social care [Tier 3] have rolled down the ravine somewhere and social services are trying to pick them up, volunteers and the workers are simply now

hanging over the edge trying to save the other [Tier 2] families from falling back down. Whereas we should be building a fence further back and not let those families ever go near that edge, but that is the problem, no one is maintaining that fence … Early intervention is the fence, not the rescue service when they fall off the ravine. (CEO, medium children's charity)

Effective early intervention is recognised as pivotal in preventative work (Allen, 2011a; Munro, 2011; Turney et al, 2011). However, the raised thresholds to access children's social services mean that while preventative services are often delivered by the wider children's workforce, the children accessing these services have heightened needs:

We are receiving referrals for what used to be a social service need. Child protection services now won't be helping and I think that we are a preventative service and what happens if we are no longer here. (Charity Worker, small children's charity)

This shift in definition of early intervention also affects the types of services many children's charities deliver, resulting in providers commonly engaging increasingly complex families with time-limited programmes. Targeting time-limited interventions at families with multiple complex needs does little to address the underlying social problems (France et al, 2010; Pithouse, 2008). The need to identify and target specific families has inevitably led to concerns expressed at the heightening needs of families and pressures put on services to deal with these needs:

There are always discussions about what does that term [early intervention] actually mean in terms of what are you doing with a family or individual young person, and generally people obviously meant dealing with issues before they escalated and as quickly as you can when they arise. But in reality, the local authority and others at the time haven't really wanted to commission that service 'cause they can't immediately evidence the value or benefit of it. So we are constantly finding the thresholds going up and up and up regarding the kind of families we are now being expected to work with, to incredibly complex needs that will take a really long time to work with and some of those needs are really ingrained in those families' generational impact. And we might have a family we can't cope with and we'll say we really feel this needs social services intervention and they would be like no that doesn't meet the threshold criteria any more … so the cases we are getting, we wouldn't call them preventative or early intervention, as they are already way passed that. (CEO, large children's charity)

While, as we shared at the start of the chapter, another commented:

Early intervention is no longer about helping the postnatally weepy mother – we don't have time for that, because there is another one over there who is threatening to put a pillow over her baby's head – and that is what we now call 'early' intervention … we have become firefighters, nothing more. (Charity Worker, medium children's charity)

Interestingly, and perhaps predictably, children's charities who actively seek to disassociate with the local authority have felt less impact concerning how they define early intervention and prevention services. As a result, they have remained more flexible about the term. For example, one charity worker commented:

I'm not sure I'd say we have a clear definition of absolutely what we class as early intervention, and we're ok with that. I think our argument is it's never early enough so we have backed away from some of the traditional arguments around it and tend to focus on what crops up for us around the needs for young people as we see it from a local community. For example, our work was originally driven by anti-social behaviour and then wanting to be clear about what we do to try to tackle some of that, so a positive futures outlook for young people approach … Our remit very much was to go into the areas where we have a lot of young people living and talk to them about what their issues were, give them that voice, let them develop themselves the issues or what they see as the things that need tackling. And that's really let them set the agenda for us in terms of what's needed around early intervention. (Children and Youth Worker, medium children's charity)

Another CEO of a small children's charity outlined this as the very reason that they refused to engage with public sector bodies:

To me, need is defined by someone saying 'I need help', the moment we turn that person away, whatever bloody tier they may be at, is the moment we have lost our way. Early intervention shouldn't be a tick box exercise, it should be responding to the needs of individuals when they need it. I will never be told who we can and cannot help by a form! (CEO, small children's charity)

The impact of shifting definitions around early intervention has affected children's charities differently, some more than others, and often largely depending on their relationship with commissioners and funding bodies. Those with more freedom to choose how they define early intervention and prevention have seemingly withdrawn from engagement with, or flexibly interpreted, the early help framework policy definitions discussed in the introduction and context setting. Such an approach chimes more with a perception that their role is to address the underlying social problems and wider social concerns (Hardiker et al, 1991). This potentially poses both opportunities and threats; opportunities in terms of traditionally Tier 2-type services of continued provision outside of the state to benefit families; and threats in terms of children's charities taking on more complex cases than they can manage and potentially being held accountable if things do not go according to plan.

There is an inherent threat across this mismatch of early intervention and prevention services that families will continue to receive disparate services, either in terms of having no access to local traditionally defined early intervention and thus their needs escalating or seeking support from children's charities who previously supported them and being turned away. Additionally, the lack of communication and engagement between those delivering early intervention outside of the early help framework (that is, those funded by sources outside of statutory funding) and those delivering early help under the framework (that is, commissioned/contracted services), potentially results in confusion and a mismatch of services, with some areas of provision overlapping and others occupying a charity desert, that is those areas with fewer charities per person than others (Mohan, 2011).

Targeting services and a loss of trust

Talking to charities on the frontline of children's services reveals a fundamental shift in how these charities work under a preventative services discourse, in terms of both services offered and beneficiaries engaged. For example, we found several instances where charities ceased working with certain beneficiaries due to changing criteria when those individuals did not 'qualify' for commissioned services:

> You are directed by the contracts or funding that you have got as to who or where your touch points are with young people. So there are contracts that we were delivering previously that we are no longer delivering as they no longer exist or we don't have that contract any more so we are not in touch with that group any more. (CEO, major children's charity)

Furthermore, frontline workers highlight this concern in terms of the definition of 'need' being too narrow, and therefore not considering the multi-level complexities of needs with which most families presented. This means that children's charities are faced with a real dilemma; they are contracted to deliver set interventions, which they feel to be inadequate to meet the family's wider needs. As a result, many charities develop a self-perception of their service delivery as a 'sticking plaster' (CEO, medium children's charity), which does not tackle the longer-term entrenched needs of a family, but rather gives a short-term fix for one member of that family. Further problematised by the focus on short-term outputs and outcomes, charity leaders are becoming increasingly frustrated with a lack of focus on real outcomes rather than metric based indicators:

> I think we throw the words early intervention and prevention around a lot but we rarely put the money into it. And if they ask what are your KPIs, what are your outcomes? Well how do I know, go back to that person in ten years' time and you'll find the outcome, how do you show somebody that actually you are making a difference within the next year, or in the next three months. One of the biggest things is, it just about the numbers, you've got to have the numbers. It's now 40 young people, then it will change again. We can help them [beneficiaries] to realise how to do things differently and help them look at things but do you really know what difference you are going to make – how can I evidence what will be different ten years later? And I think that is the difficulty; that is the challenge. (CEO, medium children's charity)

While another commented:

> I think it [commissioning] has had a negative effect in terms of relationships, altogether the whole business, how we felt in the last couple of years is that relationships mean nothing any more, nobody values relationships and it has trickled from the top down, and god forbid if we start to be like that. It feels like even relationships with families don't matter anymore, it is all about outputs, outcomes and targets and monitoring and frameworks and stuff,

and nobody looks at the relationships with families.
(CEO, small children's charity)

Furthermore, children's charities identify that time-limited interventions and under-commissioned early help services, present significant issues. Those on the frontline argue that they cannot meet the needs of their beneficiaries in the given time or holistically respond to children and families as they felt they had done in the past, or indeed effectively support their beneficiaries:

> So we have this super difficult family, all kind of crazy stuff going on and that's it, you are supposed to sort it in eight weeks … and if you don't you are hauled over the coals for it and the family will be shifted off to social care for not doing well enough. I don't feel this is helpful for us or our families, they need time and support to help them move forwards, not threats and sanctions. (CEO, medium children's charity)

While another early intervention worker commented on their involvement in a larger consortium which had been successful in securing a countywide tender:

> This isn't an improvement for us, we've gone backwards, I wish we'd never gotten involved with the contract, it now dominates everything and we are working with people we've no experience of working with. If I'm really honest we are not the best placed provider to do this work, but then who is, we've all just become unregistered social workers and they [the local authority] can't recruit enough of those, we now do their dirty work instead. And if a big case looms, and it will, we will be the ones to get the flack. (Early Intervention Worker, medium children's charity)

And:

> Eight weeks to turn a family around with multiple complex needs is just not feasible. I sometimes think

they think families are on a factory production line, do X, Y and Z and they are all turned out identical. We used to run a service which was really holistic and wrap around for the family, they dipped in and out when they needed, and we stayed in touch with them often for years. (Family Support Worker, medium children's charity)

As a result, those working within children's charities feel increasingly frustrated by problematic targeting and shifting thresholds.

Just as noteworthy was the identification by some frontline charities of the problematic approach to identifying 'at risk' families through referral processes from social services and statutory agencies. Children's charities delivering early intervention services repeatedly suggested feeling like an 'extension of social services workforce' (CEO, large children's charity), acting like social work assistants and thus conforming to statutory procedures for families (for example, Pithouse, 2008; France et al, 2010). This is especially evident, for example, in the troubled families' programme, in which commissioned voluntary organisations are tracking and monitoring families based on accessing work, health services, finances and home care. This in itself is not a new phenomenon. For example, such an approach echoes Donzelot's (1980) suggestion of the relationship between the family and voluntary action as significant in terms of the development of this 'moralisation and normalisation' strategy and Dean (2010) suggests that the 'third sector employ technologies of agency to transform "at-risk" and "high-risk" groups into active citizens' (p 199).

In contrast however, it is interesting to note that non-commissioned services reported that their services are in greater demand from children and families with multiple, complex needs, which did not 'fit' models of commissioned services. However, they suggested that they often lacked the funding and resources to deal with such issues, so felt vulnerable and isolated when attempting to support these families. Frontline service staff reflected that they used to manage these risks more holistically among themselves through partnership working, there was a shared concern among nearly all participants that competition was driving organisations to no longer work together in partnership, and that as a result children and families were receiving disparate and non-joined-up services from multiple sources.

Additionally, children's charities delivering commissioned services are concerned that families are now often unable to identify differences between the voluntary sector and the state:

> When we turn up now they think we are social services or at least reporting to social services. (CEO, large children's charity)

And:

> With all the forms now it is difficult to tell us and others apart ... we had one family who thought if they didn't keep us happy we would come in and take their children, another who thought we were part of the police ... They thought we could cut their benefits as well. They were scared of us ... we wanted to help them but we had to tell them that we do have to report to the local authority and they may follow things up. (Early Intervention Worker, large children's charity)

As a result, frontline services were concerned about a loss of trust. For example, one small charity with a 25-year history of delivery of youth services in a particularly deprived, local area, saw a sharp decrease of 20% in beneficiary engagement, which they attributed to taking over the management of a previously local authority delivered service. These issues of mistrust between voluntary organisations and beneficiaries increased through the promotion of short-term interventions (with emerging evidence of punitive sanctions that sat outside of the organisation's ethos [Peters, 2012]). This aspect was highlighted by over half of the voices included in this book as damaging trust between the beneficiaries and voluntary organisations. The first reason was because of the organisation not being allowed to invest and establish long-term relationships; and the second reason was the resulting disenfranchisement of children, young people and families who have been through multiple short-term interventions with little long-term, positive outcomes. Research highlights how children and young people value long-term relationships with organisations, which allow them to engage more or less depending on their need, but crucially provide a 'go to' point when their life hits a crisis point (Body and Hogg, 2019). However, as children's charities are delivering services which become increasingly 'managed', these frontline relationships with children and young people are diminishing and there appears to be an ongoing erosion of trust.

Finally, in terms of service delivery, almost all of the children's charities involved in the research felt that commissioning arrangements had negatively affected the overall delivery of preventative services for children and young people. Although, when it comes to challenging this positioning of early intervention services, some children's charities appeared complicit, others rejected the process and, interestingly, some appeared to selectively engage with the process in an attempt to influence the services delivered. Each identified strategies in which they could distance themselves as much as possible from state definitions of early intervention to keep doing the work they 'wanted' to do:

> It's being driven from being a necessity to being a contractual deliverer for the local authority ... one of the things we are looking at is how do we increase fundraising so that we can start to do the stuff that ethically we need to do, but actually there is no-one out there who wants to pay for it. (CEO, large children's charity)

In contrast, a smaller charity explained their reasons for refusing to engage in commissioning processes:

> Children and young people like our project. I don't want to change it. We tackle problems our way and with what works, not what we are told to do ...

People aren't looking at young people in a holistic way – the real passion is not there. (CEO, medium children's charity)

'Types' of children's charities

In a period of rapid change, children's charities survival strategies are not homogenous, instead they broadly fall under three distinct, yet overlapping, categories. It is important to note that these categories are not considered to be fixed or absolute, moreover they are suggestive of the dominant types of behaviours exhibited by groups of children's charities in relation to how they position themselves with regards to the state, local government and/or commissioning organisations. Furthermore, each of these types does not seek to represent an absolute list of each charity's behavioural traits. Instead, charities are positioned along a spectrum of these category types, are subject to change and can simultaneously occupy varying positions within different fields of activity.

These three dominant types are termed as:

- conformers
- outliers
- intermediaries

Conformers

These children's charities are centrally reliant on contract funding, with most of their funding coming from one single source (the state) and they in turn invest substantially in this relationship. As such, relationally, they are positioned in close proximity to the state. Furthermore, though involved in partnership working, they are most likely to work with other children's charities, which resemble themselves in size and type and often on quite formal, contractual terms.

Websites and premises appear predominantly professional, often with a particular corporate feel, focusing on features of the charity such as unique selling points, value for money, quantitative outputs and delivery to targets. They are most likely to be towards the upper end of the medium sized charities, large or major in size based on their financial income and have most likely experienced significant increases in income over the past ten years (2008–2018). However, they are also the most likely type to demonstrate substantial and rapid turbulence in their income. For example, based on the loss of one contract, one charity within this type had reduced its workforce by 60% in a single year, expanding it again by 50% the following year, while another had ceased to exist as loss of a single contract meant that they were 'no longer financially viable' (former CEO).

Most significantly, they are most likely to alter their services in light of funding. Such a shift often involves a re-interpretation of their mission and values. Of the children's charities engaged in this research, around one third were identified as adopting a more conformist type of approach. It is interesting to note that overall these children's charities also appeared be younger organisations of around 5 to 15 years old, suggesting that the age of an organisation matters.

Outliers

Outliers are predominantly smaller, local charities who had a long history of delivering preventative services. For example, all the children's charities who demonstrated dominant behavioural types in this category had been established for a minimum of 15 years, and often longer. Furthermore, they were commonly led by an individual, who had either been with the same charity for that length of time, or someone who had a long-established history with the organisation, for example as a former beneficiary, turned volunteer, turned employee.

Again, approximately one third of the charities we call upon in this book can be considered to demonstrate these outlier behaviours. Of these all had a local geographical coverage, they ranged from micro to medium in financial size (based on NCVO definitions), and all had received funding, support or training from infrastructure support programmes, for example the former Children's Fund programme. These organisations prioritised mission over all else, often walking away from relationships with the state based upon ideological principles. While some had held formal contractual relationships with the public sector in the past, they had either through principle or force, stepped back from these relationships, though some remained recipients of small grant-based schemes.

Intermediaries

The final children's charity type we identify in this book are what we term as 'intermediaries'. Intermediaries are most likely to have multiple sources of funding, however this does not mean the majority of funding could not come from the single source of the state, instead funding was spread across multiple state actors and commissioning organisations. These charities strategically tended to 'dip in and out of contracting' (CEO, large children's charity) dependent on how much they felt they could achieve their mission within the contract terms, or indeed influence the contract in their favour. Overall, they tended to be stable in activity, and relatively mission focused but flexible in delivery of that mission. They were most likely to informally work in partnerships and networks from across the voluntary sector and exist across all financial groupings of children's charities from small to major. Furthermore, this group either maintained stability in their size or demonstrated growth between 2008 and 2018.

Table 6.1 outlines the different 'types' of charities' relationships with key stakeholders. We consider these in terms of formal and informal relationships.

How types relate to commissioning

It is virtually impossible to take a one size fits all approach when discussing commissioning. Each charity working in the field of preventative services experienced and engaged with commissioning in different ways. However, by grouping the charities loosely by type we are able to consider the different approaches dominating state and charitable sector relationships.

For example, conformers are more likely to enter into commissioning relationships, than either of the other types, and these funding streams dominate their income. In contrast,

Table 6.1: Charity types and relationships with key stakeholders

	Conformer	Intermediary	Outlier
Relationship with commissioning bodies	**Formal:** Engage formally in commissioning processes. Engage in formal contract management processes. Relationship is economically based. Likely to be heavily funded (more than 60% (up to 100%)). Paternalistically driven relationship with clear delineation of power in favour of state. **Informal:** Whereas previously felt they had strong informal relationships, commissioning is perceived to have driven this relationship into the public sphere.	**Formal:** Engage in formal commissioning processes. Not wholly reliant upon state funding, though often engaged in significant commissioned services. **Informal:** Often engage in relationship on an informal level. Examples of bypassing commissioning processes. More likely to work informally in partnership to achieve same ends, at times, with no financial or contractual relationship.	**Formal:** Either previously had relationship with state or never engaged – feel rejected from commissioning processes. Often have had some state funding in small amounts often short-term. **Informal:** Little or no relationship – perceive themselves as 'invisible' to the commissioning organisations.
Relationship with other charities/voluntary sector organisations	**Formal:** Engage in consortiums and formal partnerships – often engage in new relationships. **Informal:** More likely to see other charities as competitors. Do not highlight informal networking as a priority.	**Formal:** Recognises the competitive nature of the voluntary sector, though more willing to consider partnership and often demonstrate several formal partnerships. Often have longstanding relationships with a wide range of charities. **Informal:** Highlight informal networking as a priority.	**Formal:** Few formal relationships, though engage with some sub-contracting. **Informal:** Highlight informal networking as a priority. Tend to have long-standing well established relationships with smaller, local organisations. Most likely to see larger organisations as a predatory threat.

Relationship with beneficiaries	**Formal:** Appear to be more formalised; often characterised by fixed term interventions of activity. **Informal:** Few informal engagements.	**Formal:** Fixed term interventions. **Informal:** Likely to have longer-term relationships with beneficiaries even when they have completed fixed term interventions. Highlight desire to build long-term relationships.	**Formal:** Less likely to have specific, set programmes of interventions. **Informal:** Focus is on long-term relationships.
Relationship with volunteers	**Formal:** Most likely to engage volunteers on formal programmes (that is, set role/job description) related to programmes of specific activity. **Informal:** Few examples of informal volunteer engagement.	**Formal:** Likely to engage volunteers on formal programmes. **Informal:** Often have informal volunteers helping the organisation.	**Formal:** Few formal volunteering activities. **Informal:** Often lack clarity between staff and volunteer or volunteers and beneficiaries, with individuals transcending both roles.

intermediaries are more selective and occasional in entering formal contracting relationships. Whereas outliers actively avoid such relationships, and instead focus on alternative sources of fundraising through philanthropy and other funding sources.

Nonetheless, while both intermediaries and conformers seek to enter commissioning relationships with the state, their experiences of commissioning, and indeed the 'rewards' they achieve in the process differ. Accepting that multiple nuances in commissioning relationships exist, at the most basic level, the commissioning approach shapes how conformers engage with and experience the commissioning process, whereas, intermediaries are more likely to attempt to shape the commissioning approach, to determine outcomes to their advantage.

Conformers and commissioning

Conformers are reliant upon the commissioning approach to secure any advantage. If a more relational commissioning approach is adopted, they have more opportunity to co-produce or influence commissioned services. However, as discussed earlier, process driven commissioning approaches increasingly dominate commissioning. As a result, there are fewer opportunities for conformers to engage in the more relational driven approaches. Essentially these organisations are stuck in a cycle where they are increasingly dependent on specific, targeted and narrow contracts, and as a result continuously reinterpret their mission and work to meet specifications and tenders dictated by commissioners. They can only influence, shape or negotiate on contracts if invited to do so through the more relational commissioning approaches.

Conformers, fuelled by this concern not 'to bite the hand that feeds them' (CEO, medium children's charity) feel unable to challenge more process driven approaches. They are less likely to challenge specifications which may not fit their ideological values and will work hard to conform to statutory approaches to early intervention, as very pointedly expressed by one CEO:

> I know the game, I have to completely stroke the commissioning people, there are people around today

that I will be completely best friends with, I work quite hard at being on the right board meeting, the right panel, the right partnership, attend the right things, be the right person. We are overly accommodating; I jump through lots of hoops. When they want some advice, I am there to give it, when they want something done yes I'm there, I will make sure my opinions are perfectly formatted in meetings, I don't say anything too far one way or the other, I am very cautious when I am at meetings with those people. I am very cautious that my opinions have to be heard in the right way ... you have to behave in a certain way at all times. (CEO, medium children's charity)

The hierarchal, imbalance of power is clearly demonstrated in this relationship, yet not uncommon within commissioning. This means conformers have less input into the expected outputs and outcomes within contracts, and highlighted feeling less commitment to these intended outcomes, but instead saw the service as a base from which they could build more meaningful services. For example, a conformer-type children's charity suggested that by securing a contract from the local authority, which they felt was too prescriptive and not reflective of local needs, they would be more likely to attract philanthropic support to deliver the services they 'really felt the area needed' (CEO, medium children's charity).

Though this intention is laudable, the reality of this additional added-value or additional funding for service delivery was a rarer occurrence among these organisations. Indeed, conformer-type charities consistently identified ways in which they felt service delivery was not meeting the needs of children and families. In spite of this, though, the competitive nature driven by commissioning appeared to silence them in voicing these concerns. As a result, this group of charities are the least likely to challenge commissioners, and inadvertently become 'an extension of the public sector'. When we relate this back to Table 6.1 the normative factors associated with bureaucratic commissioning filter through all of their stakeholder relationships. As one interviewee from a conformer charity observed:

> We haven't always been like this, for instance we used have campaigning as part of our mission but that strand of work has died away. It's frustrating as I feel we now do as we are told rather than do what needs to be done – but I have 22 staff to think about, and it is better we do some work with some groups than no work at all. (CEO, medium children's charity)

Equally, this did not come without reward, although while these charities may experience turbulence in their income, it should be noted that some of them experience substantial growth in income over the past decade (2008–2018).

Intermediaries and commissioning

Intermediaries utilise resources and tactics to help 'create' more favourable commissioning approaches (this is expanded further in Chapter 7). As a result, intermediaries are often better positioned and more able to induce more relational driven commissioning processes, even if coming from a starting point of more process driven commissioning, or indeed walk away when they felt it did not suit their mission. Intermediaries, being less dependent upon contracted funding (often due to a wider income base), can induce cooperation among actors and use this position to influence the commissioning approach in favour of a relational driven commissioning model. This beneficial positioning gives rise to negotiating a more advantageous contract within which they are likely to perform better based on the outputs and outcomes which they have co-produced. Significantly, the most influential Intermediaries tended to have relationships in which they felt they could 'by-pass' the commissioning process. Interestingly these were not isolated cases and have also been identified within previous research findings (for example, Martikke and Moxham, 2010), with both commissioners and charities identifying this as a way around the system. However, this opportunity is also not equitable, with only a small number of the charities operating in this way when they seemingly have higher levels of influence enabling them to secure advantageous positioning. For example, as one CEO of a medium children's charity angrily explained:

> The local authority are like a domestic abuser, they divide and rule, they want to separate you from your friends, it's like they say so let's not have those voluntary sector networks, let's not have everyone in the room coming together, 'cause we want to keep you isolated. All funding for those networks disappeared. We want to keep you isolated, and then we can dictate what you are going to do, they are not interested in what you want to say, and it is that divide and rule. Keeping you away from your friends, its things like all the local children's trusts boards were dismantled, the safeguarding partnership gone, we'll dismantle all partnerships so you are isolated then we got you where we want you, and that's what if feels like, it feels like a perpetrator, and we are only just starting to come out of that now. You just kind of feel that … well I have a real kind of issue when thinking of political lobbying. The children's centre outreach work that we do, um without any warning of any sort an email dropped into my inbox saying we are decommissioning the service from the 1st April. They have the right to do that. So I was absolutely fuming, so I banged out an email to all our partners and got their support. Then an email to the member for children's services, and said look this has just dropped into my email box, we are delivering these services, parent support, baby classes, outreach work, we are bending over backwards to deliver these services for the local authority, this doesn't feel like a partnership, it feels like it should be give and take but you are take, take, take and now this is the final straw and I basically threw my toys out of the pram. And she got back to me, it was Friday afternoon, she wrote back on the Saturday morning and said I'm sorting this, and on Monday afternoon I got an

email and they had reversed the position. And I just
thought I shouldn't have to do that, but what would
I have done if I didn't have those links, would that
process have happened. You have to have the guts
to go and do it.

Equally we do not mean to present intermediaries as 'better'
organisations than the previously discussed 'conformers'. Instead,
here we suggest that the commissioning system is inequitable.
Indeed, while intermediaries would challenge, they still would
'weigh up the risks before going up against commissioners'
(CEO, large children's charity). Alternatively, outliers, with no
dependency upon the state, were quick to challenge perceived
inequalities or alterations to service design (even if they were
not the provider, but it affected their beneficiary group) but felt
themselves invisible and not listened to.

From this emerges an interesting aspect around the ability of
the commissioning model approach to help influence the type
of responses from the charitable sector, with more relational
commissioning models supporting a direction of travel towards
intermediary type, and process driven commissioning further
embedding charities in the conformist category type. The reasons
that underpin this are far reaching and complex, nevertheless the
themes suggest, as other research in this field has found, that the
closer a charity situates itself to the state and the greater their
reliance on state funding, the more precarious their position may
be. They may well reap financial rewards for short-term periods
of funding, but this is often at the cost of mission.

Conclusion

This is a chapter of two halves; the first half deals with the debate
surrounding voluntary sector independence and the responses
by children's charities to the shifting paradigm of prevention,
the second half focuses on the relationship between children's
charities and their stakeholders, grouping charities broadly into
three types, conformers, outliers and intermediaries. There is
an important link between the charity type and how children's
charities perceive and develop early intervention services.

There is a strong paradox between the persuasive logic, which supports early intervention and prevention, versus the enactment and mobilisation of these concepts into preventative services for children. Underpinned by ideological concepts such as social exclusion, early intervention and identification of risk factors for problem families (France et al, 2010), preventative discourse has become a widely debated topic. As explored here and elsewhere in this book, the voluntary sector has been pulled central to this debate as a deliverer of early intervention and prevention services. The increasing emphasis on prevention represents a growing move towards children and young people being viewed as an investment by the state, emphasising the longer-term economic and social outcomes of children (Fawcett et al, 2004).

The current Conservative government approach reflects a neoliberal assumption that poor families naturally want to 'improve' their position in line with values specified by others. Those who do not are deemed as 'troubled families'. This is coupled with a rise in the policing of parenting with an increasing number of parents facing Parenting Orders (introduced under Labour) and record numbers of parents facing fines and jail due to their child or children truanting, reflects an increasing punitive and ideologically fuelled discourse taking over, disguised in the context of prevention. In the backdrop of austerity, preventative discourse has moved to a neoliberal stance, blaming parents for issues within society rather than looking at the social backdrop, which is a distinctively different path to the concept of social exclusion that dominated preventative policy during the late 1990s and early 2000s.

Early intervention and prevention work with children and young people remains a dominant and important factor in supporting them to achieve their full potential and the assumption remains that the voluntary sector has an important role to play in this (Frost et al, 2015). Nevertheless, as discussed, both in policy and practice the concept of prevention has experienced an increasing hardening towards vulnerable children and families, especially parenting. This is coupled with a shifting paradigm in terms of prevention which has witnessed an increasing effort to quantify and objectify risk factors under a 'scientific discourse' approach (France et al, 2010) and has created mechanisms in which certain children, young people and their families are specifically targeted with particular services.

This paradigm of quantifiable, measurable outputs and outcomes has translated directly into the commissioning of preventative services for children and young people. With an increasingly outcome-based focus which relies on quantified information as measurements of success, children's charities delivering commissioned services are forced to become targeted and specific with whom they support. This shifts beneficiary engagement from stakeholders who actively seek support, to those who are problematised and targeted through a risk factor, diagnostic system. As such, services are designed around this conceptualisation of 'problem families' who are both the cause of antisocial-type behaviours and the place where these problems can be solved (Parr, 2009).

Accepting and participating in this discourse children's charities are in danger of legitimising this worrying narrative. However, as we see, each 'type' takes a different approach. Conformers, accept and willingly reproduce this ideology, outliers reject this narrative and seek alternative ways to support families outside of the state's discourse, and intermediaries walk somewhere between this conformity and dissent. However, this middle ground provides a space within which actors can come together and potentially carve a new path forwards – which is the focus of our next chapter.

7

Partnership working, securing advantage and playing the game: thriving, not just surviving

> Commissioning is a game and we don't make the rules, that's way above our heads, but if you want to work for and provide services on behalf of the authority you must play that game and find ways to get around the issues. (Commissioner)

Introduction

As the commissioning culture has matured within the public sector, so too have the responses from children's charities. As explored in previous chapters in this book, commissioning and policies regarding charitable sector engagement are full of multiple contradictions, confusion and complexity. Within this, we have seen two major opposing schools of thought manifest themselves. One, often driven by politicians and social policy decision makers, advocates for the commissioning and competition agenda as increasing choice and diversifying services by placing them outside of the public sector (for example, Sturgess et al, 2011; Blatchford and Gash, 2012). Another view, often pushed by academics and practitioners, which is more critical, argues that commissioning is leading to the marketisation and privatisation of services (for example, Davies, 2008; Milbourne, 2009). Many children's charities, and indeed commissioners, feel inhibited by these difficulties, although we also identify a group of children's charities, supported by particular commissioners, who 'play the game', reinterpreting rules, and at times breaking rules, to secure what they consider the best outcomes for children. This dedication to securing their own, individual ideological bias, sets them apart from other actors in the field of early intervention and preventative services, and warrants further attention.

As we suggest earlier on in this book, while many children's charities experience significantly negative effects of commissioning, several children's charities have successfully negotiated a pathway between conformity and dissent. As a result, they have successfully negotiated contracts and tenders to their advantage or even bypassed commissioning processes altogether, to secure a mutually developed contract. This included small-scale grants which were considered to 'go under the radar' (Commissioner) to large-scale contracts. This survival does not happen in isolation, but instead requires a relational approach in which *some* children's charities deploy a range of tactics to secure additional advantage, while *some* commissioners 'bend the rules' to facilitate advantage for certain children's charities who they believe will deliver a 'better' service for children. Thus, we conclude that commissioning is neither a fair nor a rational process and suggest now is perhaps the time to reconsider this relationship.

Policy context: civil society and collaborative working

The policy context for commissioning is laid out in more detail in the previous chapters, here we draw attention to the most recent developments in the Civil Society Strategy 2018 which seeks to develop more collaborative commissioning approaches. As we noted in Chapter 2, a core strand of the government's Civil Society Strategy, and its the final and fifth theme, was the public sector, within which they outlined a commitment to more collaborative commissioning processes. In doing so the strategy states that:

> the government's vision for public services in the modern era is one of 'collaborative commissioning'. This means that in the future, local stakeholders will be involved in an equal and meaningful way in commissioning and all the resources of a community,

including but not confined to public funding, will be deployed to tackle the community's challenges. People will be trusted to codesign the services they use. (Civil Society Strategy, 2018: 106)

The government's vision for public services in the contemporary times is one of collaborative commissioning. As a result, in the Civil Society Strategy the government commits to:

- supporting the spread of Citizens Commissioners, local people supported to make commissioning decisions on behalf of their communities;
- extending support to public sector teams aspiring to form mutuals;
- reviving grant-making in order to broaden the range of funding options for community initiatives;
- increasing social value commissioning across all levels of government and improving the use of the Public Services (Social Value) Act 2012 (HM Government, 2018b).

The ideology of these ambitions is, however, not new. Indeed, commissioning from the outset and throughout the rise in prevalence over the past decade sought to adopt these collaborative approaches. In 2009, the Commissioning Support Programme produced a document entitled 'Good commissioning: principles and practice', which highlighted collaborative relationships and service user involvement in commissioning processes as a priority for successful commissioning. However, as we have seen since then, so far, this commitment has not been translated into practice. As local authorities come under increasing financial strain it is hard to see how they will innovatively lead these processes. According to the Local Government Association, between 2010 and 2020, councils will have lost 60p out of every £1, with a proposed £1.3 billion government funding cut in 2019/20.

While majority of commentators welcome the renewed commitment in the Civil Society Strategy, it cannot be achieved without adequate resourcing. Indeed, local authorities must realign their commissioning processes, to put people and services at the forefront of them. This, however, is in direct tension with the marketisation of children's services, where services are continuously pushed to deliver the most basic services at the lowest costs (a topic explored in more depth in Chapter 5). The reality is that the public services market is becoming a race to the bottom line, within which smaller, locally based organisations are faring less well. Short-term contracts do not reflect the longer-term needs of civil society, which requires investment in substantial change.

In this chapter, we discuss the spaces within which some charities and commissioners seek to capitalise on these ideas of coproduction and attempt to find innovative ways to respond to challenges posed.

Securing advantage: deploying tactics[1]

Now we discuss in depth the survival strategies adopted by some children's charities in navigating their way through austerity, policy changes and commissioning relationships. We identify some children's charities, those we refer to as 'intermediaries', as being particularly successful in securing advantageous outcomes for themselves and, indeed, their beneficiaries.

These children's charities demonstrate the purposeful and consistent deployment of particular tactics in order to secure advantage within any given field (Body and Kendall, 2020). These intermediaries appear to be the blend of the other two typologies discussed, those we refer to as 'outliers' and 'conformers', defining and framing their strategic action in a careful balance between conformity and dissent. Crucially they retain a relationship with the state, and construct this carefully both formally and informally. These charities are particularly high in social skills. In these terms, 'social skill' is defined as the 'ability to induce cooperation by appealing to and helping to create shared meanings and collective identities' (Fligstein and McAdam, 2012: 46). We identify that they deploy these social skills under four different 'tactics':

- Tactic 1: reaching out and engaging others;
- Tactic 2: development of both formal and informal relationships with state actors;

- Tactic 3: attempting to predict and influence future changes;
- Tactic 4: a focus on framing their narrative appropriately to occupy multiple areas of work, while simultaneously retaining a legitimisation of their activities.

We first suggest, however, that social skills alone cannot secure advantage, it is dependent upon the degree of two favourable conditions to promote the enactment of social skills. Nonetheless, socially skilled actors can both benefit from these favourable conditions, but also utilise their social skills to bring forth these favourable conditions. These conditions have been identified as:

- *First, more relational driven commissioning processes.* We know that commissioning processes vary widely across public sector bodies, with a recognition of a range of commissioning approaches ranging from those which are highly relational (Crouch, 2011) to those that are process driven (Martikke and Moxham, 2010). Relational approaches tend to seek a more collaborative, partnership approach between state and voluntary sector actors, whereas those that are process driven tend to be more hierarchical and bureaucratically driven by state actors.
- *Second, multiple income streams.* Children's charities who could effectively deploy these tactics were not heavily reliant on a single or small number of funding sources, and instead had strategically and purposefully developed multiple funding streams. So, for example, one children's charity that demonstrated intermediary behaviours received over 70% of their funding from the public sector, but the multiplicity of the sources from within the public sector meant that they were not wholly dependent on any one funder, commissioner or commissioning organisation. Therefore, these socially skilled actors can mobilise their ideological bias into strategic action as they are not overly dependent on a single funding body. In doing so they were able to forge new approaches and practices which due to their increased networking, can connect to stakeholder values and thus mobilise their ideological bias.

We therefore suggest that some children's charities can be identified as having increased social skills, meaning that they can more easily deploy tactics, which in certain favourable conditions, can lead to advantageous positioning within the field. As Fligstein and McAdam (2011) suggest, 'skilled social actors can help produce entirely new cultural frames for fields. They do so by building compromised entities that bring many groups along. In this process, every group's identities and interests can be transformed' (p 11). These charities are able to develop innovative and creative responses which mobilise their ideological bias (what they feel should be done) through the use of legitimacy and resource dispersion. This becomes a successive process in which one feeds into the other and increases the strength of the organisational position. Reflecting on this, we assert that they have both legitimacy and resource, which are strong positions from which to influence commissioning processes and practices often in their favour but also more widely for the voluntary sector, by deploying a mixture of the following tactics.

Tactic 1: Reaching out and engaging others

Intermediary children's charities are more likely to work formally and informally with other children's charities regardless of financial size. As discussed in the previous chapter, while commissioners hold an assumption that larger organisations would form partnerships with small local organisations, this did not appear to be a reality within the preventative services context. Instead most children's charities appear to be most likely to form partnerships with those who resemble themselves in size, scope and mission. Intermediaries, on the other hand, openly embraced working with other organisations from across the spectrum. Commissioners and the accompanying policy frameworks openly promote partnership working, although commissioners suggest that this is more due to practicality and resources required for contract management rather than an emphasis on collaborative working.

Furthermore, intermediary children's charities were most likely to highlight a desire to not only collaboratively work with other charities but also to co-produce services with beneficiaries. Co-production can be defined as delivering public services through relationships between professionals, organisations, beneficiaries, their families and their neighbours (Boyle and Harris, 2009). While our discussion with frontline services found few examples of fully co-produced models of engagement, we saw emerging examples where practices adopted more co-productive approaches. For example, this was evident in more relational driven commissioning processes when services were altered and adapted in response to the sharing of information equally between all parties, including beneficiaries. Within this more partnership working focused discourse there was also a strong recognition by intermediaries about when not to pursue a contract and when to support others to succeed instead:

> Ultimately it should all be about children and young people and we are passionate about them getting the best possible service regardless of what is happening on the funding landscape and at some points we have got capacity to help others to do that and if we have the resource and capacity to do that we will help them, better help others … Locally we are aware who our competitors are and we try to have good relationships with them. We know organisations who go for lots of contracts and we will be honest – ultimately if someone is offering a better service than we are they should get it. Our role as a charity should be to support them to achieve that. (CEO, small children's charity)

Tactic 2: Development of both formal and informal relationships with state actors

Deployment of this tactic helps children's charities retain a level of legitimacy across the field of children's services, while advantage was being sought through 'frontstage' (formal) and 'backstage' (informal) relationships. For example, one CEO of a charity commented that they would happily offer advice and support to commissioners in order to establish a positive rapport. They would invite commissioners to comment on larger strategic decisions, to ensure that 'they felt invested' in the organisation. Simultaneously, however, due to having diverse sources of income, unlike conformers, intermediaries were able to avoid and turn down commissioning arrangements and contracts which did not suit them. For example, these organisations gave a number of reasons for turning down and withdrawing from contracts including, 'the monitoring was too prescriptive', 'commissioners were uncooperative' and 'the service was not designed to really meet the needs of children and there was no room for change'. In contrast, conformers recognised these issues, but they felt unable to challenge them and thus instead conformed to the contracted delivery strategy without challenge. Crucially intermediaries relied upon commissioners adopting, or being willing to move towards, a relational driven approach. To promote this, intermediary organisations, supported by the advantage of multiple resource bases, were able to mobilise both economic resources and legitimacy to strengthen their position and encourage relational driven processes. For example, one charity was able to bypass a tendering process and secure a contract based on match funding the project with another significantly larger project. By doing this they were able to influence the monitoring and evaluation targets to suit their service, and thus increase their reputational value in delivery. Therefore, they utilise this positioning to strengthen their position politically and seek more collaborative arrangements. This resulted in these charities being able to advantageously influence commissioning processes, and/ or, bypass them entirely. For example:

> I think that has been a much more constructive way of building a relationship than just going cap in hand trying to deliver something for them under a contract when actually you can have a proper conversation about what they see as important and what we see as important. Sometimes we will have more innovative solutions to things, or see things that are a need but have never been tendered, so one of the big services we now do for local authority has never been tendered because we solved the problem before we got to the tender process. (CEO, large children's charity)

Tactic 3: Attempting to predict and influence future changes

Building on Tactic 2, intermediary charities utilised informal relationships with commissioners and other relevant stakeholders to help strengthen their positioning within the field of delivery and influence future changes. This meant that in this context intermediaries were able to use relationships with commissioners and, in some cases, relationships with political members not so much to sway outcomes in their favour (although it was suggested that this was not unheard of) but to set the discussion to one that favoured them and their allies in the wider sector, for example influencing tendering opportunities which they would be well placed to secure. As one intermediary CEO of a charity commented:

> I think under our aim if we are in the commissioning process for something we know is a big need then we have probably failed, because we should have been having, unless there is no answer or no alternative from a legal point of view they have to commission it, conversations before this. But we would certainly see our role as being involved in shaping that commissioning process by arguing what the key factors are. I don't mean that in the sense of unduly influencing the process and putting it in our favour, I just mean if there are key issues we are best equipped to support. (CEO, large children's charity)

This process of relationship building prior to commissioning processes even being decided situates these charities outside of the formal contracting relationships. The above quote illustrates both a recognition and potential tension in this of intermediary charities not wanting to be seen as unduly influencing processes, although they are nonetheless likely to be in an advantageous position through the establishment and pursuit of these relationships. Intermediaries did comment that once formal commissioning processes started their relationships with commissioners often became more formal, although the very involvement in processes early on gave these organisations potential advantage over conformers, for example.

Tactic 4: A focus on framing their narrative appropriately to occupy multiple areas of work simultaneously and retaining a legitimisation of their activities

The term 'early intervention' is wide, encompassing a range of services from emotional wellbeing, resilience and mental health services, to services such as health, housing and family support. Intermediary organisations sought to work holistically across the field, often branching out into wider services when opportunities arose, for example housing support or employment training. However, though they often expanded into these other areas of service delivery, they maintain a central position (Macmillan et al, 2013a) within their specific area of work and developed a clear story for pursuing work within other fields. This was potentially further legitimised by being selective about these decisions and also openly choosing to not pursue some contracts, and in some cases supporting other actors to pursue them instead.

An interesting tension between conformer and intermediary charities is reflected in their ability to transform and alter their central mission. Conformer type charities often employed a total reinterpretation of their mission with their service moving into new (though frequently related) themes of activities. For example, a charity who predominantly focused their service delivery around drug and alcohol support, moving to providing mental health services. What is crucial in this example is the loss of their dominant, original organisational identity, within the original area of work, that is, in this example, drug and alcohol services. Charities outside of the conformist typology would view this as 'mission drift' and with criticality.

Interestingly, intermediaries appeared to be able to make similar shifts, although they situated this move within a framework of recognised legitimate activity. In short, they framed their activity well to others, and started a narrative which supported them to secure and increase a good reputation. For example, one outlier charity commented on an intermediary, 'I don't know them personally but I do watch them and think, I want us to be like that, they are doing so well, they've got the right idea. When we were struggling with a legal issue, I rang them up and they gave me great advice' (CEO, small children's charity). The aforementioned charity commented on partnerships, 'We try and help others, well because we feel it is the right thing to do and when it comes to it everything is about reputation, look after that and the rest will sort itself' (CEO, large children's charity). This appeared to be based upon maintaining a strong positioning within their original field of activity, such as emotional wellbeing support for children, as an anchor and then extending into proximate fields, such as family intervention support or domestic abuse support. This perhaps draws us away from the notion of intermediaries being completely altruistic.

This is not to suggest the intermediaries have always retained or secured the strongest positions within their original field of work. However, they will most likely be among these actors as their reputational capital and identity remains within that initial field, while they then develop and secure positions within connected areas of activities. Relationships with stakeholders across the field ensure that they frame their narrative within legitimate action and make sure that others understand the strategic action as a legitimate and justice driven discourse. One intermediary charity commented on their competition, 'they just don't care about that service the same way we do' (CEO, medium children's charity). As these socially skilled actors recognise the strength of communication there was significant effort to involve all networks formally and informally. As such children's charities outside of the intermediary type were clearly able to communicate and retell the intermediary charities' story, and furthermore in many cases wanted to emulate them. For example, an intermediary who initially started in community development activities, shifted to develop family support services and then mental health services framing this continually in meeting needs of vulnerable individuals. Four other children's charities involved in these areas of delivery, retold this charity's story in interviews for this book, clearly understanding the action as legitimate in terms of the charity's mission. Effectively intermediaries 'frame "stories" that help induce cooperation from people appealing to their identity, belief, and interests, while at the same time using those same stories to frame actions against various opponents' (Fligstein and McAdam, 2012: 51).

This tactic, combined particularly with Tactic 1 has proved crucial when times were difficult or the intermediary faced challenges; they were able to 'call to arms' their supporters to support their cause. Here we draw on two examples which exemplify this point (examples are further discussed in Body and Kendall, 2020). First, an intermediary delivering a range of preventative services listed 104 other voluntary organisations, working both within preventative services and more widely, with which they had recognised relationships. Of these organisations, 82 attended their 2016 Annual General Meeting, varying from micro, locally based to major, national and international voluntary sector organisations. Drawing on these networks they made themselves aware of, and could quickly respond to a wide range of funding opportunities, advocate for their beneficiaries with support from their network and equally reciprocate this by providing support and advice to others, particularly to smaller children's charities. In a second example, a charity delivering a single early intervention service on behalf of the local authority, facing a massive reduction in their contract budget, explained how it successfully used such links to head off an otherwise potentially catastrophic outcome. Twenty-one local children's charities, from across the field of early intervention made common cause to challenge the decision with the commissioning organisation, ensuring a significant reduction in the cuts that would otherwise have taken place.

Succeeding in challenging times

The strength of this approach to understanding relationships between children's charities and the state is that it situates change within the organisation itself, and simply not just in response to external factors. Children's charities are pro-active players within this space, not simply passive recipients solely reliant on the world around them. External factors such as the local authority and policy changes provide the catalysts for this entrepreneurship, but the entrepreneurship itself must come from the children's charities.

This is of particular importance in terms of the concept of agenda setting. By deploying the tactics and pressure as discussed, these organisations are able to positively influence the overall agenda of the field of early intervention in favour of what they feel should be done. For example, one children's charity, who we see as embodying intermediary behaviours, walked away from a tendering process which they viewed as 'demonising certain families as problematic'. Instead, working in partnership with a particular commissioner they secured an alternative grant from the local authority outside of the commissioning processes based on match funding the project with another significantly larger project (funded by a major philanthropic organisation) and more in line with their own more holistic approach to early intervention.

This had a major impact on wider service provision within the area. It drew attention to alternative approaches to working with families. The philanthropically funded service had proven impressive outcomes and was then expanded with public sector funding. While still kept relatively local, targeting a small geographical area, it drew attention to a different way of doing things outside of the original tender which was tabled. The original tender delivered by a more conformer-type organisation ran for two years and was not renewed.

While at one level this could seem to be seen as a 'missed opportunity' in the short term of the intermediary organisation, it had positive medium- and long-term knock-on effects. The alternative funding stream allowed monitoring and evaluation targets which matched perceived service needs, confirmed the organisation's autonomy, and, as the alternative programme unfolded effectively, created a new focal point for best practice within this area of policy, of which the commissioners who had offered the original tender became aware. In the long term this then directly affected the latter's behaviour in ways that realigned with the intermediary's priorities. It had the knock-on effect of fundamentally altering part of the policy monitoring requirements for core commissioning, where preventative policy was now reinterpreted away from being about primarily a very specific target group of identified 'problem' families towards the more holistic and wider definition of families 'in need' which the children's charities collectively favoured. In this way, withdrawing from commissioning initially and being selective about opportunities taken, demonstrably adopting a successful alternative approach, and then re-engaging once core commissioning had been adapted, allowed this intermediary children's charity to simultaneously influence the agenda of early intervention and the commissioning processes in line with their priorities and agenda (Body and Kendall, 2020).

As we acknowledge, however, commissioners and their approach to commissioning is vital in intermediaries succeeding in this way. Therefore, we now turn our attention to how commissioners help create space for this more entrepreneurial activity.

Who are children's commissioners?

While 'commissioning' remains a debated, multifaceted term, the position of the commissioner has received less attention. Often referred to generically throughout literature, largely as a catch-all term for either individuals, local consortiums, organisations or collectives of organisations, and in general reference to those who manage the commissioning cycle, procure and ultimately commission a service or services, the role and remit of the commissioner remains ambiguous. We are interested in the people behind the processes, the commissioners: those individuals who help make, shape and determine policy decisions and practice. These individuals have a stake in the area of need which they represent and came to commissioning to help achieve change for children. For example, this is captured beautifully by one commissioner's account of why she became a commissioner:

> After qualifying as a teacher, I worked in education for eight years. After that I went and worked in a charity providing early intervention services for children. We specialised in anti-bullying and peer mentoring support. I loved my job, but I often felt frustrated that it always seemed the money went to the wrong places. When a job came up in the local authority's commissioning team, I went for it. I felt I'd be able to achieve and influence real change and

> I think I have. It is a job which has a lot of influence but also a lot of responsibility – and I feel that every day – a moral duty to do the right thing.

Indeed, the majority of the commissioners we spoke to all had strong practitioner- and policy-based backgrounds, anchored in services for children and young people. They were mainly qualified professionals (for example former social workers, youth workers, teachers and policy specialists), highly respected within their field of work, and well connected to locally operating voluntary sector organisations and provider networks. Their levels of passion and dedication to securing positive outcomes for children were evident, but equally so was their weight of responsibility to 'get it right', coupled with the clear awareness of the potential consequences of poor decision making. As one commissioner commented:

> It matters, you know, what we do matters, sometimes we get it right and sadly sometimes we don't, but we try, we really try … and when we get it wrong we have wasted X amount of pounds that could have gone to support children, and that is on us, children are out there not getting the support they deserve because of us.

While another added:

> Our central purpose is to protect children, decisions we make can make the difference between happiness and sadness, between danger and safety, and in the extreme cases, between life and death.

Rees et al (2017) describes commissioners as the 'lynchpin of the commissioning approach', recognising the weight of responsibility which they hold, and the importance of their role in the commissioning process. As individuals, children's commissioners operate within highly complex, multi-dimensional situations which are often externally governed by market forces, while simultaneously responding to significant social need. Furthermore, they are working within a decidedly emotive field of activity. They are not purchasing a new vending machine or procuring new cleaning contractors, they are making decisions about protecting children from harm. In this book we do not question commissioners' dedication to their cause, but we do question whether commissioning itself is fit for purpose in the provision of children's services.

Commissioners: creating the space to influence[2]

Having established that commissioners of children's services are individuals with a strong stake in the provision of services for children, we turn to looking at what 'space' do these individuals have in exercising their influence in the commissioning process? As we note in Chapter 5, this varies significantly across commissioning organisations. We start by reflecting upon three factors which each relate to the wider commissioning organisation within which the commissioner is situated and which have an impact upon the commissioners' space to influence commissioning processes:

- culture
- structure
- resources

Culture

The culture of the commissioning organisation is important as to whether it supports a more relational driven commissioning approach, and how it supports commissioners defining commissioning (see Chapter 5). As we reflect in previous chapters, many commentators on commissioning recognise a continuum of approaches to commissioning, from a process, procurement dominated approach, to a relational driven approach which prioritises cooperation between stakeholders. Process driven commissioning tends to adopt a more formal and administrational approach to commissioning. Whereas the more relational driven commissioning approaches tended to be more outcome focused and child/young person centred. These approaches were defined by co-production and partnership between the commissioning organisation, providers and beneficiaries. The commissioner sits central to this process and identifies this consistently as the preferred modus-operandi. Commissioners viewed this approach as driven by partnership, resulting in higher levels of cooperation and innovation to shared problem solving between stakeholders, even in the face of austerity:

> Since 2008 we reduced all grants and replaced them with commissioned contracts under a shared framework of priorities. We worked hard with the market to develop the framework as something we all agreed on, and then defined the priorities where we could spend the reduced amount of money. We had open and honest discussions about what would be funded by the local authority, as per its statutory duty, and where the voluntary sector was better placed to respond and as a group we supported one another to try and bring money into the area. We commissioned what we could, and the voluntary sector applied for funds elsewhere. We supported them, they supported us. (Commissioner)

Positioning of the commissioner

In terms of situational positioning within an organisation, two challenges face commissioning. The first is the level of seniority at which a commissioner should work, and second, whether a commissioner works within a team (as commonly is the set-up in local authorities), or leads joint commissioning processes across partners (for example, as we see in some health-based commissioning).

Therefore, across children's services we see a wide mix of individuals with some responsibility for commissioning, from relatively junior administration roles, to senior executive decision-making roles. Unsurprisingly the more senior an individual is within the organisation, the greater their autonomy for decision making. Equally commissioners with less seniority had less autonomy in their decision making. However, as we explore in the next section, they still sought ways in which to 'bend the rules' (Body, 2019).

The second challenge, as we identify, is that there is a distinct difference between commissioners within single teams, responsible for a wide portfolio of activity (for example, preventative services for children), and commissioners who worked across multi-disciplinary teams and who are responsible for a narrower portfolio of services (for example, commissioning school support services for health promotion). In the first case, of the single teams, commissioners tend to adopt roles more aligned with cost saving and efficiency, and more formulaic, process driven commissioning approaches dominated. There was, in short, less room for individual influence in the commissioning process.

> There is a real difference between what I feel should happen and what does happen, we have a process to follow and the process doesn't always lead to the most expected outcome, but that's what commissioning is supposed to be about. (Commissioner)

In contrast, individuals who worked across multi-disciplinary teams, often leading on joint commissioning ventures, held far greater degrees of autonomy, and were trusted as a 'lead professional' to advise and direct the commissioning process.

> I'm left to it, I advise the board of what I think it is best to do and they go with that, so I end up commissioning the people I like, the organisations I know can deliver based on what I know is needed. (Commissioner)

Resources for commissioning

Commissioners have fewer resources to carry out their roles, and fewer resources to distribute. Austerity and reduced public spending leaves virtually no area of children's services unscathed. Perhaps unsurprisingly commissioners comment extensively on shifting government priorities which they felt resulted in reductions in resources, such as funding available for early intervention support, and increased expectations on them to manage multiple services simultaneously. For example, as one commissioner expressed:

> We are continuously expected to do more with less, be agile and responsive and predict where we need to focus next, but with less and less money to distribute, and fewer people to manage it.

Within a period of diminished resources, which commissioners have experienced since 2008, as individuals, they are expected to take on more work, in many examples overseeing ten times the number of commissioning processes per year than they had previously. For example, one commissioner highlighted how in 2009/10 they were responsible for two commissioned services, both in connected services, and developed close working relationships with the providers, by 2013 they had become responsible for 28 commissioned services across a broad spectrum of provision, and by 2018 they were responsible for all early intervention provision within a district of the county, equating to managing relationships with 34 providers.

These three factors which have an impact on the individual commissioner's space for influence, can inhibit or restrict which commissioners can bend the rules. However, we found that even in the most rule-bound systems, commissioners sought ways to bypass challenging bureaucracy to secure what they felt were the best services for children and families.

Bending the rules

While many of the commissioners who engaged in this research process were keen to follow the rules of commissioning and ensure processes remained tightly rule-bound, all commissioners agreed that commissioning did not necessarily secure the best outcomes for children and young people. Deeply committed to achieving these positive outcomes, just under a third of the commissioners discussed ways and means in which they made these rule-bound processes more flexible and acted with greater autonomy than perhaps their more rule-bound colleagues. This flexibility is crucial to the success of the charities we refer to as the intermediaries and created increased opportunities for more entrepreneurial activity within the commissioning processes. We identify these as three separate strategies which we refer to as 'informal engagement', 'promoting visibility' and 'buffering'.

Strategy 1: Informal engagement

Informal engagement plays a crucial role in commissioners navigating and manoeuvring around strictly rule-bound processes. The more autonomous commissioners suggested seeking a high degree of informal engagement with certain children's charities, to inform the structuring and commissioning of particular services. They stressed the importance of relationships and partnerships in their work, relying on children's charities, to be the 'experts of what they do' (Commissioner) and to 'lead the way' (Commissioner), for example:

> Engaging providers is absolutely central to what we do, we have to work in partnership, our role is to coordinate the whole process, not be the dictator of it. (Commissioner)

Interestingly, while commissioners also emphasised the importance of running fair, open and transparent commissioning processes, this was often alongside, and in tension with, highlighting the importance of trust, prior knowledge and established working relationships with children's charities. For example, as one commissioner pointed out:

> The processes are really good for making sure it is all fair, but ... well I mean, at the end of the day it still comes down to people, doesn't it? And, well, people still comes down to relationships, there is no getting away from it, we know who we want to work with and we definitely know who we don't.

As a result, and perhaps unsurprisingly, building on this relational approach, commissioners often favoured certain children's charities over others based on prior working relationships and established trust. These charities then enjoyed positions 'close' to the commissioning organisations (both formally and informally) and as we identify in the discussion regarding intermediaries were able to secure more advantageous positions with regards to commissioning opportunities (Macmillan et al, 2013a). As one commissioner commented:

> There is a world of difference between running a formal consultation process and picking up the phone to someone you know to ask their opinion … and a lot of that goes on … so we do consult the sector, but we consult those we know … well those who know what they are talking about. (Commissioner)

These backstage, more informal relationships, were particularly prominent in situations where commissioners appeared to seek to exert high levels of personal discretion, within more process driven commissioning approaches. Thus, commissioners actively sought mechanisms to bypass the bureaucratic systems which they felt did not benefit children.

Strategy 2: Promoting visibility of preferred children's charities

As public sector cuts in children's services increased and commissioning intensified as a mechanism to increase the mixed welfare economy, there was the perception by commissioners of increased local politician's involvement in the commissioning processes, which commissioners often found problematic. For example, a commissioner outlined how a significant amount of funding had been approved by local politicians as a grant, to a group of organisations bypassing an ongoing commissioning process. Others highlighted how they felt, politically, that they could not stop funding a particular children's charity due to the connections individuals within that charity had to senior political members. Thus, commissioners frequently faced a dilemma about how to negotiate these relationships within a professional process. This was not always considered a disadvantage, however, as more than half of the commissioners highlighted how they would promote organisations who they felt were particularly effective with political members to help secure their relationship with the local authority. For example, one commissioner stated:

> I think a lot of the success of organisations is based on visibility, the more visible the better ... well for the right reasons of course. Some voluntary organisations are very good at self-promoting and having this visibility with members [the local political representatives], others not so much. Part of our role then is to promote and make visible those strong providers.

Strategy 3: Buffering

Durose (2011) identified that frontline workers working with communities articulate a narrative of 'civic entrepreneurship'. Within this research a similar narrative among commissioners was identified. Indeed, commissioners suggest that they often view their position as 'a buffer between the local authority and the providers' (Commissioner) and as we identify above develop a narrative of 'service protectors'. As one commissioner commented:

> We were not in position to lower the level of cuts – everyone blamed us but it wasn't our decision, I didn't even agree with it ... the policy the local authority was driving forward was a panicked reaction ... we couldn't stop it, but I do feel as commissioners we had an opportunity to soften the blow and we did. No one gets that, the voluntary sector moan at us and no-one gets that, yes it was bad but it could have been worse. We fought hard for slower rates of cuts. We fought hard to carry out impact exercises and continue some funding for those where we could demonstrate impact and we worked so hard with providers to show impact in a way the authority would understand ... And tried to help as many services as possible to access that damn portal ...

> honestly we worked night and day for over three
> months when that was going on. (Commissioner)

The concept of commissioners as protectors, buffering children's charities from austerity, also featured during the tendering and contract management processes. They felt a responsibility to push children's charities for monitoring information, 'which would be the type the local authority wants to see' (Commissioner), once the charity had secured the tender in order to help secure the services future, especially in situations where delivery in contracts were falling short of requirements. This immediately highlights the conflict with previous research findings (for example, Milbourne, 2013) where children's charities felt rigorous monitoring and contract management requirements were unnecessary, adversarial and unhelpful to securing positive outcomes for children.

The concept of commissioners as protectors also featured during the tendering and contract management processes. There was a general recognition of the barriers faced by children's charities seeking to engage in the commissioning process, and of the difficulties faced in contract management. There is also a general acknowledgement that the processes disadvantaged smaller charities, although commissioners appeared to present the view that accountability for this was equally shared:

> Commissioning is a game and we don't make the rules,
> that's way above our heads, but if you want to work
> for and provide services on behalf of the authority you
> must play that game and find ways to get around the
> issues. Some voluntary sector providers seem to think
> that is our job, to sort it out for them, others recognise
> they need to meet us half way. (Commissioner)

This discourse of 'game' and 'rules' is strong throughout children's charities and commissioners. This type of language is reflected throughout discussions, suggesting the concept of the collectiveness of activity as well as a sense of shared meaning among commissioner and children's charities:

> This isn't the voluntary sector we once knew, it is a new and challenging landscape, basically a whole new ball game … if you want to play, you need to learn the rules fast. (CEO, medium children's charity)

Nonetheless, commissioners recognised the difficult balancing act they had to perform, on one hand they have a responsibility to actively help create and harness a competitively driven market that can meet high expectations (Blatchford and Gash, 2012), whereas on the other they had to balance relationships especially in terms of securing market engagement to inform needs analysis. From the perspective of commissioners this area of market engagement posed the biggest differences in commissioner behaviours. Some commissioners felt that they were left to manage the market engagement process based on their individual values and perspective, while others, those who worked within more rule-bound conditions felt that they could not engage the market openly for fear of a legal challenge to the commissioning process.

The combination of these 'conditions' (which can be broadly branded under the banner of process market-orientated versus relational commissioning approaches) and 'strategies' (considered as the exercise of discretion) creates a contested and complex space for commissioning within which both constrains the potential for commissioning processes, while simultaneously providing new opportunities for civic entrepreneurship.

Opening up spaces for commissioning

As the 'lynchpin' (Rees et al, 2017) of the commissioning process, the commissioners unanimously favour more relational, social commissioning processes. However, this was constrained by the degrees of autonomy they have within their role. When this is compared to the external drivers within their wider environment, which favour more process driven or relational driven commissioning, drawing on the experiences of commissioners, we identify four distinct approaches to commissioning:

In the examples of process driven commissioning (see Figure 7.1, quadrant 1), alongside a perceived weak freedom

Figure 7.1: The four adopted approaches to commissioning

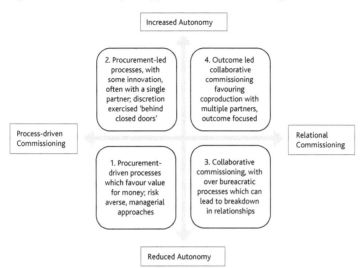

to exercise autonomy in decision making by commissioners, procurement driven, risk adverse, non-collaborative approaches to commissioning seemed to dominate. In keeping with Milbourne's (2013) findings, such approaches often led to a breakdown in the communication between commissioner and provider. For example, as one commissioner, who it could be suggested occupied this space, commented on a recent process to commission children's preventative services:

> We just didn't talk to any providers, it wasn't about lack of respect or lack of want, it was about fear. We just didn't dare, as if we did we were told that we would give unfair advantage to certain organisations and we would be open to challenge. The whole thing was about minimising risk.

Within this type of commissioning approach, there was little evidence of the systematic use of the strategies discussed.

More commonly, however, the process-driven commissioning was accompanied by commissioners who identified themselves as expert professionals and relied more extensively on their own discretion (see Figure 7.1, quadrant 2). While this could be limited or expanded by the conditions within which they worked, a common theme here was the exercising of strategies to bypass or influence the established processes, from 'behind closed doors' (Commissioner). This created something of a counterbalance to the process-driven market orientated approach, where children's charities would experience a stronger commissioner–provider relationship within the confines of a bureaucratic commissioning approach. However, within this commissioners felt 'vulnerable', 'exposed' and 'concerned about getting into serious trouble' due to the perceived risks they took in bending the rules. Such findings chime with Sellick's (2011) identification that commissioners will often work outside of the rules, 'legal or not', to secure positive outcomes for children. While the commissioners acknowledged that they followed the process to a certain extent, they used their individual relationships to develop a more relational-feeling approach to achieve what they felt was right. Thus, commissioners felt conflicted between what they felt was the 'bureaucratic driver' of the local authority, and what they 'felt was in the best interest of children's services' (Commissioner). For example, as one commissioner expressed in their interview:

> 'There is what commissioning is supposed to be, the story I am supposed to tell, and what commissioning is in reality … They're two very different things.'

The employment of the discretion strategies, particularly 'buffering', were commonplace here. However, this commissioning approach left commissioners frustrated and discontented as they felt that they had to take risks in the interpretation of the rules in order to secure the best outcomes for children, an outcome they rarely felt they fully achieved, which created tension for their relationships both within their professional role and with the communities they sought to serve. Furthermore, commissioners frequently suggested irritation at children's charities who they felt they were trying to help but would not 'play the game'.

Here however we witnessed the potential formation of exclusionary clubs, or as Osbourne (1997) referred to them, 'clans', where emphasis sits with the relational networks and social context of children's charities as social actors. A particular risk within this approach is that these clans play out behind closed doors, under the guise of a market-orientated approach. As a result, these networks remain orientated around particular social networks and there was little evidence of 'new' charities being able to enter the clan, resulting in a potential favouritism of certain providers.

Relational driven commissioning, while the poor relation of the more dominant process driven commissioning, generated some particularly interesting examples of collaborative working. However, in an example of this approach presented by a commissioner, when more policy driven relational commissioning approaches were combined with weaker freedom for commissioners to exercise discretion (see Figure 7.1, quadrant 3), a lack of flexibility to 'play outside of the rules' (Commissioner) meant that partnership eventually broke down as the commissioner had to frequently confine the process to the established rules and felt that they had 'little room to wriggle' (Commissioner).

Nonetheless, where commissioners felt policy drivers supported a relational driven approach, and they had strong freedom to exercise their own discretion, a new space for commissioning appeared to be emerging (see Figure 7.1, quadrant 4). For example, in one case a commissioner supported an established children's charity to lead a consortium of local providers, informed by data analysis and community engagement, to reconfigure the early intervention services in a particularly deprived geographical area, based on the consortium's and the commissioner's significant local knowledge. Intended outcomes were co-designed with the community and how the service was delivered in practice remained flexible. By coordinating the services across the commissioning bodies, the commissioner secured for the charity a single tendered contract, which the children's charity was able to match fund from their considerable resources, bypassing the competitive tendering part of the commissioning process altogether, and thus developed a range of widely acknowledged innovative services.

Conclusion

In this chapter we present how in a complex policy environment, some children's charities successfully deploy a range of tactics to ensure that they do not just survive, but they thrive, while remaining as close as possible to their original mission. It is the combination of these tactics which helps them mobilise their particular ideological bias, that is what they think should be done, over that of others. However, it would be too simplistic to suggest that by deploying these tactics any of the children's charities discussed in this book could be equally as successful, and indeed we do not wish to present these tactics as a magic panacea for all the challenges which charities face in the commissioning environment. Instead we come back to the importance of the central idea of favourable conditions and relationships which contribute to this picture. Approaches to commissioning can act as the enabler or inhibitor for the mobilisation of these social skills and tactics, and the responses by children's charities help reaffirm and legitimise these processes.

Where relational approaches to commissioning exist, more cooperative and innovative solutions to issues are reached, for example, the pooling of public and voluntary sector resources. More process driven approaches result in polarisation of the state and children's charities. Socially skilled actors are more able to influence the commissioning process in favour of a more relational driven approach, or indeed navigate a path around it. Conformers, on the other hand, rely on the commissioner or commissioning organisation to create that space and thus are less likely to have those opportunities available to them. Indeed, the very tensions which arise in any given field can give rise to entrepreneurial activity which socially skilled actors are able to take advantage of and set the agenda for other actors within that field (Kingdom, 1995). This draws further attention to the contested, politicised and highly relational space occupied by commissioning (Rees, 2014), and questions the assumption that commissioning is an open and transparent process. Implications for policy suggest a redefinition of the voluntary sector and commissioner relationship in favour of more collaborative and co-productive working. Such assertions place responsibility on children's charities to consider their leadership, application of social skills and dominant behaviours, alongside commissioning organisations and policy responsibility to create and facilitate this more open collaborative dialogue.

Commissioners are central to securing this more open collaborative dialogue. As children's services come under increasing strain, traditional organisational structures are breaking down, for example, education, health and early intervention support. While this breakdown of traditional institutions and subsequent blurring of the boundaries creates significant problems for vulnerable children, it provides the 'action imperative' (Hupe and Hill, 2007) to develop innovative commissioning responses which step outside of the traditional and policy rule-bound boundaries. The reality is that commissioners are largely critical of overly bureaucratic commissioning processes, and often seek to rebalance them through the employment of the strategies discussed, often at professional risk to themselves. In this chapter we have gone on to consider the 'space' available for the exercise of commissioners' autonomy and discretion, and when coupled with the organisational commissioning style we identified four broad types of commissioning approaches. Predominantly we highlight that commissioners feel motivated to act upon their own discretion. Within process driven commissioning styles this means that commissioners 'bend the rules', or 'play the game' to ensure that contracts are secured at a local level by those children's charities in which they have faith to deliver the required services. Thus, even process driven commissioning often becomes more relational, but 'behind closed doors', favouring certain charities over others.

Finally, however when a commissioner's skills and desire for professional autonomy aligns with an organisational cultural support for collaborative approaches, a new space for commissioning emerges (see Figure 7.1, quadrant 4). Here we see commissioning approaches redefine the role of commissioner under what we're terming 'civic entrepreneurship' and create a more co-productive space. However, we must be careful to note here, that while we acknowledge these more co-productive spaces as positive, they too are susceptible to favouritism, inappropriate contract selection and poor programme implementation. We pick this theme up further in Chapter 8.

Notes

[1] This section draws upon published research by Body and Kendall (2020), examining the same data set as used for this book specifically through the lens of strategic action fields theory.

[2] This section expands upon published research by Body (2019), examining the same data set as used for this book.

PART IV

Concluding thoughts

8

The action imperative to do things differently?

The relationship between the voluntary sector and the state has come under significant scrutiny within this book. The formalisation of the relationship between state and children's charities has intensified contestation among some actors, while simultaneously securing collaboration among others. In this concluding chapter we seek ways in which we may reduce the former and build on the latter.

As we have discussed in this book, there is a tendency among some researchers to position commissioning as either positive or negative for the voluntary sector, with significant focus placed upon the power relationship between the state and the sector. Such a discussion is important, although it risks there being a one-dimensional focus on the impact of one actor on another. This is an over-simplification of the nuances and complexity of the multi-dimensional and multi-faceted aspects surrounding voluntary sector and state relationships. A focus on the relational factors which underpin this is a more appropriate mechanism for both understanding what is going on and how to move forwards.

Discussing these tensions, at the start of this book we presented three significant arguments which we hoped to make. First, how children's charities have evolved considering the changing environment, presenting three typologies of responses, conformers, outliers and intermediaries. Second, we sought to extend our understanding of commissioning beyond the binary divide between process and relational driven processes. Instead, in keeping with some previous colleagues' work (Checkland et al, 2012; Harlock, 2014; Rees, 2014; Rees et al, 2017), we propose a much more nuanced, richer understanding of the realities of commissioning service provision. One which is multifaceted, complex and often awkward, driven by individuals' professional and emotional responses to multifarious situations. Third, we argue that children's services are in crisis and change is an imperative. Traditional institutions such as health, education and social care, alongside our political institutions under the weight of Brexit (Britain's intended departure from the EU), ongoing austerity and funding cuts, are in crisis. While this breakdown of traditional institutions and subsequent blurring of the boundaries creates significant problems for vulnerable children and those who seek to support them, it now provides the 'action imperative' (Hupe and Hill, 2007) to develop innovative commissioning responses. We therefore conclude this book by proposing commissioning approaches which step outside of the traditional and policy 'rule-bound' boundaries to find collective solutions.

Children's services are in crisis

Children's early intervention and child protection support services are in crisis. While the state retains statutory responsibility for children's social care, increased responsibility is being placed upon schools and children's charities to stop children moving up the thresholds of intervention. However, the financial and infrastructure support for schools and children's charities to achieve this has significantly diminished.

Local authorities up and down the country have suffered a 29% cut in government funding for children's departments since 2010, which is equivalent to a cut of £3 billion. Simultaneously, however, demand for services is rising across a range of services from early intervention support to child protection services. Austerity is putting children's lives and happiness at risk. An open letter to the Prime Minister and Chancellor in 2018, signed by 120 charities working with and on behalf of children, stated the following:

> We are writing to you because there is compelling evidence that the services and support that children and young people rely on are at breaking point. We believe this is because children and young people are being ignored in the government's spending plans.

- Ninety children are being taken into care every day – this is a record high;
- Fewer than a third of children and young people with a diagnosable mental health problem will get access to NHS funded treatment this year;
- Only three in a hundred families of disabled children think the health and care services available to their children are adequate;
- Almost three-quarters of school leaders expect they will be unable to balance their budgets in the next financial year;
- The number of children with special educational needs who are awaiting provision has more than doubled since 2010;
- Up to 3 million children are at risk of going hungry during school holidays.

We have come together at this crucial time to urge you to put children and young people at the heart of government spending.

As pressure grows on services to respond to this groundswell of need, children's charities are both frustrated and struggling. Local authorities have been forced to prioritise looked after children's budgets and late intervention work, at the cost of early intervention. According to a report published by the Children's Services Funding Alliance, which comprises Action for Children, National Children's Bureau, Barnardo's, The Children's Society and the NSPCC, local authority spending on early intervention services for children and young people has fallen from £3.7 billion to £1.9 billion between 2010/11 and 2017/18. This is a 49% decrease. Simultaneously, local authority spending on late intervention services for children and young people has risen from £5.9 billion to £6.7 billion between 2010/11 and 2017/18. This is a 12% increase. The shift in focus from early to late intervention, means more children are receiving support too late and ending up in a 'revolving door' of social care. In short, in the UK, children's services are failing. Council spending on early intervention services for children including Sure Start centres and youth clubs fell by 49% to £1.9 billion since 2012. More than 1,000 children's centres and 600 youth clubs have closed. Spending on disabled children fell by 11%.

In this book we sought to provide a place where children's charities working in these circumstances could voice their concerns and experiences. Focusing heavily on the relationship between these charities and the state we do not paint any rosier a picture. Children's services, and indeed education, are at breaking point, and many charities and schools are struggling to survive. Small and micro charities working in the field of preventative services have been particularly hard hit with almost a third ceasing to exist since 2008. Successive governments are playing a devastating funding game which threatens the very heart of children's early intervention services.

Voices from the frontline highlight a multitude of concerns, which primarily centre around the relationship between local authorities, clinical commissioning groups and children's charities, under the auspices of commissioning. Children's charities delivering or engaging in commissioned service provision are concerned about rising thresholds of intervention, meaning that children do not get help and families are reaching crisis point before services can intervene. As charities work hard to stop children and families 'falling into the ravine of social care', schools are increasingly forced to tackle rising holiday hunger, poverty and emotional wellbeing issues which are affecting their school community. This means that frontline workers are left to manage increasingly complex families, on less funding, as social services struggle to cope with rising demand. Both schools and charities increasingly turn towards fundraising and volunteers to help bridge these gaps, but as we have seen, this support is not evenly dispersed, meaning that the children in the most disadvantaged communities often have access to the least resources. In short, philanthropic activity cannot effectively distribute resources equitably. That is the job of state funding, but state funding is so diminished, that local authorities and councils are forced to focus on reactive late interventions, and early intervention becomes the poor relation. As we have discussed throughout this book, children's charities also voice a growing concern about problematic targeting of services, which provide a 'factory style approach' of short-term intervention programmes. Indeed, as early intervention services provided in the charitable sector become 'more managed', there is a perceived erosion of trust between charities and beneficiaries as families struggle to identify differences between the charities and social services.

This formalisation, of the relationship between children's charities and the state via commissioning as the dominant mechanism for managing this process, is not perceived by many actors from state, sector or schools to be improving or enhancing the lives of vulnerable children and young people. When considering the partnership between the voluntary sector and the state, we are left to question whether the voluntary sector is primarily a vehicle for social change or social control. The context of early intervention and prevention services provides a helpful backdrop to address this. In this book we observe the tension between how the local authorities define early intervention prevention services as targeted interventions to support identified 'problem families', and voluntary sector actors who overall reject this definition of early intervention, citing it as too targeted and too late. Instead, many of the children's charities opted for a more universal approach in which these services should be used to address wider social concerns (Hardiker et al, 1991). However, the dominant, more process driven commissioning, resulting in prescriptive contracts, punitive contract management and hierarchical relationships, means that many children's charities (particularly those we defined as conformers in Chapter 6), operating in this constrained space, struggle to act independently and speak out with a critical voice. Effectively, by engaging in these processes, these children's charities could be accused of legitimising this discourse, actively subscribing to the delivery of more punitive, targeted approaches which would normally be considered to sit outside of the charitable sector's ethos (Peters, 2012). As these charities become more entrenched in this activity, these behaviours become more self-fulfilling, as the activity continually reproduces itself. The process of commissioning contributes therefore to hardening the approach on 'problem' families, and some children's charities become part of the legitimisation of this narrative.

Whereas conformers have fallen in line with this narrative, outliers have rejected it, some precluded by the process and others as an act of dissent against the relationship between the state and the voluntary sector (Ryan, 2014). This is not to say that the identified outliers have not continued to deliver early intervention services; the majority continued with their mission, turning to non-state funding sources such as community fundraising, charitable trusts and selling services instead. However, this activity is ad-hoc, and not evenly spread or accessible to all families referred for early help. Intermediaries fall somewhere between this state conformity and dissent. They are, to some extent, part of the legitimisation of this approach as they bend and accommodate contractual obligations posed by the state. However, they are also able to utilise social skills and tactics to both secure more advantageous positions for themselves and also to mobilise their particular ideological bias, that is, what they feel should be done. The ability to mobilise this ideological bias results in these children's charities being able, under the right specific circumstances of more relational driven commissioning approaches, not only to set themselves up in advantageous positions but also to influence the agenda for the wider field of activity of early intervention services.

It is not only the relationship between the state and children's charities that was under investigation within this book. As we discuss in Chapter 5, the breakdown in trust is not only limited to the relationship between charities and the state, and charities and beneficiaries, but extends to the intra-relationships between charities, as relationships become increasingly formalised and managed under commissioning arrangements. Children's charities are likely to view one another suspiciously and with caution. Although evidence of partnership working was seen, in terms of charities of similar size and service delivery focus, on the whole, partnership working is perceived to have decreased and the sense of competitiveness between children's charities has increased. Intermediary organisations discussed efforts to transcend the boundaries between size and type, although outliers were consistently the most likely type of charity to be marginalised in these processes. Furthermore, in historic pre-established collaborative working arrangements, partnerships appeared to survive beyond the tendering processes, whereas partnerships brought together in order to compete for a tender opportunity, appeared to only last for the contractually obligated period of time, especially when those children's charities did not share the same ideological base. The importance of social skills in managing these relationships was paramount.

Challenges posed by current commissioning approaches

As Crouch (2011) identified, commissioning itself is not the problem per se, rather it is how the commissioning process plays out which creates tension. Within this book we support this assertion and thus the second factor to be considered in our conclusion is the relationship between commissioners and children's charities.

We have identified a spectrum of commissioning approaches from process to relational driven (see Part III). More process driven relationships rely heavily on a hierarchical, top down enforcement of power from commissioners, and often left children's charities feeling vulnerable and powerless. Furthermore, the more process driven commissioning was characterised by confrontational and adversarial relationships which stifled innovation, creativity and partnership working. In contrast, the more relational driven commissioning processes encouraged higher levels of cooperation and partnership working between commissioners and the children's charities, redistributing power, leading to innovation and shared problem solving. Nonetheless, the experiences shared by children's charities and commissioners alike suggested that poorly executed, process driven approaches dominated their commissioning experiences. As such, children's charities are frequently left out of needs analysis and service design, and often engaged only formally through the procurement process. If successful in securing the tender, children's charities in these more process driven approaches identified contract management as problematic and stifling, highlighting that the push for quantified targets failed to demonstrate their true value. As a result, there is decreasing confidence in the commissioner–provider relationship.

Responding to this there is a need to re-define the commissioner–provider relationship to one that focuses on a more relational, collaborative based approach. However, before that can be achieved there needs to be a shared consensus on the role and purpose of commissioning. As identified by previous research (Rees, 2014), the fragmented approach to commissioning across individuals, teams, departments and organisations needs to be addressed. Within this book alone, commissioners defined their role broadly under three competing definitions (see Chapter 5) and children's charities recognised the multiple approaches taken by different public sector bodies. In agreement with Checkland et al (2012) this fragmentation can only be achieved if there is a shared consensus about the role of the commissioner and the purpose of commissioning. The ongoing shifts in the public sector policy and funding (Gough, 2011) prevent commissioners from engaging voluntary sector organisations as they would like to, often citing fear of job insecurity, shifting policy and overt interference from political members as challengers. Indeed, commissioners highlight a desire to draw more upon their relational values, although they acknowledged that this was often inhibited by the environment from within they operated.

The inequality of access within the commissioning processes needs to be addressed. Thus, another significant criticism of commissioning processes is that it openly favours larger organisations. Based on the children's charities in this book, we see this playing out in children's early intervention services. Further consideration for different and more equitable models of commissioning which embrace the wider sector would result in wider engagement and potentially more innovative and creative solutions to local issues. Within this, however, the tension between the drive for community empowerment promoted by commissioning policy, and the practice of centrally directed services by the local authority and other public sector organisations needs to be resolved.

To achieve this redefinition of the relationship, commissioners and commissioning organisations need to create the space and opportunities for voluntary sector organisations to be part of this redefinition, this essentially suggests a whole system change from a predominantly hierarchical approach to one of co-production, collaboration and partnership. This needs not to simply exist within policy, as it currently does to some extent, but needs a clearer translation into practice if such models are going to work.

If successful in this, commissioning of children's services has the potential to achieve positive results for children and families by bringing together the skills, knowledge and capacity of the voluntary sector with the resources and political capital of the state in models of partnership and co-production. However, commissioning has not yet achieved a fully diverse model of services being delivered outside of the public sector and of increasing choice, as some advocates of commissioning would like (Blatchford and Gash, 2012; Sturgess et al, 2011). Nor, fortunately from our point of view, has it led to full marketisation and privatisation of services and overall loss of independence of children's charities as critics suggest (Benson, 2015; Davies, 2008). The complex and contested picture we are left with is far more relationally driven and messy.

Instead, we find entrepreneurial commissioners and children's charities carving out a specific space within which they can collaborate and define service provision for children between them. Individuals and organisations are passionately committed to securing positive outcomes for children and keen to find alternative ways. This calls for a more collaborative commissioning approach. In Chapter 7 we discuss how commissioners and charities alike seek to engage in relationships outside of the formal rule-bound contracted spaces. Furthermore, as we explore in Chapter 4, schools are feeling the financial strain and they themselves are seeking collaborative alternatives to address the needs of their most vulnerable children. However, within commissioning relationships we have highlighted that much of this entrepreneurial activity happens 'backstage', behind closed doors, and exists despite the commissioning processes in place, rather than because of them. This is problematic, as certain organisations are further favoured over others. Yet bringing collaborative commissioning into the open, where it is freely acknowledged and pursued by all actors, requires a whole system change, the sharing of power and investment in establishing long-term trusting relationships. It cannot be achieved in the short-term, three-year cycles of funding proposed by many commissioning organisations or the short-term economic focused strategies proposed.

Is collaborative commissioning the new hope?

The final iteration of this book was completed in December 2019. It is important here that the date is noted, as changes in the UK political discourse have been so frequent. On Friday 13th December 2019, the Conservative government won a significant parliamentary majority in the general election. Given the previous almost decade of funding cuts and austerity in children's services, this was greeted with some apprehension by many within the education and charitable sectors, raising concerns about continued negative impacts for the most vulnerable children and young people. Indeed, the Resolution Foundation predicts the Conservative manifesto risks child poverty reaching a 60-year high of 34% by 2023 (Gardiner, 2019), whilst the Association of Chief Executives of Voluntary Organisations calls upon civil society leaders to hold 'the government's feet to the fire on addressing social, environmental and community issues which have been neglected for too long' (Whitehead, 2019). The Conservative manifesto at least makes some promises of increased funding in education and early years, along with a review of the Troubled Families programme and care system. However, concerns are not unfounded. Under the Conservative government the 2010s have been heavily marked by the UK's intended departure from the European Union. It has created deep divisions across all parts of society and continues to dominate debates. No significant societal development work has happened in Whitehall, as social care, education, children's services, policing and national health service are all on their knees, crushed under the weight of demand, lack of resources and uncertainty about their future. Civil society is operating in a period of division, inequality, austerity and fragmentation. This has led to a somewhat defensive voluntary sector, with former cabinet members telling the sector to 'stick to their knitting', the Charity Commission urging charities to not get too involved in politics and charities embroiled in scandals amplified by the media. With significant threats to our economy forecast, it is hard to find hope. However, hope there is.

The first and most important strand of hope comes from the very people featured in this book, the practitioners, the professionals, the volunteers, the charity leaders, the teachers, the community members and headteachers, all of whom work tirelessly to secure better outcomes for children. The charitable sector and civil society are central to this. From the large charities coming together in a shared mission to advocate for children's services, to the community groups on the ground fundraising and recruiting volunteers to continue to deliver their mission, to the school teachers who turn up to their classrooms with spare food for hungry children. We have a society, voluntary sector and children's workforce who continually seek to improve outcomes for children. The hundred plus voices represented in this book highlighted this continuously. While they each felt that services faced increasing challenges, they continued to rise to those challenges. However, without infrastructure and financial investment from the state, these services will remain patchy and unevenly dispersed.

The second strand of hope comes from the growing recognition of the importance of civil society. Over the 120 pages of the 2018 Civil Society Strategy (HM Government, 2018b) a glimmer of hope emerges which signals the potential recognition of government towards the challenges of commissioning, many of which we reflect in this book. There is a recognition that commissioning has created a system which propels process driven approaches, favouring economic narratives which support the success of larger organisations who can deliver to scale – favouring process over impact. As a solution the strategy promotes collaborative commissioning as a way forward, although it lacks a clear sense about what this means in practice or indeed where the resources for this shall be found. Furthermore, the idea of collaborative commissioning is not new and has long been promoted as best practice. In 2009, the Commissioning Support Programme produced a document entitled 'Good commissioning: principles and practice' (DfE, 2009), which highlighted collaborative relationships and service user involvement in commissioning processes as a priority for successful commissioning. So, we must ask what provides an imperative for change now. My response is that it is the weaving together of these two strands of hope which help produce change.

The UK has been locked in a long-term austerity project that has dominated the last decade. Faced with year on year cuts, by 2015 the Institute of Fiscal Studies stated that all easy efficiency savings had been made and now councils needed to make radical changes. Local authorities first sought to meet these challenges through scale, bundling together contracts and tenders into large single contracts and tendering these out to large organisations. As a result, local authorities and organisations were tied into inflexible, output focused contracts which provided in many cases little more than a tick box service, and resulted in expensive legal proceedings if things went wrong.

As budgets tighten, schools and services have reached breaking point. Charities have come together in an attempt to place pressure on government to increase funding for children's services, headteachers have taken to the pavements of Downing Street to protest against school cuts and parents have launched numerous campaigns to increase services and support for children. This has provided a renewed action imperative to look to do things differently. Simply put, those who care about children's futures feel that there is nowhere else to turn and so come together to seek new ways to solve local and national issues. While most public services remain the responsibility of the statutory sector, there is a renewed recognition of the role of civil society, epitomised by local action and captured in the Civil Society Futures and Civil Society Strategy 2018. With this comes an energy to look for ways to empower local communities to help solve local problems.

Indeed, collaborative approaches have the opportunity to offer a multiple of positive impacts including driving down long-term pressures on services, supporting a re-investment in early intervention to achieve this, and creating a more joined-up approach in commissioning services which seek to be place-based and address the cause of local issues, rather than simply the consequences. Collaborative commissioning can spread the risk of commissioning across multiple, smaller, simpler contracts. There are additional benefits, we know for example, that local organisations most commonly employ local people, investing in these organisations supports the local economy to grow.

To achieve this though, we must radically change our approach to commissioning. We have seen cuts to children's services provide barriers to change, but also enabling change through both commissioners and children's charities coming together to seek to do things differently. However, this is a real challenge for children's charities. Children's charities remain fragmented, damaged by years of hardening, marketisation and competition. They need to re-establish trust in the local authorities, and in many cases, in one another. A whole system change is needed to place relationships once again at the forefront of services, relationships which prioritise outcomes for children over cost. Furthermore, while we suggest in this book that commissioners of children's services demonstrate a willingness to change, unless this is matched by cultural change within commissioning organisations, and from central government, along with significant investment, change is unlikely to happen.

In short, collaborative commissioning is good in principle, yet there remain many unknowns. While we suspect that it presents a case for better value and impact, the evidence in children's services is simply not there yet. Collaborative commissioning requires a longer-term outlook than the common two- or three-year tenders offered in early intervention at present, meaning that children's charities rarely invest in tracking long-term impacts. Collaborative commissioning also relies on the involvement of citizens and service users, that is, children and families, at the heart of service design, provision and impact evaluation. Models of this type are emerging but are ad hoc at best. Concepts of transferring responsibility are also contentious, relying on the voluntary action of citizens to solve local issues. When we apply this model to education, we are immediately confronted with the situation that voluntary action in communities is unevenly dispersed, with wealthier areas able to mobilise voluntary action more than areas of deprivation. Collaborative arrangements, and particularly local community organisations, have a distinct role here to find ways of engaging those most excluded from such processes.

So, while collaborative commissioning offers a new hope, it remains an emergent process. This must become a research and practice priority over the coming years. How collaborative commissioning differs from what commissioning is intended to be at present remains unclear and what collaborative commissioning means in terms of the market remains uncertain. What is more important is that we are still steering unchartered waters as we consider what success looks and feels like. Is this a way of improving services for children, or a mechanism by which the state seeks to shift responsibility, and cost, of children's futures onto local communities with reduced resources and infra-structure support?

The final note of hope, though, comes from returning to the voices of the individuals to whom we have spoken about children's services and the realities of delivering early intervention for children. While we have a workforce of both paid and unpaid individuals, in children's charities, schools, statutory agencies and commissioning organisations, passionate about achieving and advocating for the best services and outcomes for children and young people, hope on finding a shared way forwards remains a real possibility:

> I can't remember a period of time when the role of civil society and the voluntary sector was so imperative. We need to be dynamic, we need to be inclusive and we need to unite – we need to challenge the government every step of the way about how we support children and we need to hold them to account. The future of children's lives now lies firmly in the hands of civil society – we need to stand up together, we need to work with the local authorities and commissioners to really think about the country we want post Brexit. Our country, and the world, is facing the biggest global challenges of our time, we must ensure children's futures are at the heart of the response. (CEO, Medium Children's Charity, December 2019)

APPENDIX

Data and methods: voices from the frontline

There is a plethora of texts relating to the commissioning of voluntary sector organisations. However, there is a lack of discussion in the literature about a) the lived experience of engaging in these processes from the point of view of charities, and b) the voices and views of commissioners themselves.

We draw this data from a multi-method approach, through multiple conversations with CEOs of children's charities, staff and volunteers working within those charities and commissioners, with whom some of the charities featured had ongoing relationships.

Sampling children's charities

Sampling of these children's charities was based upon broadly delivering some form of early intervention or preventative services within a single local authority area in the South East of England. While all children's charities delivered within this single local authority area, many worked across multiple local authorities and so were able to draw on wider experiences. The initial sample of children's charities was drawn from a mapping exercise undertaken by the local authority, and further children's charities were added via knowledge gained through discussions within local networks. In total, 235 children's charities were identified as delivering services which broadly fell under this categorisation within the local authority area. Of these children's charities only 231 could be tracked, therefore four were omitted from the sample due to a lack of information. Thus, the final sample size for the research for this book was 231.

The research process for this book started with desk-based data collection, which resulted in a quantification by financial size of children's charities that have increased, stayed the same or decreased over the period (2009/10 to 2013/14) under investigation. The aim of this was to provide some descriptive information to identify any key characteristics and trends. The goal of this exercise was to collate an overview of the relationship between organisational size, geographical coverage and success in terms of maintaining or increasing income over a period of five years.

Using a combination of research tools, a database was drawn up to collect data for the following themes:

- organisational size based on financial income in 2009/10 (based on the NCVO definition of Micro < £10,000; Small £10,001–£100,000; Medium £100,001–£1 million; Large £1 million–£10 million; Major > £10 million);
- organisational geographical coverage based upon the geographic spread of services:
    - local: service provision coverage within a single district/ local borough but not across the entire district/local borough;
    - district: service provision coverage across at least one single district but less than coverage across the whole of the local authority area;
    - county: service provision coverage across the whole of the county but not beyond;
    - regional: service provision coverage across local authority and in other local authority areas within the south east;
    - national: service provision coverage across the south east and/or national international coverage;
- the difference in actual income between 2009/10 and 2013/ 14, recorded as increased, decreased, merged or ceased to exist.

The data collection mechanism varied for each individual organisation. Where organisations were registered charities, information was drawn directly from the Charity Commission website. Where this information was not available due to financial income, legal status, cessation or merging into another

Table A1: Financial size of children's charities included in the quantitative data

Size of children's charity	Number of children's charities
Micro	39
Small	75
Medium	71
Large	28
Major	18
Total	231

Table A2: Geographical service coverage of children's charities included in the quantitative data

Size of children's charity	Number of children's charities
Local	125
District	41
County	26
Regional	13
National	26
Total	231

organisation, information was drawn from relevant websites and networks.

The final descriptive of those children's charities used within this quantitative exercise are outlined in Tables A1 and A2. Most commonly, children's charities were either small or medium, with a local coverage.

The analysis of the changes experienced by children's charities during the period of 2009/10 to 2013/14 is detailed and discussed in Chapter 5.

The second phase of sampling was from those children's charities who wished to lend their voice to this research through interviews. In November 2014, with follow-up emails sent in December 2014 and January 2015, scoping questionnaires were sent to all 231 children's charities. Interestingly, 12 children's charities

Table A3: Financial size of children's charities represented in the qualitative data

Size of children's charity	Number of children's charities
Micro	8
Small	12
Medium	12
Large	6
Major	2
Total	40

immediately declined participation in the research as they felt current, or former contracts, prevented them discussing the commissioning process. A total of 42 voluntary sector organisations completed the questionnaires, resulting in a response rate of 24.4%. This was considered a relatively satisfactory response rate. Analysis of the questionnaires was used to inform the structure of the semi-structured interviews. A total of 28 children's charities volunteered to participate in the first wave of semi-structured interviews in 2015/16. Further interviews via snowball sampling and introductions via children's charities and commissioners resulted in conversations and interviews with 12 more charities over the following three years. In over half of the charities multiple individuals shared their voices. In 2018, we revisited all the past conversations and had short follow-up discussions with the majority of those still working within the sampled charities.

In terms of size, micro to medium sized organisations (as of 2018) make up the majority of the sampled qualitative voices in this book (see Table A3).

Interviews with those working in children's charities

We have spent three years (2015–2018) talking to individuals working on the frontline of children's charities. Over this period of time we have spoken to over 80 individuals, across 40 different charities. Initial interviews carried out in 2015/16 were followed up by ongoing conversations up until the summer of 2018.

Interviews were based upon discussions under six main headings:

1 *Services for children and young people* These focused on exploring the changing concepts of early intervention and prevention, how this affects individual organisations and services delivered.
2 *Background to the organisation* These were about understanding the 'story' of the organisation and how it has developed and changed over time, particularly in relation to the state and other voluntary sector organisations.
3 *Key drivers and stakeholders* These looked at the aims, key drivers and motivators for the organisation and definitions of success, and key stakeholders.
4 *Strategic positioning* These covered the concept of strategic positioning of the organisation and 'power and influence' in the sector, including working in partnership with others and the impact that decisions by other organisations can have on individual organisations to understand what makes an organisation more influential/ powerful than another.
5 *External factors* Here the focus was on the impact of external factors on an individual organisation, such as changes in political leadership, social policy shifts and the economic downturn.
6 *Political influence* These discussions centred around the influence in local decision making, the identification of needs and the relevance of organisational specialism/expertise in wider decision making.

The majority of the initial interviews were carried out face to face at the children's charity's main office. For those with multiple venues this was within the head office, for smaller children's charities this included temporary venues. Further interviews and discussions took place over the telephone and through meeting face to face over the following years.

Interviews with commissioners

Commissioning officers (or those with equivalent responsibility) were engaged through snowball sampling through the organisations engaged. All commissioning officers interviewed had a current or former connection to the children's charities involved in the research and either were a commissioner for the local authority or involved in joint commissioning partnerships with the local authority and thus using the commissioning framework. A total of 20 commissioning officers were interviewed between 2016 and 2018. The interview schedule reflected that of the one used for the children's charities. Each interview lasted between one and two hours, took place at a mutually agreed venue. The participants included both those currently working within commissioning and individuals who had left commissioning but not more than one year previously. For the purpose of this research, to ensure anonymity, all individuals will be referred to as commissioners although their titles varied widely depending upon their host organisational structure and approach to commissioning.

Interviews discussed topics under the six following themes:

1 *Services for children and young people* This theme focused on exploring the changing concepts of early intervention and prevention, and how this affects commissioning and the role of the commissioning officer.

2 *Background to commissioning* This theme was about understanding their perception of the 'story' of commissioning and how it has developed and changed over time, including exploring who have been the key decision makers and the impact of changes in funding source.

3 *Key drivers and stakeholders* The aims, key drivers and motivators for commissioning and commissioners, definitions of success and key stakeholders were the topics for this theme.

4 *Strategic positioning* This theme concerned the concept of strategic positioning of children's charities and the exploration of 'power and influence' in the sector both in terms of the role of commissioners and how they felt influenced by children's charities and other external factors. It also explored how working in partnership with others and the impact that decisions by other organisations can have on individual commissioning processes helped us to understand what makes an individual or organisation more influential/powerful than another.

5 *External factors* This theme looked at the impact of external factors on commissioning processes, such as changes in political leadership, social policy shifts and the economic downturn.

6 *Political influence* Here, the focus was on their influence in local decision making, the identification of needs and the relevance of drawing upon organisational specialisms/expertise in wider decision making.

Research with schools

In Chapter 4 we focus on how schools and charities work together to meet the needs of children. At the very forefront of universal services for children, schools are commonly the first port of call for children and families in need of help. This chapter uses secondary data and summarises research completed by the author of this book, Alison Body, and her colleague Eddy Hogg, to help contextualise how schools operate in this changing environment.

Analysing the data

The data analysis followed five distinct stages of analysis:

1 *Data preparation* This included the complete transcription and anonymisation of interviews utilising the qualitative data analysis computer software package, NVivo.

2 *Familiarity with data* This included immersion within interviews and repetitive listening, recording observational notes and working inductively to begin identify collective themes.

3 *Interpreting data* Interpreting data was done through coding and theme identification. Data were sorted, through NVivo, and encoded into a list of preset codes, drawn from the literature review, for example, 'relationships', 'tactics' and 'collaborations'.

4 *Verifying data* This included circulation of a short preliminary report outlining key findings to participants for feedback, and children's charities provided supplementary information including case studies of commissioning processes, tendering

documents, minutes of meetings, evaluations, business plans and reports to corroborate interviews. Supplementary information was not coded, but instead used to help provide depth of understanding of specific examples of commissioning raised in the interviews.

5 *Representing the data in terms of themes, quotes and examples in preparation for this book* All quotes and examples, and the context in which they are used in this book have been sent to and approved by the participants concerned.

Representing the data

An important focus in this book is on the direct voices of those working at the frontline of children's services in the charitable sector, and the state actors working within commissioning organisations. Therefore, after setting the policy context in Chapters 1 and 2, we continuously draw on quotes and experiences of those individuals working within these charities and the commissioners with whom they work.

We have deliberately anonymised the quotes throughout only indicating the position of the individual being quoted, and, if relevant, the size of charity within which they work. This decision was taken in partnership with the children's charities who have taken part in this research and the commissioners of children's services. Perhaps an interesting reflection on the current risk adverse and challenging culture that dominates state and sector relationships is that many participants felt that they could not discuss their experiences openly if they could be identified. We have honoured our agreement and sought to ensure that no quotes or examples used are traceable to individuals or individual experiences. We have only used recognisable examples where specific consent was given from the participant. Finally, all quotes are verbatim, unless they revealed identifiable information, in which case we have edited slightly.

References

Action for Children (2019) *Choose Childhood:* building a brighter future for our children. London

Adonis, A. (2012) *Education, education, education: Reforming England's schools.* London: Biteback

Aiken, M. (2014) 'Ordinary glory: Big surprise not Big Society': The changing shape of voluntary services. How this affects volunteer-based community groups, *Working Paper* 2, London: National Coalition for Independent Action (NCIA)

Albrow, M. (2012) 'Big Society' as a rhetorical intervention, in A. Ishkanian and S. Szreter (eds) *The Big Society debate: A new agenda for social welfare?.* Cheltenham: Edward Elgar, 105–115

Alcock, P. (2010) Building the Big Society: A new policy environment for the third sector in England, *Voluntary Sector Review*, 1(3): 379–389

Alcock, P. (2011) Voluntary action, New Labour and the 'third sector', in M. Hilton and J McKay (eds) *The ages of voluntarism: How we got to the Big Society.* Oxford: Oxford University Press/British Academy

Alcock, P. and Kendall, J. (2010) Constituting the third sector, *Third Sector Research Centre (TSRC) Working Paper* 42, Birmingham: TSRC, Birmingham University

Alcock, P., Kendall, J. and Parry, J. (2012) From the third sector to the Big Society: consensus or contention in the 2010 UK General Election? *Voluntary Sector Review*, 3(3): 347–363

Allcock, A (2019) *ESSS Outline:* Schools, safeguarding and early intervention. Iriss

Allen, G. (2011a) *Early intervention: The next steps.* London: HMSO

Allen, G. (2011b) *Early interventions: Smart investment, massive savings.* London: HMSO

Allen, R. and Allnutt, J. (2017) The impact of Teach First on pupil attainment at age 16, *British Educational Research Journal*, 43(4): 627–646

Andrews, J., Robinson, D. and Hutchinson, J. (2017) *Closing the gap: Trends in educational attainment and disadvantage.* London: Educational Policy Institute

Anheier, H. and Kendall, J. (2002) Interpersonal trust and voluntary associations: Examining three approaches, *British Journal of Sociology*, 53(3): 343–362

Artaraz, K. and Thurston, M. (2005) *Evaluation of the Branches Project: A family support service in Halton.* Chester: Centre of Public Health Research

Artaraz, K., Thurston, M. and Davies, S. (2007) Understanding family support provision within the context of prevention: A critical analysis of a local voluntary sector project, *Child and Family Social Work*, 12: 306–315

Axford, N. and Berry, V. (2017) Perfect bedfellows: Why early intervention can play a critical role in protecting children – a response to Featherstone et al (2014) 'A Marriage Made in Hell: Child Protection Meets Early Intervention', *British Journal of Social Work*, 48(1): 254–273

Bach, S. (2012) Shrinking the state or the Big Society? Public service employment relations in an era of austerity, *Industrial Relations Journal* 43(5): 399–415

Ball, S. and Youdell, D. (2008) *Hidden privatisation in public education.* Brussels: Education International

Barker, R. (ed) (2009) *Making sense of Every Child Matters multi-professional practice guidance.* Bristol: Policy Press

Bartlett, J. (2009) Getting More for Less Efficiency in the Public Sector. DEMOS, London

Benson, A. (2010) Hackney Advice Forum: taking back the power. *Voluntary Sector Review*, 1 (2): 233–38

Benson, A. (2014) 'The Devil that has come amongst us': The impact of commissioning and procurement practices, *Working Paper* 6, London: National Coalition for Independent Action

Benson, A. (2015) *Fight or fright: Voluntary services in 2015. A summary and discussion of the inquiry findings, NCIA Inquiry into the Future of Voluntary Services*, London: National Coalition for Independent Action (NCIA)

Biesta, G. (2013) Interrupting the politics of learning, *Power and Education*, 5(1): 4–15

Billis, D. (1981) At risk of prevention, *Journal of Social Policy*, 10(3): 367–379

Billis, D. (2001) Tackling social exclusion: The contribution of voluntary organisations, in M. Harris and C. Rochester (eds) *Voluntary Organisations and Social Policy in Britain*, Basingstoke: Palgrave, 37–48

Billis, D. and Glennerster, H. (1998) Human services and the voluntary sector: towards a theory of comparative advantage, *Journal of Social Policy*, 27(1): 79–98

Blair, T. (1997) 'The will to win', Speech, 2 June. Aylesbury Housing Estate, Beveridge Lecture, [Online] http://www.bbc.co.uk/news/special/politics97/news/06/0602/blair.shtml

Blair, T. (1998) *The third way: new politics for the new century* (No. 588). Fabian Society

Blair, T. (1999) Beveridge Lecture. http://www.bris.ac.uk/poverty/downloads/background/Tony%20Blair%20Child%20Poverty%20Speech.doc, www.bris.ac.uk/poverty/downloads/background/Tony%20Blair%20Child%20Poverty%20Speech.doc

Blake, G., Robinson, D. and Smerdon, P. (2006) *Living values: A report encouraging boldness in third sector organisations.* London: Community Links

Blanden, J. (2006) 'Bucking the trend': What enables those who are disadvantaged in childhood to succeed later on in life? *DWP Working paper* 31, London: Department for Work and Pensions (DWP)

Blatchford, K. and Gash, T. (2012) *Commissioning for success: how to avoid the pitfalls of open public services.* London: Institute of Government

Body, A. (2017) Fundraising for primary schools in England: Moving beyond the school gates, *International Journal of Nonprofit and Voluntary Sector Marketing*, 10.1002/nvsm.1582

Body, A. (2019) The commissioner's perspective: the lived realities of commissioning children's preventative services in England and the role of discretion. *Voluntary Sector Review.*

Body, A. and Hogg, E. (2018) *A bridge too far? The increasing role of voluntary action in primary education.* Canterbury: University of Kent

Body, A. and Hogg, E. (2019) What mattered ten years on? Young people's reflections on their involvement with a charitable youth participation project, *Journal of Youth Studies*, 22(2): 171–186

Body, A. and Kendall, J. (2020) Expansive opportunity makers but selective opportunity takers? Positional agility and tactical social skill in English third sector social service, *Journal for Civil Society*, 1–20.

Body, A., Holman, K. and Hogg, E. (2017) To bridge the gap? Voluntary action in primary schools, *Voluntary Sector Review*, 8(3): 251–271

Bonefield, W. (2015) Big society and political state, *British Politics*, 10: 413–428

Bovaird, T. and Loeffler, E. (2012) From engagement to co-production: The contribution of users and communities to outcomes and public value, *Voluntas: International Journal of Voluntary and Nonprofit Organizations*, 23(4): 1119–1138

Bovaird, T., Dickinson, H. and Allen, K. (2012) *Commissioning across government: Review of evidence*. Research Report 86, Birmingham: Third Sector Research Centre

Boyle, D. and Harris, M. (2009) *The Challenge of Co-production*. London: New Economics Foundation

Breeze, B., Halfpenny, P. and Wilding, K. (2015) Giving in the UK: Philanthropy embedded in a welfare state society, in P. Wiepking and F. Handy (eds) *The Palgrave Handbook of Global Philanthropy*. Basingstoke: Palgrave, 285–306

Brown, E.A. and Dillenburger, K. (2004) An evaluation of the effectiveness of intervention in families with children with behavioural problems within the context of a Sure Start Programme, *Child Care in Practice*, 10(1): 63–77

Buckingham, H. (2011) Capturing diversity: A typology of third sector organisations' responses to contracting based on empirical evidence from homelessness services, *Journal of Social Policy*, 41(3): 569–589

Bruer, J. (2011) Revisiting 'the myth of the first three years'. Special briefing for monitoring parents: Science, evidence, experts and the new parenting culture, http://blogs.kent.ac.uk/parentingculturestudies/files/2011/09/Special-briefing-on-the myth.pdf

Cabinet Office (2006) *Partnership in Public Services: An Action Plan for Third Sector Involvement*. London: Cabinet Office

Cabinet Office (2008) *Think Family: Improving the Life Chances of Families at Risk*. London: Social Exclusion Task Force, Cabinet Office

Cairns, B. (2009) The independence of the voluntary sector from government in England, in M. Smerdon (ed) *The first principle of voluntary action: Essays on the independence of the voluntary sector from government in Canada, England, Germany, Northern Ireland, Scotland, United States of America and Wales*. London: The Baring Foundation, 35–50

Cairns, B., Harris, M. and Young, P. (2005) Building the capacity of the voluntary nonprofit sector: Challenges of theory and practice international, *Journal of Public Administration*, 28(9–10): 869–885

Cameron, D. (2009) 'The Big Society', Hugo Young Memorial Lecture, 2nd April 2014, www.conservatives.com/News/Speeches/2009/11/David_Cameron_The_Big_Society.aspx

Carrington, D. (2002) *The Compact: The challenge of implementation*. London: Active Community Unit, Home Office

Charity Commission (2007a) *Stand and deliver: The future for charities providing public services*. London: Charity Commission

Charity Commission (2007b) *Charities back on track*. London: Charities Commission

Checkland, K., Harrison, S., Snow, S., McDermott, I. and Coleman, A. (2012) Commissioning in the English National Health Service: What's the problem? *Journal of Social Policy*, 41(3): 533–555

CIPFA (Chartered Institute of Public Finance and Accountancy) and NSPCC (National Society for the Prevention of Cruelty to Children) (2011) *Smart Cuts? Public spending on children's social care*, A report produced by the Chartered Institute of Public Finance and Accountancy (CIPFA) for the National Society for the Prevention of Cruelty to Children (NSPCC), London: NSPCC

Civil Society Exchange (2016) Independence in Question: the voluntary sector in 2016, The Baring Foundation & Tudor Trust

Civil Society Futures (2018) *Civil Society in England: Its current state and future opportunity*. Civil Society Futures

Clarke, M. and Stewart, J. (1997) Handling the wicked issues: A challenge for government, *Discussion Paper*, Birmingham: Institute of Local Government Studies, Birmingham University

Clifton, J. and Cook, W. (2012) *Closing the attainment gap in England's Secondary Schools: A long division*. London: Institute for Public Policy Research

Commission on the Future of the Voluntary Sector (1996) *Meeting the challenge of change: Voluntary action in the 21st century*. London: NCVO

Contaldo, M. (2007) *Building the evidence base: Third sector values in the delivery of public services*. London: Charity and Third Sector Finance Unit, HM Treasury

Coote, A. (2011) *Big Society and the new austerity*. The Big Society challenge, 82. London: Key Stone Trust

Couldry, N. (2011) *Why voice matters: Culture and politics after neoliberalism*. London: Sage

Crees, J., Davies, N., Jochum, V. and Kane, D. (2016) *Navigating change: An analysis of financial trends for small and medium-sized charities*. London: NCVO

Cribb, J., Norris Keiller, A. and Waters, T. (2018) *Living standards, poverty and inequality in the UK: 2018* (No. R145). IFS Report.

Crouch, G. (2011) A new age of interdependence: managing relationships between the voluntary sector and government. *Voluntary Sector Review*, 2(2): 247–256

Crozier, M. and Friedberg, E. (1995) Organisations and collective action: Our contribution to organisational analysis, in S. Bacharach (ed) *Research in the Sociology of Organisations*. New York: Elsevier Science, 71–92

Cunningham, I. (2008) A race to the bottom? Exploring variations in employment conditions in the voluntary sector, *Public Administration*, 86(4): 1033–1053

Cunningham, I. and James, P. (2017) Analysing public service outsourcing: The value of a regulatory perspective, *Environment and Planning C: Politics and Space*, 35(6): 958–974

Children and Young People's Unit (2001) *Learning to listen: Core principles for the involvement of children and young people*. London: Department for Education and Skills

Davies, S. (2008) Contracting out employment services to the third and private sectors: A critique, *Critical Social Policy*, 28(2): 136–164

Davies, C. and Ward, H. (2012) *Safeguarding Children Across Services Messages from Research*. London: Jessica Kingsley

Davis, J.M. (2011) *Integrated Working in Children's services*. London: Sage

DCSF (Department for Children, Schools and Families) (2004) Children Act. Guidance on Duty to Cooperate, http://webarchive.nationalarchives.gov.uk/20100402141602/http://dcsf.gov.uk/everychildmatters/about/guidance/dutytocooperate/

DCSF (Department for Children, Schools and Families) (2007) *The Children's Plan: Building brighter futures*. St Clements House, Norwich: HMSO

Deakin, N. (1994) *The politics of welfare: Continuities and change* (2nd edn). Hemel Hempstead: Harvester-Wheatsheaf

Dean, M. (2010) *Governmentality: Power and rule in modern society*. London: Sage

DfE (Department for Education) (2008) Initial Teacher Training (ITT) Census for the academic year 2018 to 2019, England. London: HMSO

DfE (2009) *Good Commissioning: Principles and Practice*. Commissioning Support Programme, England. London: HMSO

DfE (2010) White paper: The importance of teaching. London: HMSO

DfE (2018) *Supporting excellent school resource management*. London: DfE

DfE (2019) Keeping children safe in education Statutory guidance for schools and colleges, England. London: HMSO

DfES (Department for Education and Skills) (2003) *Every child matters*. London: HMSO

DfES (2004) *Every child matters: Change for children*. London: HMSO

DfES (2006) *Safer children and safer recruitment in education*. London: HMSO

DoH (Department of Health) (2003) The Victoria Climbié Inquiry: Chairman Lord Laming CM 5730. Norwich: HMSO

DHSS (Department of Health and Social Security) (1985) *Review of Child Care Law*. London: DHSS

DHSS (1988) *Working together: A guide to inter-agency co-operation for the protection of children from abuse*. London: HMSO

Diamond, N. (2007) *Compact funding study: Central government grants for the voluntary and community sector and the extent to which they comply with the Compact*. Birmingham: Commission for the Compact

Dickinson, H. (2014) *Performing governance: Partnerships, culture and New Labour*. Basingstoke: Palgrave Macmillan

Dingwall, R. and Eekelaar, J.M. (1988) 'Families and the state: An historical perspective on the public regulation of private conduct', *Law and Policy*, 10(4): 341–361, Oxford: Basil Blackwell

Dingwall, R., Eekelaar, J.M. and Murray, T. (1983) *The protection of children: State intervention and family life*. Oxford: Blackwell

Donzelot, J. (1980) *The policing of families: Welfare v the state*. London: Hutchinson

Durose, C. (2011) Revisiting Lipsky: Front-line work in UK local governance, *Political Studies*, 59(4): 978–995

Ecclestone, K. and Hayes, D. (2009) *The dangerous rise in therapeutic education*, Abingdon: Routledge

Edwards, R., Gillies, V. and Horsley, N. (2016) Early intervention and evidence-based policy and practice: Framing and taming, *Social Policy and Society*, 15(1): 1–10

EIF (Early Intervention Foundation) (2013) *Right for children, better for the economy*, www.eif.org.uk/

EIF (2018) *Realising the potential of early intervention*, London: Early Intervention Foundation

Eisenstadt, N. (2011) *Providing a Sure Start: How government discovered early childhood*. Bristol: Policy Press.

Eisenstadt, S.N. (2001) The vision of modern and contemporary society, *Identity, Culture and Globalization*. Leiden: Brill, 25–47

Ellis, V., Maguire, M., Trippestad, T.A., Liu, Y., Yang, X. and Zeichner, K. (2016) Teaching other people's children, elsewhere, for a while: the rhetoric of a travelling educational reform, *Journal of Education Policy*, 31(1): 60–80

Emirbayer, M. (1997) Manifesto for a relational sociology 1, *American Journal of Sociology* 103(2): 281–317

Entwhistle, T. and Martin, S. (2005) From competition to collaboration in public service delivery, *Public Administration Review*, 83: 233–42

Evans, K. (2011) 'Big Society' in the UK: A policy review, *Children and Society*, 25: 164–171

Evans, R. and Pinnock, K. (2007) Promoting resilience and protective factors in the Children's Fund, *Journal of Children and Poverty*, 13(1): 21–36

Evans, R., Pinnock, K., Beirens, H. and Edwards, A. (2006) *Developing preventative practices: The experiences of children, young people and their families in the Children's Fund.* London: Department for Education and Skills

Fawcett, B., Featheston, B. and Goddard, J. (2004) *Contemporary child care policy and practice.* Basingstoke: Palgrave Macmillan

Featherstone, B., Morris, K. and White, S. (2013) A marriage made in hell: Early intervention meets child protection, *British Journal of Social Work*, 44(7): 1735–1749

Feinstein, L. (2003) Inequality in the early cognitive development of British children in the 1970 cohort, *Economica* 70: 73–97

Ferguson, H. (2011) *Child protection practice.* Basingstoke: Palgrave Macmillan

Fearn, H (2014) Brooks Newmark's knitting comment undermines the very essence of charity, *Guardian*, https://www.theguardian.com/voluntary-sector-network/2014/sep/05/brooks-newmark-knitting-politics-undermines-charity (accessed 15.12.2019)

Fitzgerald, D. and Kay, J. (2008) *Working together in children's services.* Abingdon: Routledge

Fledderus, J., Brandsen, T. and Honingh, E. (2015) User co-production of public service delivery: An uncertainty approach, *Public Policy and Administration*, 30(2): 145–164

Fligstein, N. and McAdam, D. (2011) Toward a general theory of strategic action fields, *Sociological Theory* 29(1): 1–26

Fligstein, N. and McAdam, D. (2012) *A theory of fields.* Oxford: Oxford University Press

Fonagy, P., Steele, P., Steele, H., Higgitt, A. and Target, M. (1994) The theory and practice of resilience, *Journal of Child Psychology and Psychiatry*, 35: 231–257

France, A. and Utting, D. (2005) The paradigm of 'risk and protection-focused prevention' and its impact on services for children and families, *Children and Society*, 19(2): 77–90

France, A., Freiberg, K. and Homel, R. (2010) Beyond risk factors: Towards a holistic prevention paradigm for children and young people, *British Journal of Social Work*, 40: 1192–1210

Frost, N. and Parton, N. (2009) *Understanding children's social care politics, policy and practice.* London: Sage

Frost, N., Abbott, S. and Race, T. (2015) *Family support: Prevention, early intervention and early help.* Hoboken, NJ: Wiley

Frumkin, P. (2002) *On being nonprofit: A conceptual and policy primer.* Cambridge: Harvard University Press

Furedi, F. (2001) *Paranoid parenting.* London: Allen Lane

Fyfe, N. (2005) Making space for 'neo-communitarianism'? The third sector, state and civil society in the UK, *Antipode*, 37(3): 536–557

Garrett, P. (2014) *Critical and radical debates in social work: Children and families.* Cambridge: Polity Press

Gardiner, L. (2019) *Conservative manifesto risks child poverty reaching record highs while no manifesto will reduce it.* 26th November, 2019, Resolution Foundation

Giddens, A. (1979) *Central problems in social theory: Action, structure, and contradiction in social analysis.* Berkeley, CA: University of California Press

Giddens, A. (1984) *The constitution of society: Outline of the theory of structuration.* Berkeley, CA: University of California Press

Giddens, A. (1998) *The third way: The renewal of social democracy.* Cambridge: Polity Press

Gill, C., La Valle, I., Mai Brady, L. and Kane, D. (2011) *The ripple effect: The nature and impact of the children and young people's voluntary sector.* London: National Children's Bureau

Gillies, V. (2005) Meeting parents' needs? Discourses of 'support' and 'inclusion' in family policy, *Critical Social Policy*, 25(1): 70–90

Gillies, V. (2014) Troubling families: Parenting and the politics of early intervention, in S. Wagg and J. Pilcher (eds) *Thatcher's grandchildren? Politics and childhood in the twenty-first century.* Basingstoke: Palgrave Macmillan

Gilligan, R. (1999) Enhancing the resilience of children and young people in public care by mentoring their talents and interests, *Child and Family Social Work*, 4: 187–196

Glass, N. (1999) Sure Start: The development of an early intervention programme for young children in the United Kingdom, *Children and Society*, 13: 257–264

Gough, I. (2011) From financial crisis to fiscal crisis, in K. Farnsworth and Z. Irving (eds) *Social policy in challenging times: Economic crisis and welfare systems*. Bristol: Policy Press

Gove, M. (2012) Speech to Institute of Public Policy Research, 'The failure of child protection and the need for a fresh start', 19th November

Gray, M. (2013) The swing to early intervention and prevention and its implications for social work, *British Journal of Social Work Advanced Access*, 44(7): 1750–1769

Grover, C. (2008) *Crime and inequality*. Cullompton: Willan

Halfpenny, P., & Reid, M. (2002) Research on the voluntary sector: an overview. *Policy & Politics*, 30(4): 533–550(18)

Hansen, K., and Plewis, I. (2004) *Children at risk: How evidence from British cohort data can inform the debate on prevention*. London: Institute of Education, University of London and National Evaluation of the Children's Fund

Hardiker, P., Exton, K. and Barker, M. (1989) The social policy contexts of prevention in child care. *British Journal of Social Work*, 21: 341–59

Hardiker, P., Exton, K. and Barker, M. (1991) *Policies and practices in preventive child care*. Belfast: Avebury

Harlock, J. (2014) From outcomes-based commissioning to social value? Implications for performance managing the third sector, *Third Sector Research Centre (TSRC) Working Paper* 123, Birmingham: TSRC, Birmingham University

Harris, M. (2001) Voluntary organisations in a changing social policy environment, in M. Harris and C. Rochester (eds) *Voluntary organisations and social policy in Britain – perspectives on change and choice*. Basingstoke: Palgrave Macmillan

Harris, M. and Rochester, C. (eds) (2001) *Voluntary organisations and social policy in Britain*. Basingstoke: Palgrave

Hayden, C., Goddard, J., Gorin, S. and Van Der Spek, N. (1999) *State child care: Looking after children?*. London: Jessica Kingsley

Hendrick, H. (1997) *Children, childhood and English society, 1880–1990*. Cambridge: Cambridge University Press

Hensmans, M. (2003) Social movement organisations: A metaphor for strategic actors in institutional fields, *Organisation Studies* 24(3): 355–381

Hilton, M. (2011) Politics is ordinary: Non-governmental organizations and political participation in contemporary Britain, *Twentieth Century British History*, 22(2): 230–226

HM Government (1989) *Children Act 1989*: London: HMSO

HM Government (2004) *Children Act 2004*: London: HMSO

HM Government (2006) *Working together to safeguard children: A guide to inter-agency working to safeguard and promote the welfare of children*. London: HMSO

HM Government (2011) *Open Public Services White Paper*. London: HMSO

HM Government (2015) *Working together to safeguard children: A guide to inter-agency working to safeguard and promote the welfare of children*. London: HMSO

HM Government (2018a) *Working together to safeguard children: A guide to inter-agency working to safeguard and promote the welfare of children*. London: HMSO

HM Government (2018b) *Civil society strategy: Building a future that works for everyone*. London: Cabinet Office

HM Treasury (2002) *Spending Review*. London, HMSO

Home Office (1998) *Compact on relations between government and the voluntary and community sector in England*. Cm. 4100, London: Home Office

Hood, C. (1995) The 'new public management' in the 1980s: Variations on a theme, *Accounting, Organizations and Society*, 20(2–3): 93–109

Howard, E. (1961) The Ingeby Committee report, *British Journal of Criminology*, 1: 264–278

Howard, S., Dryden, J. and Johnson, B. (1999) Childhood resilience: Review and critique of literature, *Oxford Review of Education*, 2 (3): 307–323

Hupe, P. and Hill, M. (2007). Street-Level bureaucracy and public accountability, *Public Administration*, 85(2): 279–299

Independence Panel (2015) *An independent mission: The voluntary sector in 2015*. London: The Baring Foundation

Ingleby Report (1960) *Report of the Committee on Children and Young Persons, by the Chairman, the Rt. Hon. Viscount Ingleby,* London: Home Office

Institute for Fiscal Studies (IFS) (2018) *Comparing school spending per pupil in Wales and England,* 12 July 2018

Jas, P., Wilding, K., Wainwright, S., Passey, A. & Hems, L. (2002) *The UK Voluntary Sector Almanac.* London: NCVO Publications

Jenson, J. (2010) Diffusing ideas for after neo-liberalism: The social investment perspective in Europe and Latin America, *Global Social Policy,* 10(1): 59–84

Jones, G.W. (2002) *Modernising governance: New labour, policy and society.* Old Bailey Proceedings Online (www.oldbaileyonline. org, version 7.0, 24 February 2014), May 1895, trial of Emily Rosina Burrell (32) (t18950520-482)

Kane, D., Clark, J., Wilding, K. and Wilton, J. (2010) *The UK civil society almanac 2010.* London: National Council for Voluntary Organisations

Kellett, M. (2011) *Children's perspectives on integrated services: Every child matters in policy and practice.* Basingstoke: Palgrave Macmillan

Kendall, J. (2000a) The mainstreaming of the third sector into public policy in England in the late 1990s: Whys and wherefores, *Policy and Politics,* 28(4): 541–562

Kendall, J. (2000b) Measuring the performance of voluntary organizations, *Public Management: An International Journal of Research and Theory,* 2(1): 105–132

Kendall, J. (2003) *The Voluntary Sector.* London: Routledge

Kendall, J. (2009) The UK: Ingredients in a hyperactive horizontal policy environment, in J. Kendall (ed) *Handbook of third sector policy in Europe: Multi-level processes and organised civil society.* Cheltenham: Edward Elgar, 67–94

Kendall, J. and Knapp, M. (1995) *Voluntary means, social ends.* Canterbury: PSSRU

Kingdom, J. (1995) *Agendas, alternatives, and public policy.* New York: HarperCollins College Publishers

Kirton, D (2009) *Child social work policy and practice.* London: Sage

Krumer-Nevo, M. (2003) From 'a coalition of despair' to 'covenant of help' in social work with families in distress, *European Journal of Social Work,* 6(3): 273–282

Laming, L. (2009) *The protection of children in England: A progress report*. London: The Stationery Office

Levitas, R. (2005) *The inclusive society? Social exclusion and New Labour*. Basingstoke: Palgrave

Levitas, R. (2006) The concept and measurement of social exclusion, in C. Pantazis, D. Gordon, and R. Levitas (2006) *Poverty and social exclusion in Britain*, Bristol: Policy Press

Levy, D. and Scully, M. (2007) The institutional entrepeneur as modern prince: The strategic face of power in contested fields, *Organisational Studies*, 28(7): 971–991

Lewis, J. (1999) Reviewing the relationship between the 'voluntary sector' and the state in Britain in the 1990s, *Voluntas*, 10(3): 255–270

Little, M., Morpeth, L. and Axford, N. (2003) Children's services in the UK 1997–2003: Problems, developments and challenges for the future, *Children and Society*, 17(3): 205–214

Lister, R. (2003) Investing in the citizen-workers of the future: Transformations in citizenship and the state under New Labour, *Social Policy and Administration*, 37(5): 427–443

Lister, R. (2004) *Poverty*. Cambridge: Polity Press

LGA (Local Government Association) (2010) *Local authorities' approaches to children's trust arrangements*. London: LGA

LGA (Local Government Association) (2018) *Children's services funding – facts and figures*. Available at https://www.local.gov.uk/about/campaigns/bright-futures/bright-futures-childrens-services/childrensservices-funding-facts

Lloyds Bank Foundation (2016) *Commissioning in crisis: How current contracting and procurement processes threaten the survival of small charities*. London: Lloyds Bank

Mackey, R. (2003) Family resilience and good child outcomes: An overview of the research literature, *Social Policy Journal of New Zealand*, 20(1): 98–118

Macmillan, R. (2011) Seeing things differently? The promise of qualitative longitudinal research on the third sector, *Third Sector Research Centre (TSRC) Working Paper* 56, Birmingham: TSRC, Birmingham University

Macmillan, R. (2013a) Decoupling the state and the third sector? The 'Big Society' as a spontaneous order, *Voluntary Sector Review*, 4(2): 185–203

Macmillan, R. (2013b) Making sense of the Big Society: Perspectives from the third sector, *Third Sector Research Centre (TSRC) Working Paper* 90, Birmingham: TSRC, Birmingham University

Macmillan, R., Taylor, R., Arvidson, M., Soteri-Proctor, A. and Teasdale, S. (2013) The third sector in unsettled times: a field guide, *Third Sector Research Centre (TSRC) Working Paper* 109, Birmingham: TSRC, Birmingham University

Mair, J. and Hehenberger, L. (2013) Front-stage and backstage convening: The transition from opposition to mutualistic coexistence in organizational philanthropy, *Academy of Management Journal*, 57(4): 1174–1200

Martikke, S. and Moxham, C. (2010) Public sector commissioning: Experiences of voluntary organizations delivering health and social services, *International Journal of Public Administration*, 33: 790–799

Middleton, L. (1999) The social exclusion of disabled children: The role of the voluntary sector in the contract culture, *Disability and Society*, 14(1): 129–139

Milbourne L. (2009) Remodelling the Third Sector: Advancing collaboration or competition in community based initiatives?, *Journal of Social Policy*, 38: 277–297

Milbourne, L. (2013) *Voluntary sector in transition: Hard times or new opportunities?*. Bristol: Policy Press

Milbourne, L. and Cushman, M. (2013) From the third sector to the Big Society: How changing UK government policies have eroded third sector trust, *Voluntas*, 24: 485–508

Milbourne, L. and Murray, U. (2014) The state of the voluntary sector: Does size matter?, Paper 2, *Working Paper* 10, London: National Coalition for Independent Action (NCIA)

Milbourne, L. and Murray, U., (eds) (2017) *Civil society organizations in turbulent times: a gilded web?*. UCL Institute of Education Press.

Miller, R. (2013) Third sector organisations: unique or simply other qualified providers?, *Journal of Public Money and Management*, 31(4): 279–286

Milligan, C. and Fyfe, N.R. (2005) Preserving space for volunteers: Exploring the links between voluntary welfare organisations, volunteering and citizenship, *Urban Studies*, 42(3): 417–433

Mohan, J. (2011) Mapping the Big Society: Perspectives from the Third Sector Research Centre, *Third Sector Research Centre (TSRC) Working Paper* 62, Birmingham: TSRC, Birmingham University

Mohan, J., Kendall, J. and Brooks, N. (2016) Third Sector Impact: Towards a more nuanced understanding of barriers and constraints. Supplementary analysis to UK Work Package 5 Third Sector Impact, *BARRIERS: Briefing* 2 03/2016. Birmingham: Third Sector Research Centre, Birmingham University and Canterbury: University of Kent

Moriarty, J. and Manthorpe, J. (2014) Controversy in the curriculum: What do we know about the content of the social work qualifying curriculum in England?, *Social Work Education*, 33(1): 77–90

Morris, D. (2011) Building a Big Society: Will charity's creeping reach generate a new paradigm for state schools?, *Journal of Social Welfare and Family Law*, 33(3): 209–226

Morris, K. and Barnes, M. (2008) Prevention and social exclusion: New understandings for policy and practice, *British Journal of Social Work*, 38: 1194–1211

Morris, K., Hughes, N., Clarke, H., Tew, J., Mason, P., Galvani, S., Lewis, A. and Loveless, L. (2008) *Think family: A literature review of whole family approaches.* London: Cabinet Office Social Exclusion Task Force

Morris, K., Barnes, M. and Mason, P. (2009) *Children, families and social exclusion: New approaches to prevention.* Bristol: Policy Press

Munoz, S.A. (2009) Social enterprise and public sector voices on procurement. *Social Enterprise Journal*, 5(1): 69–82

Munro, E. (2007) *Child protection.* London: Sage

Munro, E. (2010) *The Munro review of child protection. Part One: A systems analysis.* London: Department for Education

Munro, E. (2011) *The Munro review of child protection. Final report: A child centred system.* London: Department for Education

National Education Union (NEU) (2018) Teachers and Workloads, https://neu.org.uk/media/3136/view

NCVO (2014) *UK Civil Society Almanac 2014.* London: NCVO

NCVO (2015) *UK Civil Society Almanac 2015.* London: NCVO

NCVO (2016) *UK Civil Society Almanac 2016.* London: NCVO

NCVO (2017) *UK Civil Society Almanac 2017.* London: NCVO

NCVO (2018) *UK Civil Society Almanac 2018*. London: NCVO

NECF (National Evaluation of the Children's Fund) (2004) *Prevention and early intervention in the social inclusion of children and young people*. London: DfES (Department for Education and Skills)

Ofsted (2015) *Early help: Whose responsibility?*. London

Osbourne, S. (1997) Managing the coordination of social services in the mixed economy of welfare: Competition, cooperation or common cause?, *British Journal Of Management*, 8(4): 317–328

Painter, C (2013) The UK Coalition Government: Constructing public service reform narratives, *Public Policy and Administration* 28(3): 3–20

Parr, S. (2009) Family intervention projects: A site of social work practice, *British Journal of Social Work*, 39(7): 1256–1273

Parton, N. (1991) *Governing the family: Child care, child protection and the state*. Basingstoke: Palgrave Macmillan

Parton, N. (2006) *Safeguarding childhood: Early intervention and surveillance in late modern society*. Basingstoke: Palgrave Macmillan

Parton, N. (2008) The 'Change for Children' programme in England: Towards the 'prevention–surveillance state', *Journal of Law and Society*, 35(1):166

Parton, N. and Williams, S. (2017) The contemporary refocusing of children's services in England, *Journal of Children's Services*, 12(2): 85–96

PASC (Public Administration Select Committee) (2008) *Public services and the third sector: Rhetoric and reality*. Eleventh Report of Session 2007–08. London: The Stationery Office

PASC (Public Adminstration Select Committee) (2011) *The Big Society*. Public Administration Committee – 902-I Seventeenth Report. London: The Stationery Office

Percy-Smith, J. (2000) *Policy responses to social exclusion towards inclusion?*. Buckingham: Open University Press

Peters, E. (2012) Social work and social control in the third sector: Re-educating parents in the voluntary sector, *Practice: Social Work in Action*, 24(4): 251–263

Pierre, J. and Peters, G. (2000) *Governance, politics and the state*. New York: St Martin's Press

Pithers, D. (1986) Focus: A trust betrayed, *Marxism Today*, January

Pithouse, A. (2008) Early intervention in the round: A great idea but..., *British Journal of Social Work*, 38: 1536–1552

Powell, T. (2019) House of Commons Library briefing paper: Number 7647, 11 July 2019: Early Intervention.

Prout, A. (2000) *The body, childhood and society*. London: Palgrave

Pugh, G. (2007) 'Policies in the UK to promote well-being of children and young people', in A. France, A. and R. Homel (ed) *Pathways and crime prevention: Theory, policy and practice*, Cullompton: Willan Publishing

Reay, K.M. (2012) *Toxic divorce: A workbook for alienated parents*. eBookIt.com

Rees, J. (2014) Public sector commissioning and the third sector: Old wine in new bottles?, *Public Policy and Administration*, 29(1): 45–63

Rees, J. and Mullins, D. (eds) (2016) *The third sector delivering public services: Developments, innovations and challenges*, Third Sector Research Series. Bristol: Policy Press

Rees, J., Miller, R. and Buckingham, H. (2014) Public sector commissioning of local mental health services from the third sector, *Third Sector Research Centre (TSRC) Working Paper* 122, Birmingham: TSRC, Birmingham University

Rees, J., Miller, R. and Buckingham, H. (2017) Commission incomplete: exploring the new model for purchasing public services from the third sector, *Journal of Social Policy*, 46(1): 175–94

Reich, R. (2018) *Just giving: Why philanthropy is failing democracy and how it can do better*. Princeton, NJ: Princeton University Press

Respect Taskforce (2006*) Family intervention projects: Respect guide*. London: Home Office

Ridge, T. (2002) *Childhood poverty and social exclusion: From a child's perspective*. Bristol: Policy Press

Rochester, C. (2014) The impact of contracting and commissioning on volunteers and volunteering in Voluntary Services Groups, *Working Paper* 8, London: National Coalition for Independent Action (NCIA)

Ryan, L. (2014) Outsourcing and the voluntary sector, *Working Paper* 3, London: National Coalition for Independent Action (NCIA)

Sage, D. (2012) A challenge to liberalism? The communitarianism of the Big Society and Blue Labour, *Critical Social Policy*, 32(3): 365–382

Salamon, L. and Anheier, H. (1992) *In search of the nonprofit sector 1: 'The question of definition', Working Paper No. 2.* The Johns Hopkins University Institute for Policy Studies.

Scott, M. (2011) Reflections on 'The Big Society', *Community Development Journal*, 46(1): 132–137.

Scott, R. (2004) Institutional theory, in Ritzer, G. (ed) *Encyclopedia of Social Theory*. Thousand Oaks, CA: Sage, 408–414

Sellick, C. (2011) Commissioning permanent fostering placements from external providers: An exploration of current policy and practice. *British Journal of Social Work*, 41(3): 449–466

SEU (Social Exclusion Unit) (1998) *Truancy and social exclusion*, London: Jessica Kingsley Publishers

SEU (2000) *National strategy for neighbourhood renewal: Report of Policy Action Team 12: Young People.* London: SEU

Social Services Committee (1984) *Children in care* (HC 360) (Short Report). London: HMSO.

Stone, L. (ed) (1994) *The education feminism reader.* London: Routledge

Sturgess, G., Cumming, L., Dicker, J., Sotiropoulos, A. and Sultan, N. (2011) *Payment by outcome: A Commissioners toolkit.* London: 2020 Public Service Trust

Taylor-Gooby, P. and Wallace, A. (2009) Public values and public trust: Responses to welfare state reform in the UK, *Journal of Social Policy*, 38: 401–419

Tinson, A., Ayrton, C., and Petrie, I. (2018) *A quiet crisis: Local government spending on disadvantage in England.* London: Lloyds Bank Foundation

Turney, D., Platt, D., Selwyn, J. and Farmer, E. (2011) Social work assessment of children in need: What do we know? *Messages from research*, Pdf, London: Department for Education

UNICEF Office of Research (2007) *Child poverty in perspective: An overview of child-wellbeing in rich countries*, Report Card 7. Florence: UNICEF Innocenti Research Centre

UNICEF Office of Research (2013) *Child well-being in rich countries: A comparative overview*, Innocenti Report Card 11, Florence: UNICEF Office of Research

Waldegrave, H. (2013) *Centres for excellence?*. London: Policy Exchange

Walters, R. and Woodward, R. (2007) Punishing 'poor parents': 'Respect', 'responsibility' and parenting orders in Scotland. *Youth Justice*, 7(1): 5–20.

Whitehead, H. (2019) *Charity Sector reacts to massive Tory majority*. 13th December 2019. Civil Society News

Whitfield, D. (2012) *In place of austerity: Reconstructing the economy, state and public service*, Nottingham: Spokesman

Whyte, S.R. (1995) Constructing epilepsy: Images and contexts in East Africa, in B. Ingstad and S.R. Whyte (eds) *Disability and culture*, Berkeley, CA: University of California Press

Zimmeck, M. (2010) The Compact 10 years on: Government's approach to partnership with the voluntary and community sector in England, *Voluntary Sector Review*, 1(1): 125–133

Index

Note: Page numbers for tables appear in italics.